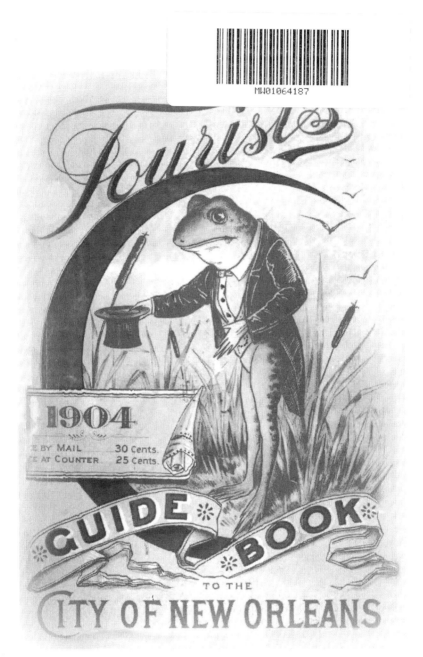

Tourist's

1904

E BY MAIL   30 Cents.
E AT COUNTER   25 Cents.

GUIDE ✺ BOOK ✺

TO THE

CITY OF NEW ORLEANS

by the:

Picayune Editors

The Picayune's

Guide to New Orleans

Revised and Enlarged.

SIXTH EDITION

Price, By Mail, - - - 30 Cents.

At Picayune Counter, - 25 Cents.

THE PICAYUNE, NEW ORLEANS, LA.

CHAPTER I.

"New Orleans has a personality," so a poet-lover declared, 'way back in those dim and dreary days when the old French and Spanish City, glorying in her title of "Le Petit Paris," carried the New World's commerce on the broad river that rushed past her shores, and the New World's romance and poetry in her heart.

"New Orleans has a personality, and studying her in all her changeful moods and phases one might almost say that New Orleans has a soul." To-day, with the crown of one hundred years of American progress encircling her brows, this fair child of two centuries and two continents, this imperial daughter of France and Spain, flings her beautiful banners to the breeze, and with the fine, true impulse born of her historic descent and proud ancestral heritage, gives to the world in the revival of the songs and stories and traditions of Louisiana, the grandest note ever struck in this American Continent since the pæan of American liberty was sounded amid the fire and smoke of Bunker Hill.

With far greater truth may it be said to-day that this great, glorious, intelligent, sentient city of New Orleans has a soul. Existing apart from and superior to all the other cities that have been founded in this immense area of which she was one hundred years ago the central thought and figure, New Orleans stands to-day amid the vast aggregation of cities of the Union peculiar, unique, charming and gracious, speaking to the tourist as only a city with her history and traditions may speak, and holding them under the spell of a fascinating charm that is always felt, but which one vainly seeks to analyze or understand.

Into this ancient city of varied lights and colors, of strange contrasts and fine individuality, this new city of high hopes and promises and fulfilled pledges, the Picayune Guide invites the tourist, and whether you wander leisurely through the old French Quarter, teeming with the songs and stories of other days, and reflecting a quaint life unlike that of any other city of the American continent, or whether you drive through the rose-scented roadways of her beautiful American section catching the fragrance of orange blossoms and magnolias, you will at once understand by intuition, how the heart of the poet was moved, when it brought forth that fine tribute "New Orleans has a soul."

You will realize more and more the mystery of her nameless charm when you study her wonderful complexity of life, her ever changing moods, the smiles that now ripple over her beautiful face, the tears that anon dim her eyes in sympathy and thought. See her old French and Spanish streets, and queer houses with quaint tunnel-like entrances peculiar to the architecture of the Spanish settlers in the latter portion of the seventeenth century. Visit her old curiosity shops and read in the many rich and rare objects exposed for sale the stories of the heart aches and tragedies and sacrifices of a once regal people. Turn to her main thoroughfare, and here you will see the dazzling spectacle of a great modern street, blazing with lights and astir with the gay life that circles and crosses and dashes along like a splendid moving picture; and within a stone's throw, in the twinkling of an eye, all is changed and you will find amid ruined homes, the stately dignity of the old Spanish days, and the quaint customs of a period that has passed forever, but which stand out in striking contrast to the customs of this busy, rushing age, and which have for the poet and student the soft and tender glow of an autumnal twilight's lingering adieu.

Such is New Orleans, rich in her history, her traditions, her poetry, her lore. New Orleans, fair and fragrant as the beautiful roses that bloom in her open gardens; sweet and stately as the maidens in the old world pictures that smile in the homes of the ancient Latin quarter.

It may truthfully be said that the New Orleans of to-day is not the New Orleans of yesterday; neither will it be the New Orleans of to-morrow. The year 1903 especially marked an era of prosperity that rivalled the palmiest period of ante-bellum days. Everywhere the busy hum of activity was heard on the streets, everywhere the march of improvements still goes on. New and handsome buildings are being erected, some for public others for private uses; but all indicating the capital is flowing in the direction of the city, and the taste and culture of the people who are coming to make their home among us. Even the dreamy old French Quarter has been invaded by the spirit of progress, and one of her most historic squares has had its buildings demolished to make way for a magnificent new Courthouse.

Long ago it was said that in the rubbish of the old Spanish city Aladdin's lamp was hidden. So it seems, and the people themselves are the Magician: their earnest work for the advancement of New Orleans challenges admiration.

OLD COLONIAL HOME.

From Southport to Port Chalmette, every change, since the Picayune Guide Book was last issued, has been carefully noted. The present edition is therefore thoroughly up-to-date and reliable, and as such commends itself to the tourist.

New Orleans is not to be seen in a day. Visitors must linger here beneath the sunny skies and tropical palms, must wander at will through the old French streets and get a glimpse into those old Creole homes that strangers generally only see from the streets, they must visit the French Market. they must go to West End and have a fish breakfast looking over the waters of Lake Pontchartrain, they must see the wonderful Carnival pageants and gorgeous balls, and even then they will not know New Orleans till they have known its people, its generous warm-hearted sunny people. Whatever of changes takes place in the city itself, there is one thing that does not change, and that is the heart of the people. True as the beautiful skies that hover over their ancient homes, they are like those homes themselves, tender and faithful, with love and memory dwelling with gracious charm upon the past, and hope and promise pointing brightly to the future. They bid you come and loiter here, as the old saying goes, "till you have drank the waters of the Mississippi." and perhaps when you will know them better, you too will do as many another tourist has done, come back some day to make your abode in this dear old city of infinite charm and infinite promise, that lays her lavish gifts at your feet, and bids you come and "be at home" with her.

CHAPTER II.

A Short History of New Orleans.

In order to properly see and appreciate New Orleans the stranger must know something of its history.

Louisiana was discovered by the Chevalier Robert de La Salle, who explored the Mississippi River from its source to the sea in 1682, taking possession of the entire country in the name of Louis XIV, King of France. He called the country Louisiana in honor of his King. Louisiana comprised all that country extending from British America on the north to the Gulf of Mexico on the south, and west of the Mississippi to the Pacific slope above California.

The first French colony was founded in Biloxi in 1699, by Iberville, a Canadian of French extraction, who with his brother, Bienville, was the next to enter the Mississippi River. They ascended the river as far as the mouth of Red River, and then separated. Iberville passed through Bayou Manchac, and discovered several lakes, one of which he called Lake Pontchartrain, in honor of Count Pontchartrain, a Minister of France, the other Lake Maurepas, after another Minister, and the third, Lake Borgne, which he called for a French word meaning "one-eyed," as he found that it was not a complete lake. He passed from Lake Pontchartrain into a beautiful bay which he called "Bay St. Louis," after Louis IX, who was such an excellent King that he was cannonized as "Saint Louis." Continuing his route Iberville passed into Biloxi Bay, and finding the Indian village of Biloxi at this spot, he made a settlement there.

Meanwhile, Bienville continued down the Mississippi River to the mouth where the French fleet was moored. Before reaching the mouth he met an English vessel, under command of Captain Bar. The Captain told him that he was examining the banks of the river in order to select a good site for an English colony. Bienville told him that the French had already taken possession of the country and made it a dependency of Canada. Captain Bar then turned back and sailed into the ocean. The point was called by Bienville "Le Detour Anglais," or the English Turn. All these original names still remain. Bienville then joined Iberville at Biloxi, and found him on the point of leaving for France. He had appointed his brother Sauvolle Governor of the colony of Louisiana.

Among the arrivals in the French colony at this time were twenty young girls who were sent by the King of France to be married to the colonists. The Bishop of Quebec was charged with selecting good and pious young women for this purpose, and as a proof of her respectability each young woman was provided by the Bishop with a curiously wrought casket. Fond of giving nicknames, these twenty were called by the Creoles "The Casket Girls." In 1706 these girls, becoming indignant at being fed on corn bread, held the first public meeting of women on the American Continent. They threatened that if things were not better they would return home at the first opportunity. In a few days they quieted down and remained loyal and faithful wives. The uprising is laughingly called "The Petticoat Insurrection."

Sauvolle was killed by the Indians shortly after Iberville's departure, and Bienville became Governor of the Colony. He is known as the "Father of Louisiana History."

Noting the inaccessibility from the sea of the Biloxi settlement, and dreaming of a great port near the mouth of the Mississippi River, in 1718 Bienville determined to select a more suitable site for the capital of the colony. Taking with him fifty picked men he came upon the site of the old deserted Indian village "Tchoutchouma," which was located 110 miles from the mouth of the river. Here he decided to build his city. He called it New Orleans, after the Duc d' Orleans, who afterwards became Louis XVI of France. Owing to opposition from the Company of the West, to whom Louis XIV had granted a charter, Bienville did not remove the colony to the new capital till 1723. It was then that the real history of the city began. That same year New Orleans was visited by a terrible hurricane that lasted three days. It destroyed many houses, the church and hospital and the shipping in the harbor. The crops were utterly ruined. Many of the settlers were so discouraged they determined to leave New Orleans, but Bienville persuaded them to remain and rebuild the city. In 1727 the first boys' school in Louisiana was established. That same year the Jesuit Fathers and the Ursuline nuns, on invitation from Bienville, came to labor in the colony.

In 1743 the romantic history of New Orleans began, under the administration of the Marquis de Vaudreuil, a nobleman and high-toned gentleman, who established a miniature court called "Le Petit Versailles," or the "Little Versailles." He introduced court balls and state dinners, costume de rigueur and polite speeches. Many titled noblemen and French officers also came over with their families and settled in the colony. Marquis de Vaudreuil is called in Louisiana history "Le Grand Marquis." His administration was the beginning of that aristocratic coterie which a century later made New Orleans famous in the cities of the Union. In 1757 Louisiana was ceded by France to Spain. The colonists bitterly resented the cession, and sent the Spanish Governor back to his country. Then the most influential citizens rose in revolution against Spain and declared the independence of the colony. This was the first declaration of independence on American soil. The leader of the revolution was a planter named Lafréniere.

Spain sent a fleet and three thousand picked men to punish the conspirators. Lafréniere and his compatriots were sentenced to be hanged. The public hangman cut off his arm rather than fulfill his duty, and not a man in the colony could be found willing to act as hangmen. Finally, Lafréniere and his associates were shot in the Place d' Armes, now Jackson Square. The other conspirators were sent to confinement in Moro Castle, Havana, and New Orleans was made a dependency of the Island of Cuba.

Don Luis Unzaga, the next Spanish Governor, completely won the colonists. He married a Creole lady and the officers of his court and army also married Creoles. Finally the reconciliation and amalgamation of the races became complete, and both worked in harmony for the upbuilding of the city. In 1788 the city was visited by another disastrous fire, which destroyed the Cathedral, Charity Hospital, and almost the entire residence section. New Orleans was laid bare. From the ashes of the old, irregularly-built French city arose the stately Spanish city—old New Orleans practically unchanged as we see it to-day.

In 1791 the insurrection of slaves against their masters in San Domingo brought to New Orleans many titled and wealthy refugees. They introduced a wealth and luxury unknown before in the colony. In 1794 the most important agricultural event in the history of Louisiana occurred when Etienne de Boré succeeded in making the first sugar crop in Louisiana. The cultivation of the cane was introduced by the Jesuits in 1751, but up to 1792 no planter had ever succeeded in making the syrup granulate. The cultivation of cane has contributed more to the prosperity of Louisiana than any of her other products. Many titled visitors came to New Orleans about this time; among others Duc d' Orleans, who afterward became Louis Philippe of France, and his brother, the Duc de Montpensier and the Count de Beaujolais came in 1798. They were magnificently received and royal entertainments were given in their honor. When he became King of France Louis Philippe remembered by beautiful presents many of the families who had treated him so kindly when he was in exile.

In 1793 the Episcopal See of New Orleans was founded.

In 1803, by the treaty of Ildefonse, New Orleans was ceded back to France. Only for a few weeks did the French flag wave. Following quickly came the news that France had sold Louisiana to the United States. The American Government took possession Dec. 23, 1803. The people bitterly resented being "sold like a lot of cattle," and appealed to France. But Napoleon was too busy changing the map of Europe. As our historian says, "Louisiana was a gift never intended for Kings to keep." April 30, 1812, Louisiana was admitted into the Union as a State. January 8, 1815, General Andrew Jackson and his band of Creole and American soldiery won the famous victory over the British on the Plains of Chalmette. This great conflict is called the "Battle of New Orleans." With the American domination a marvelous period of prosperity began. Ancient walls were demolished, forts torn down and the city spread away up and out beyond her ancient limits. Differences growing out of

LANDING OF THE URSULINE NUNS — 1727.

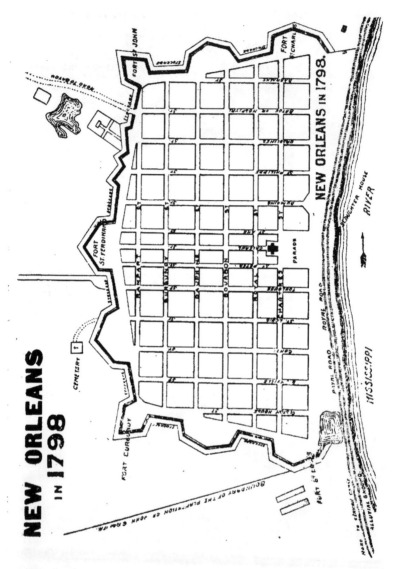

trade arose between the Creoles and Americans, and the latter built the American city above Canal street. The greatest rivalry prevailed. At one time there were three distinct municipalities, all united under one mayor. But as time passed on, Creoles and Americans, seeing the necessity of union, laid aside their differences and were reunited under one government.

In 1861, along with her sister States, Louisiana seceded from the Union.

In 1862 the Federal fleet, under Admiral Farragut, succeeded in forcing the passage of Forts Jackson and St. Philip. Appearing before New Orleans the city surrendered on April 25. General Butler came with his troops April 30, and martial law was declared. This condition of affairs remained to the close of the memorable struggle. New Orleans suffered severely during the war and still more so from the misgovernment of carpet-baggers during the so-called days of reconstruction. Her commerce was virtually destroyed and for many years after the war business seemed at a standstill. The revival in trade began less than twenty years ago, and has been astonishingly rapid. Every year finds New Orleans further advanced in its career of prosperity. To-day Louisiana exists among her sister States as free as the freest of them all. She is in the Union, of the Union, for the Union.

CHAPTER III.

How to see New Orleans—Street Numbers and Names—Distances.

New Orleans, in its social customs and aspects differs radically from all other cities of the Union. Indeed, we have here two cities, the one lying below Canal Street, called the "French Quarter," or "down-town section," the other lying above Canal Street, called the "American Quarter," or "up-town section."

The American section is best seen from the street cars; to properly see the French Quarter the tourist must make up his mind to walk. It is practically impossible while "doing the French Quarter," to lose one's way in New Orleans despite the winding streets and queer little alleys that appear so unexpectedly at a fresh turn of the main thoroughfare. Every cross street leads to the river, every other street eventually leads to Canal Street, which is the central thoroughfare of New Orleans.

In Canal Street cars may be taken to any part of the city, and one has only to remain long enough in any car to find himself again in the heart of New Orleans within walking distance of any of the hotels. New Orleans has 173.2 miles of Street Railway; this includes the Spanish Fort Line, which is a steam road, but is classed as a street railway. All these lines converge to Canal Street, running across or from and back to that thoroughfare. The cars are marked conspicuously, so that there need be no mistake. A full list of the car lines and the streets they traverse will be found in the chapter devoted to "Car Routes and Ferries and Railroads," in the rear of this Guide.

Street Numbers.

Throughout New Orleans the streets are numbered on the decimal system. The numbers begin at Canal Street and run up or down as the case may be on the streets running parallel with the river. The cross streets are numbered from the river. There are supposed to be 100 numbers in each block, so that at every intersection a fresh hundred is begun. In this way the visitor will know that if a house is situated at No. 1100 — Street, that it is eleven squares from Canal Street, or from the river. By consulting the Picayune's Street Guide, also to be found in the rear of this book, it can easily be found if a street runs up and down, parallel with the river, or from the river, across the town and parallel with Canal Street.

In the streets running parallel with the river, the even numbers are on the river side of the street, and the odd numbers on the lake side. In the streets running across the town parallel with Canal Street the even numbers are on the left hand side going from the river and the odd numbers are on the right hand side. Street names are posted conspicuously on every corner.

It often puzzles the visitor to hear the names of "Jefferson City," "Lafayette," "Carrollton," "Algiers," etc. In former days the city was surrounded by a number of small towns and villages, each with a distinct municipal government. Jefferson City and Lafayette were then quite populous little corporations, the limits of which correspond roughly to those of the present Fourth and Sixth Districts. All the city above Upperline Street was then the municipality of Carrollton, while intervening between Lafayette were the little towns of "Greenville," "Bouligny," and "Napoleonville." The uninhabited spaces which separated these towns from one another, were gradually built up, and then the towns were absorbed by New Orleans, of which they now form an integral part. Algiers lies across the river and is now the Fifth District. There are still a number of suburbs not yet annexed, although immediately adjacent to the city. Of these McDonoghville, Mechanicsville, and Gretna, lie on the southeastern bank of the river, above Algiers. "Bucktown" is a negro settlement at West End.

The curious circumstances that attended the growth of the city and her historic, religious, artistic and material development are suggested at every turn by

The Names of the Streets.

New Orleans has in fact the most picturesquely named streets of any city in the Union, and there are character and thought in all. For instance, all through the old French Quarter the streets suggest the city's royal descent and ancient faith and customs. We have Bourbon and Orleans, Dauphine and Burgundy, St. Louis, St. Peter, St. Ann. Bayou Road, now a well paved street, bespeaks the once fashionable drive of old New Orleans, and Rampart Street, in which there are no fortifications to-day, the city's ancient fortified line. We have memories of Dukes and Princes galore, such as Chartres, Condé, Du-Maine—Marquises and Generals, as Casa Calvo, Marigny, Moreau, Lafayette. We now cross Canal Street on dry land, and find that Americans pitched tents in Union Street, within sight of the old Spanish Government "Magazine," that gave to this street its name. Camp Street was once the "Campo de Negros," or Negro Camp, the space allotted to the free negroes who came to New Orleans after the San Domingo revolution; and this land opened upon the "Terre Commune," or "Common" ground. Indian herb doctors once lived in Tchoupitoulas Street and sold the "millet seed," for which the street is named, and which grew in abundance there. Further on we find the Nine Muses all in a row, leading gracefully into Felicity Street. All the Generals of the Mexican War are drawn up in soldierly array, and Napoleon is commemorated not only by the avenue which bears his name, but by a half dozen streets, christened after his most famous battles, such as Jena, Austerlitz, etc. Calhoun, Henry Clay and Webster march along side by side; Cato and Brutus confer in close proximity to Socrates, who looks with calm philosophy over at the passionate Byron in the curious vicinity of Vienna and Dublin. Passing through the "Vieux Carré," into the "Faubourg Marigny," Love leads you gently on into Elysian Fields, while just beyond Science and Art clasp hands, Agriculture and Industry yield Abundance and Independence, and Congress stands near ready to enact any Law necessary for the good of the Union, and to back it up by Liberal Force. And what is there lacking in poetry and romance when you are told that a beautiful prima donna once lived in Music Street, that a French King in exile occupied a mansion in Victory Street, that "Greatmen" passed in review while bad boys played "Craps" and gave the name of the game to the adjoining street; that the band of children trooping gaily on are going to play on the campus in "Good Children Street," and that the sweet-faced, black-veiled nun leading the little orphan by the hand dwells in an old convent in Piety Street.

All through the city you will find that history, romance, religion, the times have been exhausted for characteristic street names. Every now and then a petition is introduced into the City Council to change the names of the streets to North, South, East, West and add the numerical distance of squares from the river or from Canal Street, the dividing line of the city; it is represented that such change in nomenclature would greatly facilitate the efforts of the business community, as well as afford a better guide to strangers who are here for commercial purposes. But these resolutions are invariably voted down in accordance with public sentiment. What would West Forty-fifth or East Twenty-seventh Street mean to us in comparison with these old names that express the life, the growth, the thought of the city from its foundation to the present. And so there has been comparatively little change in the names of any streets since they first received their titles. This fact has been made the subject of many pleasant magazine articles.

The terms "Vieux Carré," "Faubourg Ste. Marie," "Faubourg Marigny," are often used throughout this Guide. It may be said

The "Vieux Carre,"

or "old square," is that interesting section of the French Quarter that was laid out by Bienville when he came from Biloxi to build his city in 1718. The cleared space had a frontage of twelve squares, and comprised all the land that

, OLD VIEW IN CHARTRES STREET—"VIEUX CARRE."

lay between Esplanade Street on the north, Canal Street on the south, the Levee on the east and Rampart Street on the west. The names of the streets running parallel with the river were Levee, Chartres above the Cathedral, Condé below it; Royal, Bourbon, Dauphine, Burgundy, Rampart, so-called because being the city limit on the west, ramparts were erected all along the line. Crossing these streets from the river, were Bienville, Conti, St. Louis, Toulouse, St. Peter, Orleans, St. Anne, Dumaine and St. Philip. Later, when the Ursuline Nuns came over, the old street on which was their property received the name of Ursuline, from their convent in Chartres Street. The "Barracks," or soldiers' quarters, were located two squares from the convent, hence the name, "Barracks Street," or "Quartier." Intervening was the Military Hospital, which gave to the street directly below Ursuline the name "Hospital." "The

Esplanade" was located in the beautiful street that runs below Barracks, from the river to the woods. The names of these original streets have remained unchanged through all these years. They are dear to the people, because they are the living reminders of a beautiful historic past.

The "Faubourg Ste. Marie"

lies on the upper side of Canal Street. It was the first distinct "America·n" section of New Orleans, and extended from the "Terre Commune" or Government Reservation (now Common Street) outside the walls of the ancient city to the line marked by Delord Street. It was owned by a wealthy planter named Jean Gravier, and was first called the "Ville Gravier." After the cession of Louisiana to the United States and the Americans came pouring into the city from the West, there was a contest for mastery between the Creoles with their elegant manners and luxurious homes, and the hardy, thrifty band of invaders. Finally, there grew so much jealousy and distrust that the Governor and State officials began to feel the difficulties of their position, and trouble seemed imminent. At this juncture the coolness of the American Governor and the foremost American citizens prevailed. The Americans decided to have a city of their own, beyond the ancient French limits. Gravier was willing to divide his land into lots and streets, and found a ready sale among the discontented Americans. Gravier changed the name of the section to the "Faubourg Ste. Marie," in honor of his mother, whose name was Mary. This was the beginning of the beautiful American city that lies above Canal Street, and which now stretches to the verge of Southport.

The "Faubourg Marigny"

was the ancient plantation of Philippe Mandeville de Marigny, a provincial magnate, who entertained Louis Philippe and his brothers when they were exiles in New Orleans. The Faubourg extended from Esplanade Street to St. Ferdinand and from the river to St. Claude Street. When Marigny decided to build his own city, that should outrival either the "Vieux Carré" or the "Faubourg Ste. Marie," he cut up the plantation into lots and streets. A portion became one of the most fashionable residence centres of old New Orleans, but the tide of progress flowed upward, and the dreams of Marigny were never realized.

Algiers.

Algiers was known in early Creole days as the "Plantations of the King." This was the name given by Bienville. In time swarms of negro slaves alone inhabited it. They were constantly at work and all day their quaint negro ballads could be heard. The Creoles showing their propensity for giving nicknames, rechristened the "King's Plantation" "Algiers," and the name clings to this day. It is now the Fifth District of New Orleans, and has a large population of thrifty white people.

Municipal Boundaries.

The city exercises jurisdiction over the whole Parish of Orleans, an area of 187 square miles. The populated section embraces about 50 square miles. The city slopes gradually from the river to Lake Pontchartrain, which is in the rear. The levee system has been perfected to a degree that excites the wonder and admiration of strangers. New Orleans is surrounded on all sides by huge walls of earth called Levees, the height of which along the river front averages from twenty to twenty-five feet. With these preliminary details so necessary to the stranger who would see and understand New Orleans, the Picayune leads the tourist into the old French Quarter.

VIEW OF OLD COURT—"FAUBOURG MARIGNY" (2712 ROYAL).

CHAPTER IV.

The "French Quarter," or the Down-town Section of New Orleans.

The most picturesque and interesting part of the city is that termed colloquially the "French Quarter." Here every square has its story of realistic or legendary lore. The tall, brick buildings looking dreamily over the narrow streets teem with facts of historic or romantic interest. Down the dim ages come the stories of the high-bred dames and gallant knights, who laughed and sang and danced and loved while the "fleur-de-lis" of France floated from the flagstaff 'in the old Place d'Armes. Then comes the stately echo of the Spanish domination, the days of the grand senors and high-born ladies of Spain; the days of the influx of French and Spanish noblesse, and the gradual amalgamation of the two races into that peculiar type of American civilization, the Creoles of Louisiana.

ANCIENT SPANISH ROW, RUE DUMAINE—MME. JOHN'S HOUSE.

Amid the echoes of the music and the dance and the first notes of the drama that marked the complete reconciliation, we hear the sound of the axe and the saw, the anvil and the hammer, and the rumble of bricks and mortar all over the Faubourg, and there stands out the "Vieux Carré," or the old "French Quarter," practically unchanged, as we see it to-day.

This is the city of Gayarre and Lafcadio Hearn, the city around which Cable wove his wonderful romances. Their genius has made the Quarter famous wherever the name of New Orleans is known.

Poetry and romance, beautiful traditions and legends have combined to cast an air of unreality over the history of this old section, but truth is stranger than fiction and the legends associated with points of interest in the old "Carré," as indicated in this Guide, have been verified by careful historians.

In order to see the French Quarter at its best, and breathing in these latter days all the quaint poetry and foreign atmosphere of early days in New Orleans, the tourist must make up his mind to rise early and loiter lazily through the quaint Faubourg, for he will want to stop at every parrot call, at every "clang of wooden shoon," at every note of a gay bacarole floating down from the dormer windows set in the queer tile roof; he will want to peep into the quaint old Spanish courtyards, fresh and fair and cool, with sunny marble-flagged pavements and palms and olives and magnolias growing within; to stop a moment to listen to the soft musical French of the passers-by, to catch a glimpse of the fair Creole girls as they stand in the fragrant old-fashioned gardens, wafting a kiss on a rose to "mamma," sitting on the jalousied veranda or at the jasmine-twined window above; or see them as they pass demurely out of the grim buildings, prayer-book and rosary in hand, on the way to early mass in the old Cathedral.

It is in the morning that the dreamy beauty of this old city dawns upon you, and you see in the dull gray belfries and tall steeples and gilded crosses of her sanctuaries, the roses climbing over the beautiful wrought iron work of the old verandas, and the lovely women you meet, with their sweet foreign ways, the things that have given thought and inspiration to poets and romancers of old New Orleans.

OLD ABSINTHE HOUSE.

All through this old Latin Quarter the houses retain many of the characteristics of the French and Spanish dominations, and all along the narrow, ill-paved streets will be heard a Babel of tongues and there will be seen convents and chapels and cemeteries, mostly of the Catholic faith. These appeal to the imagination with extraordinary charm; each has its history, its tradition, its lingering memory of other days.

In early Creole days, Royal Street was the main street of the city. The fashionable section was in the vicinity of Jackson Square. Bearing in mind this fact, the tourists will do well to begin his explorations in

Royal Street,

diverging every now and then, as this Guide will indicate, a square or so to right or left, to view some interesting landmarks just within the radius then receiving attention.

As you walk along do not fail to note the hand-wrought balconies of iron work, the beautiful courtyards, the tunnel-like entrances to houses enriched with arched mullioned windows, and the spiked galleries that project over the sidewalks.

At the corner of Royal and Iberville Streets is a large building, ornamented with handsome granite columns. It was erected for bank purposes, and was occupied for many years by the Citizens' Bank.

In the vicinity of Royal and Iberville, in the same square as the old bank building, stood formerly the Merchants' Exchange, where the United States Court held its sessions previous to the building of the Custom-House.

TYPE OF COURTYARD—FRENCH QUARTER.

The old postoffice was in the centre of the square bounded by Exchange Alley, Customhouse, now Iberville, Royal and Canal Streets.

Just around the corner from Iberville, in a building the precise location of which is not known, Lopez organized an expedition against Cuba, the disastrous result of which aroused a great deal of public attention in 1851.

The square on the river side, between Iberville and Bienville, was once the site of Bienville's country house.

In the vicinity of Bienville Street will be found a number of quaint auction marts, where the wares chiefly sold are old furniture, antiquated bric-a-brac, and dingy family relics of various kinds. It is amusing, indeed, to look through these places, where many curious things will be found. New Orleans has been for years a favorite stamping ground for the relic hunter, and scores of valuable finds have awarded his search. The prizes are all gone now.

At the corner of Bienville Street diverge one square toward the lake and see the old Absinthe House. It dates from the year 1798, and has been doing business since 1826.

Returning to Royal Street, at 403, was housed the first Bank ever organized in the Mississippi Valley. The three corners of Royal and Conti Streets were formerly occupied by banks—the Bank of Louisiana, the Louisiana State Bank and the United States Bank. They have long since removed, although one of the buildings is now a branch depositary of the State National Bank.

The large building on the upper, river corner of Conti is the Mortgage Office. Admission is unrestricted. It is a curious sight to see the interior filled with desks, upon which repose hundreds of huge folios containing the real estate records.

In the middle of the block, between Conti and St. Louis, at 417 Royal. Paul Morphy, the celebrated chess player, once made his residence. He died

FRENCH OPERA HOUSE, BOURBON STREET.

in his bathroom, on the second floor. The building may be recognized by the beautifully worked iron balcony, and by the circular lunettes piercing the wall, just under the eaves. The ground floor is now occupied by a plumbing establishment. One of the most picturesque courtyards in New Orleans is in the rear.

During the year 1903, some of the most historic buildings in New Orleans were demolished in the square bounded by Royal, Chartres, Conti and St. Louis Streets, to make way for the erection of the new Court House which will be situated in this square. The most interesting of the buildings destroyed was that in which Gen. Jackson made his headquarters in 1815, and from which point he directed his preparations for meeting the English army under Packenham. For many years, till the period of its demolition, the building was the residence of the distinguished Southern writer, Mrs. Mollie E. Moore Davis. Mrs. Davis now resides at No. 505 Royal Street.

At the corner of Toulouse diverge one square toward the lake, and at the corner of Bourbon and Toulouse see the

French Opera House.

This immense structure was built in 1860 from a design by the noted local architect, Gallier. It seats about 2,800 persons. There are four tiers, each of which retains its peculiar name. For instance, the dress circle is called "les loges;" the balcony, "les secondes;" while the gallery is popularly known as "le paradis." The boxes on the parquet floor are termed "baignoires grillées." There is a handsome "foyer," capable of holding 1,000 persons, on the second floor.

The central part is the theatre proper, or "la salle," as it is technically termed. There are small courtyards on either side, and on the outside, wings occupied by dressing-rooms and administration offices. The office of the "comptrolleur" is at the foot of the double staircase.

The origin of the opera in New Orleans is exceedingly curious and interesting. Between 1808 and 1811 there were two French theatres in successful operation, one in St. Peter Street and one in Royal Street. At the latter period John Davis, a French emigrant from San Domingo, built the Orleans Theatre, on the square behind the St. Louis Cathedral. In 1813 Davis engaged in Paris, the first French Opera Company ever brought to this country, and many of the great classics of the operatic stage were produced for the first time in America in New Orleans. On the death of Davis his son assumed management of the opera, and most ably conducted it for twenty-two years. Under his management Fanny Elssler and Damoreau were brought to New Orleans.

In 1859 Charles Boudousquie formed a stock company, by whom the present splendid building was erected. During the Civil War the opera was suspended. It was revived in 1868. From 1871 to 1872 Placide Canonge, a distinguished Creole journalist and playright, obtained a lease of the opera house and re-established the ancient brilliant traditions of this temple of the lyric art. The opera has continued almost uninterruptedly ever since. The enterprise is under the auspices of the French Opera House Association, composed of leading capitalists.

It is impossible to review in this space, even briefly, the history of the French Opera House. Here Adelina Patti made her début in "Le Pardon de Ploermel." Here, too, were heard the dying notes of another great Italian artist, Mme. Frezzolina. Etelka Gerster sang here; so did Fursch-Madi, Devoyod, Dumestre, Delabranche, Ambre, Picot, Michot and Orlins. The house contains many curiosities, including magnificent collections of music in MSS., and scenery, among others the original sets for "Aida," as produced in Egypt before the Empress Eugenie.

New Orleans is the only city in America which has maintained uniformly an operatic troupe. The great carnival balls take place in this building.

Returning to Royal Street, the next point of interest is the

Old St. Louis Hotel.

It stands in the heart of the French Quarter. The original building, erected in 1835, at a cost of $1,500,000, was completely destroyed by fire in 1841, but another palace was immediately erected on the same site, and soon reached a meridian of splendor almost unparalleled in the history of the United States. The building still stands a monument to the elegance, wealth and prosperity of those days. The hotel was the resort of the wealthiest planters and largest slave-holders in the South. The lower rotunda was frequently used by the negro slave traders as an auction mart. The names of the auctioneers may still be seen carved in the walls. The place is in rather a dilapidated condition just now (January, 1903), but it has recently been purchased by a strong corporation, at the head of which is Mr. J. A. Mercier, and it will be thoroughly renovated. Tourists should not fail to see the beautiful domed banqueting hall nor the famous old ballroom, in which were inaugurated the grand subscription balls of ante-bellum days. The frescoing in the hall was done by a nephew and pupil of the great Canova. In this hall Henry Clay delivered the only speech he made in Louisiana. famous "bal travesti," the most magnificent entertainment, it is said, that ever occurred in New Orleans, was given in honor of Henry Clay's visit, and the supper served cost $20,000. General Boulanger and the Prince of Brazil, grandson of Dom Pedro, were entertained magnificently here, and a few years ago the late President McKinley sat down to a supper there after an evening's arduous campaigning. The hotel has seen many singular vicissitudes. It has been a statehouse and a besieged fortress. In reconstruction days it was the headquarters of the Radical Government. In 1874, when the people of New Orleans rose against Packard and his oppressive administration, the Radicals were confined to the hotel for several months, fighting taking place outside the building. When the garrison capitulated the building was found in a terrible state of ruin and desolation. Before the war entrance was had through the stately portico in St. Louis Street, but now the entrance is in Royal Street.

Between St. Louis and Toulouse, at 517 Royal Street, is an archway flanked by cannon embedded in the ground. This was the Commanderia, or headquarters of the army during the Spanish domination.

In the vicinity will be found a number of curio and second-hand shops, where the antiquarian and bibliophile have often picked up treasures. These stalls are extremely inviting, reminding one, in the nature and value of their possessions, of the book stores along the Seine in Paris. It is said that more rare French and Spanish volumes are to be found at these places than anywhere else in the country.

At the corner of Royal and St. Peter Streets will be found a four-storied structure of stuccoed brick. It was built in 1819, and was the first four-storied

ENTRANCE TO ST. LOUIS HOTEL (ONCE HOTEL ROYAL),
ST. LOUIS STREET.

building ever erected in New Orleans. It figures in one of Cable's romances as " 'Sieur George's House." By this name it is almost universally known. It is a handsome specimen of the old city residences of the great Louisiana planters.

The next point of interest in Royal Street, is in the square between Orleans Place, on the south side, and St. Anthony's Place on the north. Immediately behind the pretty garden, so gracefully laid out in palms and ferns, and magnolia trees, stands the historic

St. Louis Cathedral.

Turn into the dim Cathedral Alley, past the quaint brick buildings looking down so silently over the entourage of vines and flowers, and enter through the side door the famous old shrine, whose history may indeed be said to be the history of New Orleans. The Cathedral occupies the site of the first church ever erected in the great expanse known afterward as the "Louisiana Purchase." This church was erected by Bienville when he laid out the city in 1718, and named St. Louis, after the patron saint of the then reigning monarch of France.

ST. LOUIS CATHEDRAL.

This primitive Church was destroyed by fire and a new church was erected in 1721. This, too, was burnt to the ground in the memorable conflagration of Good Friday, 1788. As the entire city almost was consumed the disaster seemed to preclude the possibility of erecting a new church, when Don Andres Almonaster y Roxas, a wealthy Spanish nobleman, erected at his own expense this Cathedral Church at a cost of $50,000, on condition that a mass would be said in perpetuity every Sunday for the repose of his soul. The design was the usual Spanish style, with three round towers in front. In 1851 the building was remodelled, and steeples were raised on the towers. The present portico, with its columns and pilasters, dates from that period. The beautiful frescoing was done by the famous painter, Humbrecht. The large mural painting above the high altar represents "King Louis of France proclaiming the Ninth Crusade." The statues which surmount the high altar are Faith, Hope and Charity. To the left of the sanctuary is the archiepiscopal throne, surmounted by the symbols of episcopal authority, the miter and the crossed keys and crozier. On the walls of the sanctuary appear many tablets inscribed to the memory of the dead Bishops and Archbishops of New Orleans, most of whom are buried in the crypt beneath the grand altar. A reproduction of the famous grotto of Lourdes forms one of the side altars; the water which trickles perpetually over the rocks is supplied from the miraculous shrine at Lourdes. The side chapel on the north side is dedicated to the Sacred Heart of Jesus. Don Andres Almonaster sleeps beneath a large slab on which is inscribed in Spanish his many deeds. Many quaint institutions maintain at the Cathedral, not the least curious of which is the sexton or "Suisse," who attends with cocked hat, sword and halbert all the services. Notable events in the history of New Orleans have been linked with the Cathedral, most important perhaps of which was the solemn high mass offered by Bishop Dubourg at the request of General Jackson after his famous victory on the plains of Chalmette. It was attended by General Jackson and his army and a solemn "Te Deum" of Thanksgiving was sung. In 1893 the centennial of the Cathedral was celebrated with great pomp and ceremony, and in December, 1903, were held in the Cathedral the religious services incident to the Louisiana Purchase Centennial celebration.

In the St. Louis Presbytery, facing the Cathedral Alley, may be seen curious old portraits, among them the only one in existence of Don Almonaster, Mgr. Penalver, the first Bishop of New Orleans, and Père Antoine, whose memory is so linked with early days in the French Quarter. His name was given to the pretty garden fronting on Royal Street, with the Cathedral as a background. Père Antoine was a Spanish priest who came to New rleans toward the close of the eighteenth century and who worked many years at the Cathedral. He died beloved by all. His name is given to the beautiful little square in the rear of the Cathedral. For many years, too, his name was associated with a palm tree that stood until recently in a woodyard at the corner of Bourbon and Orleans Street. This yard formed part of the land on which Père Antoine lived. Innumerable tales were told of how this strange palm came to be there, not the least romantic of which was that it sprang from the heart of a young girl who was buried in this spot, and who died dreaming of her native palm-befringed shore. At 625 St. Anthony Place are kept the ancient archives of the Cathedral.

Crossing into Orleans Street, is a large brick building, with handsome walls covered with brown stucco. A cross surmounts the roof. This is the Convent of the Holy Family. In other days it was the famous

Quadroon Ballroom

of New Orleans. Adjoining is a three-story brick building, an orphanage connected with the convent. It stands upon the identical spot on which stood the old Orleans Theatre. No section of New Orleans is invested with more romance than the square in which these buildings stand. As mentioned above, in the building now the Convent of the Holy Family took place those "Quadroon balls," at one time celebrated throughout the world. No women were more beautiful than the quadroon women of New Orleans. The slight negro taint was betrayed only in the soft olive skin and the deeply increased brilliancy of the eye, while no one, not versed in the signs by which the Louisianian recognizes at once the person of mixed blood, could distinguish in feature, hair or form any resemblance to the African type.

It was while the quadroon women were in the zenith of their unsavory glory that there rose, clam and serene, like a star of promise for the colored race, the Sisterhood of the Holy Family. It was founded by the Abbe Rousselon in 1835, with the hope of regulating a condition of affairs that saddened the hearts of the Archbishops of New Orleans. Among those who went to confession to the old Abbé were three colored women who were slaves; one was a quadroon, another a griffe, a third a mulatto, representing the various grades of evolution from the African proper. They were good, virtuous, pious, Christian women, reared in Christian households by noble masters and mistresses. They felt keenly the degradation of their race. The Abbe Rousselon knew this,

A COLORED SISTER OF THE HOLY FAMILY.

and in his far-seeing wisdom knew, too, that religion alone could give these women the right conception of the duties imposed by God. He conceived a great plan, and obtaining the freedom of the three slaves, he sent them to a convent in Europe to be trained and educated. After seven years they returned to New Orleans and he founded the Sisterhood of the Holy Family. It was a struggling little community; it had the sympathy of the white ladies of New Orleans and the unfailing support of the Bishops and priests. The war came and then the work of the Sisterhood began in earnest. They gathered in the orphans and the aged and afflicted of their race, now freed and thrown upon the world. The South had been beggared; it was a race for subsistence everywhere. But all shared with the humble Sisterhood, for the men and women of

Louisiana appreciated their work. The old Orleans Theatre had long been burned down; the ancient quadroon ballroom still remained. In 1881 this place was offered for sale. Before the day was out the Sisterhood had gathered in the means to purchase it. And here, in the very house where folly once reigned and music sounded and graceful figures floated dreamily to and fro, the Sisters have erected their chapel, and above the doors are inscribed the words: "Silence, my soul, God is here." The old ballroom, so long used as a chapel, but now as a community room for the sisters, is said to have the finest dancing floor in the world. It is made of cypress three feet in thickness. Above the stairway the Sisters have placed the significant inscription: "I have chosen rather to be an abject in the house of the Lord than to dwell in the temple with sinners." Silence and prayer and work now reign in these halls, and no community is more esteemed than the Sisterhood of the Holy Family, which has done more than any other body for the elevation and education of the colored race in Louisiana.

Turning again into the dreamy Rue Royale, just along the Cathedral line, are the Catholic book stores for the sale of religious articles. The

Workers in Wax and Flowers

also have their abode along this section. On the approach of All Saints' Day, Nov. 1, the day set apart in New Orleans as sacred to the dead, the windows in Royal Street are aglow with wonderful beaded wreaths and flowers, wax and paper flowers, enriched with various mottoes: "À Mon Père," "À Ma Mère," "À Une Epouse Chérie," as the sacred thread of memory runs. Very quietly all the year round the flowermakers sit at work in the rear of these ancient stores so that at All Saints' time they may rival one another in the beauty, the variety and the skill of their productions."

The Café des Exiles," made famous by Cable, stood at the corner of Royal and St. Ann Streets. On Dumaine, between Royal and Bourbon Streets, is a low-browed frame house, with dormer windows and a long veranda supported by a brick pavement. This is the house bequeathed by M. John, of the "Good Children's Social Club," to "Zalli and 'Tite Poulette," as veraciously set forth in Cable's story of " 'Tite Poulette."

At 1122 Royal Street are quaint courtyards surrounded by old Spanish portals. They are all that remains of the cld Spanish Barracks. The place is now used as a seltzer water factory.

Just around the corner from Royal Street, at 817 St. Philip Street, is the Convent of the Missionary Sisters of the Sacred Heart. They are devoted to the work of elevating to the dignity of true citizenship the swarm of Italian and Sicilian emigrants which pours into New Orleans. The Sisterhood came to New Orleans shortly after the lynching of eleven Italian prisoners in the old Parish Prison of New Orleans, twelve years ago. The deadly work of the Mafia had been gaining ground day by day; scarcely a month passed without chronicling some terrible secret murder, directly traceable to this society. At length the members became so bold as to defy justice and secretly shot down the Chief of Police of the city while engaged in the discharge of his duties. The murderers, strange to say, were six of them acquitted and a mistrial entered as to the other three, but the citizens rose in arms and slew the prisoners in the Parish Prison. The Sisterhood is doing a noble work in instructing these emigrants and their children in their duties to God, their neighbor and country. They have the cordial support of the citizens, and many ladies of the finest families have joined their order. The courtyard and garden of the convent are very quaint, and the institution itself well repays a visit.

A half square further on, at the corner of St. Philip and Bourbon Streets, once stood the famous smithy of the Lafitte brothers, the

"Daring Pirates of Barataria,"

whose romantic history and bravery form one of the most interesting chapters of the life of old New Orleans. Here these polished gentlemen, under the guise of blacksmiths, smuggled goods into New Orleans and established such an enormous trade that the United States Government stepped in and sought to apprehend them, But it was all of no avail. The old Creoles, smarting under the unjust mercantile laws of Spanish colonial days, had learned to love the Lafitte brothers, who brought such beautiful and expensive wares to New Orleans and sold them so cheap. They sought to shield them from arrest. As soon as the United States revenue cutter was spied in the distance coming up the river, the brothers were notified. At once the great piles of smuggled goods were hidden away, usually in the fastnesses of the woods of Barataria Bay; the smithy was in full blast, and Jean and Pierre Lafitte the busiest and most industrious of workers. At last they were forced to take up their residence in Barataria Bay altogether, for the United States made it very hot for them in New Orleans. At this time the war with Great Britain broke out. Lafitte was offered a large sum by the British if he would allow them to land at the pirate's trysting place in the Barataria woods and steal quietly into New Orleans. The two brothers were also offered commissions as officers in the British Army. But Lafitte was a brave patriot and a true Louisianian, despite his piratical inclinations. He scornfully rejected the British offer, told General Jackson of the approach of the enemy, placed all the documents in his hands, and then, advancing to the defense of New Orleans, he himself organized his pirates into a regiment for the defense of the city. No braver service was rendered on the day of the great battle of New Orleans than that of Lafitte's Regiment. In consideration of his services the United States, upon the recommendation of General Jackson, granted the brothers and their men full and free pardon for past offenses on condition that they would give up smuggling and lead the lives of respectable American citizens. The offer was accepted and Lafitte was welcomed into the best society in New Orleans. The stories told of the Barataria pirates would fill a volume.

The headquarters of the Italian organ grinders are a half square further on in St. Philip Street. These people live in an old and dilapidated tenement building opening upon a great yard. They spend the day eating macaroni and singing songs, and at evening emerge in numbers, with their hand organs on their backs, and go from corner to corner of the old Faubourg, playing their tunes, to the delight of the little children, who dance to the music and to the dismay of the older folks, who like not the twanging instruments.

At 1140 Royal Street, corner of Hospital, stands a fine old house which has a story as strange and terrible as any German castle. This is the famous

"Haunted House,"

which every visitor to New Orleans wishes to see, and whose singular history caused Cable to embody it in his "Strange True Stories of Louisiana." Here, in 1831, lived Mme. Lalaurie, who moved in the most wealthy and aristocratic Creole circles of her time. She was beautiful, educated, accomplished; she was a member of one of the most ancient and honored families of Louisiana. She inherited numerous slaves, whom she treated with the most abominable cruelty, starving and torturing them to death, until, her barbarities becoming known to the public, she was compelled to flee for her life. The indignant populace rose in its wrath, wrecked the house, threw the most costly mirrors and cabinets from the windows and smashed them into atoms on the banquette below. The imprisoned and half-starved slaves, many of whom were found held in chains fastened to the dungeon below, were released. Three old slaves, tortured almost to death, were taken in a dying condition to the "Cabildo." Human bones were found in the well and a curious old trap door, still to be seen in the wall, is said to have been the avenue by which Mme. Lalaurie let down these slaves into gloom and darkness and death. Ever since the house is said to have been haunted. It is said that no tenant can occupy it for any length of time. The Creoles tell the most wonderful stories of how at times the ghosts of the murdered slaves hold high carnival in the old mansion. The principal ghost haunting the house is said to be that of a little negro girl, who, being pursued by her mistress with a lash, fled up and up the winding stairs to the belvidere and committed suicide by leaping from the roof into the courtyard below. On dark and stormy nights it is said the little girl appears

Walking Round and Round the Belvidere,

her moans and sobs being heard above the storm, and on moonlight nights, when the atmosphere is very rare, her wraith, fleeing from her infuriated mistress, is seen leaping with a wild shriek from the cupola to the flag-stoned courtyard below. Many are the stories told of how Mme. Lalaurie effected her escape on that awful night away back in the thirties. Some say that after the mob had wrecked the house she caused herself to be nailed in a coffin, gave out that she had died of fright and was taken out in a hearse to the Metairie Road, whence she made her escape to France. But the true manner, learned by the writer from an eye-witness to the scenes, was that Mme. Lalaurie saw that a crisis had come and nothing but a bold effort would save her life. She dressed herself beautifully for her evening drive, ordered her coachman to drive her carriage to the main entrance of the house, and, smiling radiantly, she bowed like a queen to the infuriated mob. Taken unaware, the crowd fell back, wondering

THE HAUNTED HOUSE.

what would happen next. This was the opportunity that Mme. Lalaurie had calculated upon. She bowed again with her sweetest smile, stepped through the crowd into her carriage, and ordered her coachman to drive at breakneck speed out the ancient fashionable route of Bayou Road. It had all happened in the twinkling of an eye. The crowd recovered itself, realized that it was to be cheated out of its victim and followed in close pursuit. It was a race for life, and Mme. Lalaurie won. She reached the Half-way House a few moments ahead of the crowd. A schooner stood in the bayou. She thrust a purse of gold into the Captain's hand and he steered out toward the lake. Mme. Lalaurie made her way to Covington, thence to Mobile, where she embarked for France. She became noted in Paris for her many charities. She was killed in a boar hunt in the forests of Versailles For many years after her departure the house remained closed. The people said the house was haunted and would show the well in the courtyard where Mme. Lalaurie buried her victims, the murder of whom had been perpetrated in the loft immediately beneath the roof.

Turning from this eerie spot, just two squares beyond, is the Rue Esplanade, and in the section bounded by Decatur, the Levee and Barracks Street, is the

United States Mint.

It occupies the site of the old Fort St. Charles. The building cost $182,000. The Mint is capable of turning out $5,000,000 per month. Admission to the Mint is easily effected, and a polite official is always ready to show the visitor through the various departments. In December, 1814, General Jackson stood on the rampart of Fort St. Charles to review his army as it marched past on its way to meet the British at Chalmette. In 1862 Willliam Mumford was hung in front of the Mint, by order of General Benjamin F. Butler, for tearing down

THE UNITED STATES MINT.

the United States flag from the roof of the building after the Union Army had taken possession of the city. For years after, a sad, gray-haired woman wandered aimlessly about the Faubourg. "Hush!" the little children would say as she approached; "that is Mumford's mother." "No, she is not," others would answer; "she only thinks she is." And the old Creole grand dames would take up the thread and say, in hushed voices: "Yes, children; she is Mumford's mother."

The Old Slave Quarters,

where slaves were brought from all sections of the Southern States, but principally from Virginia and Maryland, to be sold at auction in New Orleans, were located at the corners of Chartres and Esplanade Streets. The large brick building, now one of the finest residences on the avenue, was erected on the site of the long row of brick buildings which stood on the river side of Chartres Street, from Esplanade to Peace Street. On the side toward the woods, in the same boundary, stood a long row of frame buildings (two-story), with iron balconies reaching to the banquette, and a three-story kitchen with little pigeon-hole windows guarded in by iron bars. Both of these sides of Chartres Street were known as the slave quarters, and millions of dollars changed hands in this slave traffic.

Adjoining almost all the ancient homes in this section are two and three-storied kitchens separated from the main house. These were the quarters used by the family servants, or the slaves who were attached directly to the household departments.

On the corner of Elysian Fields and the levee, and visible from Chartres Street where it crosses Esplanade, is the massive brick building, with a lofty smokestack, used as a power-house by the Claiborne Street Railroad. The power-house occupies the site of the old Mandeville de Marigny residence. This was the residence of Philippe Marigny, who is buried before the altar in the St. Louis Cathedral. Marigny, as mentioned in the historical chapter of this Guide, was a grand seigneur in every sense, and when Louis Philippe was in America, before his accession to the French throne, he entertained the exiled Prince for some time in magnificent fashion. Lafayette, Moreau and other celebrated personages were his guests at other times. All this portion of the city was, in those times, known as the "Faubourg Marigny."

Many are the stories told of his magnificence and lavish use of money, among others the common story that he used to light his cigar with $10 bills and carelessly throw away the burning fragments.

CHAPTER V.

Chartres Street—The French Market and Vicinity.

Having explored the old Rue Royal and caught a glimpse of the ancient Faubourg Marigny, turn from the United States Mint into picturesque Chartres Street, and return to Canal Street along this route.

Chartres Street was the great business thoroughfare of old New Orleans, the street in which millions of dollars changed hands; it was in early days as great a promenade as the grand boulevard Canal is in our own.

Everything is old, very old, in Chartres Street, and the street itself seems like a bit of old time frescoing, left to ruin and decay amid the busy progress of another age.

The grim houses and odd balconies appear to be in endless confab with one another, but there is a hush as you approach, and they look stern and stolid, as though defying your curious gaze. The inhabitants, however, are very kind; they see at a glance that you are a stranger by your eyes, and they smile graciously, while with a pretty air of mingled reserve, they motion you to look your fill.

Thus encouraged you may peer shyly into the tunnel-like entrances of old paved courtyards, with arched porticos such as one may see in Venice under the shadow of St. Mark's or the old Palace of the Doges. In most of these courtyards you will see plants in huge pots, geraniums, pomegranate trees and flowering shrubs; sometimes you will catch a glimpse of a battered statue of bronze or marble, or immense yellow earthenware jars that remind one of the "Forty Thieves," or which are as big as that in which Ali Baba hid in the wonderful romance of the Arabian Nights.

Chartres Street opens from Canal Street four blocks from the river, but for the purpose of this Guide follow the old street from Ursuline Avenue after you have gotten a glimpse of the quaint life of the oyster and fruit dealers in the vicinity of Esplanade and Barracks, and see the ancient Archbishopric, which is

The Oldest Building in Louisiana.

This historic edifice stands in the center of the square between Hospital and Ursulines Streets. Entrance may be had through a quaintly constructed portal, defended by double gates, piercing the wall in the middle of the Chartres Street front. The porter's lodge is within this portal. The buildings face a spacious lawn. They were erected between 1727 and 1734 for the use of the Ursuline nuns. The nuns resided here from 1734 to 1824, when they removed to their present domicile, in the extreme lower part of the city. The old building has seen various uses, not the least interesting of which is that in 1831 it was the State Capitol, and the Legislature held its sessions within its walls. The building was at that time leased by the State of Louisiana from the Ursuline nuns. Shortly afterward, the lease having expired, the Ursulines presented it to the then reigning Archbishop of New Orleans as

THE ANCIENT ARCHBISHOPRIC—FRONT VIEW.

a place of residence for the archbishops of the diocese. It was so used until 1899, when a new residence for the archbishops was purchased in Esplanade Avenue. The historic old site in Chartres Street, however, is still retained as the "Archbishopric," and is used for the transaction of all the official business of the archdiocese. The Archbishop and the Chancellor have their offices here, and it is the official place designated for all important ecclesiastical meetings. No one should leave New Orleans without visiting this ancient building. It remains exactly as when first erected. The visitor should remark the ancient staircase, the steps of which are single, massive pieces of timber, deeply worn by the feet of many generations. The chapel contains a little oratory and shrine. The reception room, on the lower floor, is beautifuly paneled in cypress, and contains a curious old clock. The shutters of cypress over the main entrance are over 100 years old and are still perfectly sound. In the dining-room hang portraits of all the Bishops and Archbishops who have presided over the See of New Orleans. On the third floor of the building may still be seen the quaint little cells used by the Ursuline nuns in 1734, the old-fashioned desk in the community room, at which the superioress sat and presided when the nuns were assembled for meditation and prayer. In another room are the quaint, heavy benches on which the slaves sat as they were gathered together morning and evening for instruction and prayer. In the building are preserved all the most ancient archives which are a part of the history of Louisiana from the beginning. A beautiful old garden is in the rear of the convent.

Adjoining the Archbishopric is St. Mary's Church. It was the ancient Ursuline Chapel, and is the oldest church in Louisiana.

At the corner of Hospital and Chartres Street, where a small grocery now stands, was the ancient burying ground of the Ursuline nuns. From 1727 to 1824 all the departed members of the community were buried in this spot. When the convent was removed to the new quarters near the Barracks, the remains of the nuns were disinterred and reburied in the present graveyard attached to the ancient convent. The remains of the slaves they owned, and who were buried in the spot on the corner of Chartres and Hospital Streets, however, were not disturbed. It is interesting to note here that the slaves owned by the Ursulines chose to remain with them rather than accept freedom after the emancipation of the black race, and that, some eight

REAR VIEW OF ANCIENT ARCHBISHOPRIC.

or nine years ago, the devoted nuns buried the last of their slaves, a negress a century old.

Bishop Dubourg, who occupied the episcopal chair of New Orleans in 1812, lived in a house belonging to the Ursulines, on a part of their Chartres Street property nearest the river. Its site is now occupied by Sambola's macaroni factory. Bishop Dubourg used to spend his winters in New Orleans and his summers in the northern portion of his vast diocese, which extended from the Gulf of Mexico to the great lakes, from the Mississippi River to the Pacific coast above California.

In the vicinity bounded by Ursuline, Chartres Street and the Levee are the shops of the macaroni-makers and basket-weavers. At the corner of Ursuline and Chartres pause a moment to look at the queer old tiled roof building, one of the few that remain as specimens of Spanish colonial architecture previous to the great fire of 1788.

. On Chartres Street, between Dumaine and St. Philip stood the famous old "Café des Emigrés" or Emigrants' Café. It was the favorite headquarters of the San Domingo refugees and their famous liquer "Le Petit Gouave," was concocted here to perfection.

Walking slowly toward Canal Street, you pass the front of the old Cathedral and the famous

"Cabildo,"

where the ancient Municipal Chapter of Spanish times met. The picturesque structure stands at the corner of Chartres, between St. Peter and Orleans Alley. Within its walls all but one of the transfers of the country from one government to another were effected. Here, representing the King of France, Governor Aubrey absolved the colonists from their oath of allegiance to France and handed them over to the swarthy delegate of His Catholic Majesty of Spain. Here was effected the transfer back to France, and here again the transfer of the country to the United States was made, and from the balcony Claiborne announced the event and displayed the American flag. In 1826 General Lafayette was received here, and in later days President McKinley was formally welcomed to Louisiana just prior to his

THE "CABILDO."

death. In December, 1903, the civil ceremonies connected with the celebration of the Louisiana Purchase Centennial took place in the Cabildo. At present the lower floor of the building is used as the Second Recorder's Court and police jail; on the second floor the Supreme Court of Louisiana holds its sittings. The ancient "Spanish Calaboose," or jail, is in the building. In one of the cells can be seen a pair of old-fashioned stocks, a relic of the Spanish domination.

At No. 613 Orleans Place, is the ancient Spanish Arsenal, still used, despite the dilapidated appearance of the building, as the State Arsenal. The massive building, a fac simile of the old "Cabildo," standing on the lower side of the Cathedral, between St. Anthony's Alley and St. Ann Street, is the lower court building. The Civil Court sits on the upper floor and the Civil Sheriff has his office on the lower floor. It is a very ancient building, but not as old as the Cabildo. It occupies the site of a former Capuchin monastery, the monks of which were charged in early days with the care of the St. Louis Cathedral. The gardens of their convent extended back several squares. Père Antoine resided here for many years, as did also the famous Père Dagobert, who is canonized among the sweet memories of old New Orleans. He was called "the singing Père," and it is said in old traditions that even now at night, passing through St. Louis Cemetery, one can hear his sweet voice chanting the grand "Te Deum" or caroling the sweet lullabies that Creole mothers sang to their children. The people are not afraid of his ghost. They stop to listen, and still again the old tradition runs, "Blessed is he who hears Père Dagobert singing the 'Te Deum' at the midnight hour."

The venerable Cathedral, Cabildo and Courthouse overlook

Jackson Square, or the old "Place d'Armes."

It is a noted spot in Louisiana history and was the place that Bienville marked out for the review of the French troops, hence the name, "Place d'Armes." Here were held from the beginning all the most important public meetings in Louisiana. Here Don Antonio Ulloa received the keys of the city and took possession of it in the name of the King of Spain; here met the resolute band of patriots under Lafréniere, and right here may be said to have been made the first declaration of independence on American soil, for Lafréniere declared the independence of the colony in 1768 and sent the Spanish Governor back to his

THE JACKSON MONUMENT.

own country. Here a few days later the brave French patriots were shot as traitors, and here Don Bernardo Galvez, one of the most heroic figures in Louisiana history, appeared before a popular meeting of the citizens in 1779 and completely won their hearts. In the old square General Jackson, the hero of New Orleans, was received in 1815, and passing through a bevy of beautiful Creole girls, representing the different States of the Union, one of them, personating Louisiana, crowned him as her victor and hero.

When the monument was erected in the center of the square, taking the place of the flagstaff from which had been unfurled successively the flags of France, Spain and the United States, the name of the hero of Chalmette was bestowed on the square by the grateful citizens. The Jackson monument, in the middle of the square, was made by Clark Mills, at a cost of $30,000. The artist has been highly praised for the manner in which he succeeded in balancing such a mass of metal—20,000 pounds—without any support or prop beneath. In this position the statue has withstood the storms and hurricanes of half a century. The incription on the granite base of the monument was cut by General Butler's orders during the Civil War. It runs: "The Union must and shall be preserved."

Jackson Square is one of the few remaining public places which are inclosed. It is shut to the public at 9 o'clock at night. It has long been under the management of a special Board of Commissioners, who have greatly beautified the parterres by planting them with tropical fruits and flowers. The fountain near the Chartres Street entrance is equipped with a mechanism by which the jet may be illuminated at night.

The two long rows of quaint buildings, drawn up like twin regiments of red-coated soldiers, on either side of the square, are the Pontalba Buildings, erected in the early part of the century by the Baroness de Pontalba, daughter of Don' Andres Almonaster. They are still owned by her descendants. It was a great mark of gentility in early days to reside in the Pontalba Buildings. The tide of fashion has, however, long since flown away. The long, narrow courtyards, the grand old stairways, the curious transoms and brass knockers, whose click reverberates through the ancient halls, are worthy of notice.

And now you are in sight of the famous You know it by the busy rush, the noisy rumbling of carts and wheels, the ceaseless clatter of foreign and native tongues combined, the outlandish garbs, the curious faces, the strange cosmopolitan scene to be nowhere else witnessed on American soil. The market is open daily from 5 a. m. to 12 m. The "meat

JACKSON SQUARE—CATHEDRAL AND CABILDO IN THE DISTANCE.

French Market.

market" was erected in 1813 at a cost of $30,000, and stands on the exact spot where the first market was built in New Orleans, according to the plan of Le-Blond de La Tour, in 1723, and which was destroyed by a hurricane in that same year. The best time to visit it is in the early morning, and Sunday morning of all others. It is the most remarkable and characteristic spot in New Orleans. Under its roof every language is spoken, and this will be noted through its four divisions, the fish, the meat, the vegetable and the fruit market. The buyers and sellers are men and women of all races. Here are the famous coffee stands, where one gets such delicious "café noir" or "café au lait," with a "brioche" or "cala," as the taste may suggest. There are the Gascon butchers, and the Italian and Spanish fruit vendors, and the German and Italian vegetable women; there are Moors, with their strings of beads and crosses, fresh from the Holy Land; peddlers and tinners and small notion dealers; the "rabais men," with their little stores on wheels; Chinese and Hindu, Jew and Teuton, French and Creole, Spanish and Malay, Irish and English, all uniting in a ceaseless babel of tongues that is simply bewildering. The old Creole negresses are there, with quaint bandana and tignon, offering for sale "pralines" and "pain patates" and "calas," the latter a species of soft doughnut made of rice and flour. Squatted about the ground between the markets are strange, half-civilized beings, with queer little papooses strapped to their backs or rolled up in shawls and blankets. You catch the odor of wild herbs and

OLD SPANISH TILED BUILDING.

woodland leaves, and get a glimpse of the dried sassafras leaves from which the famous "gumbo filé" is made. These patient, dark-skinned women, with their straight, flowing hair, are the last remnants of the once powerful tribe of Choctaw Indians, who were once the very owners of the soil on which New Orleans stands. They have come all the way from the old Indian settlement of Bayou Lacombe, across Lake Pontchartrain, to the French Market, where they always find a ready sale for their "gumbo filé" and fragrant "tisanes." And in the French market, above all, there is the charm of local life and color, especially of a Sunday morning, when the Creole belles and beaux saunter leisurely through, buying roses and jasmines, after hearing mass in the old Cathedral.

These Indians

deserve more than a passing notice. The history of this tribe is one of peculiar interest. They were the only Indians who never once rose in arms against the United States. They were bound by ties of deepest friendship to the early settlers of Louisiana, and called the good Bienville, their "father." In all the early troubles of the infant colony they were always at the side of the colonists, and when Jackson led the Americans against the British, on that memorable Eighth of January, 1815, they followed the fortunes of the Americans and merited a compliment from the famous "Old Hickory" in his report to the Government.

In token of their fidelity, they were never sent to the Indian reservation; but years since they were crowded out of New Orleans by the superior and cultured race, and they have lived quietly on the ground allotted to them by the United States at the Indian settlement of Bayou Lacombe, over in St. Tammany Parish. Twice a week, on Sunday and Thursday, they come to the city, crossing, free of fare, on the steamer that plies between Old Landing and New Orleans, and then walking from Lake Pontchartrain to the French Market, where they always find a ready sale for their good "gumbo filé" and

MORNING IN THE FRENCH MARKET.

bunches of herbs from which the Creoles concoct such fragrant "tisanes" for the sick.

The amenability and docility of the Choctaws have been attributed by historians to the wonderful influence exercised over them by the Catholic priests who labored among them in the beginning, from generation to generation in

VIEW OF FRENCH MARKET.

Louisiana. Very sweet among them, especially, is the memory of Father Rouquette, a famous poet and scholar of Louisiana, who devoted nearly sixty years of his life to unremitting labor among these simple untutored children of the

TAKING A CUP OF CAFE NOIR—FRENCH MARKET.

forest. When he died the tribe came all the way from Bayou Lacombe bearing their bunches of sassafras and "laurier" to lay upon his grave.

You turn from the market, with its singular complexity that interests while it challenges admiration, and

Emerge upon the Levee.

The scene along the Levee is at all times extremely animated, especially in the vicinity of the French Market.

The Levee in front of the fish market is called the "Picayune Tier" or Lugger Landing.

GROUP OF INDIANS—FRENCH MARKET.

The "Dago" fishermen from the lower coast land their cargoes of orange and oysters here, and here gathers a swarm of luggers, with their sails tied down on their long booms or flapping idly in the breeze to dry, while their motley

BARRELS OF SWEETS OVERFLOW THE LEVEE.

crew of traders through the bayous and lakes of the lower Louisiana coast— Greeks, Italian, Dagoes, Gascons, negroes and nondescripts—bustle about unloading cargoes of oranges, oysters, fish, vegetables and all the various produce of the land and water of their section; or else, while waiting for some sort of a cargo to set sail again, loiter idly about, smoking their cigarettes and cooking

A DAGO FRUIT STALL—FRENCH MARKET.

their meals over queer little furnaces fired with charcoal. The "Picayune Tier" is always a picturesque sight.

PICAYUNE TIER.

Walking up the levee one or two squares, you reach the site of the old "Government House;" this stood at the corner of Levee and Toulouse Streets in the old colonial days. It was burned in 1826, after the sale of Louisiana to the United States.

One square further up, between St. Louis and Customhouse Streets, are the Sugar Sheds. At this point one gets a fine view of the shipping. The Sugar Exchange, where the merchants conduct many of those operations which regulate the price of sugar throughout the country is on the corner of Front and Bienville Streets.

One cannot pass this section of the Levee without realizing the greatness and importance of the sugar industry of Louisiana. Block after block along about midwinter is packed and crowded with barrels and hogsheads of sugar and molasses. Large as the area is, it scarce affords room for the product that seeks this greatest sugar market in the United States. The barrels of sweets overflow the sheds, crowd all the warehouses in the vicinity, block the sidewalks and overrun the Levee. There is sugar everywhere.

A word right here about the cultivation of sugar cane in Louisiana will be of interest. In 1794 Etienne de Boré, a planter living about six miles above New Orleans, in the spot where Audubon Park now stands, succeeded in making the first crop of sugar ever made in Louisiana. He disposed of his crop for

THE SUGAR EXCHANGE.

$12,000. The cultivation of cane was first introduced by the Jesuit Fathers in 1751, but up to 1792 no planter had ever succeeded in making the syrup granulate, and so convert it into sugar in sufficient quantities to make the culture profitable. To Etienne de Boré belongs this honor. His portrait hangs in the Sugar Exchange in this city. The cultivation of sugar cane has contributed more to the prosperity of Louisiana than any of her other products.

Close by the Sugar Exchange are several great refineries where the crude products of the sugar-houses on the plantations is changed into the beautiful white sugar seen upon our tables.

Continuing up Chartres Street, to Canal, one passes many quaint old courtyards and dilapidated mansions telling of the glory of departed days.

In Chartres Street, near Canal, are some famous antique shops and wonderful bird stores, where the chatter of magpies and parrots, mingling with the songs of mocking birds and canaries, and the crowing of roosters and cackle of fine breeds of chickens, and the squealing of monkies, seem to transport one into a South American forest. The gay plumaged birds from the tropics always to be found in these quaint stores give them a tropical color and beauty that fascinate strangers.

CHAPTER VI.

Rampart Street and Its Vicinity—St. Louis Cemeteries—Congo Square—The Voudoos—The Barefooted Nuns.

North Rampart Street is the handsome Avenue, with a neutral ground shaded by trees, beginning four squares beyond the Rue Royal at Canal Street. It was the ancient limits of the city laid out by Bienville, and was called "Rampart" because a strong redoubt ran along it in old Creole days.

As the city spread beyond its primitive limits, Rampart Street became a fashionable residence avenue. The moat which ran along the center of the neutral ground, or present car track, was filled in, and beautiful shade trees were planted along the way on either side, as far as the intersection of Esplanade Avenue.

Rampart is an interesting street, not only in itself, but on account of the many curious old side streets which cross it, and whose songs and stories read like wild romance in these realistic days. From the quaint old mortuary chapel where Père Antoine used to chant the litany of the dead, to the cloistered monastery, where barefooted nuns, by night and day keep vigils of prayer for the sins of the "Vieux Carré," Rampart Street is full of historic interest and legendary lore.

Though it was such an ancient Creole boundary, as time went on Rampart Street became a fashionable residence quarter, and "Americans," too, sought to have their homes in the old street. On the lake side, just adjoining the large pharmacy on the Canal Street corner, there dwelt for many years, while she made New Orleans her home, Mrs. Sallie Ward Hunt, the famous Kentucky belle of old Southern days. The house may be known by the curious old porch jutting out on the banquette with a spiral iron stairway leading up.

Adjoining it is the home in which the celebrated Madame Octavia Walton Levert, the feminine literary genius, of ante-bellum days, lived when visiting New Orleans.

At 203 North Rampart Street, the Eye, Ear, Nose and Throat Hospital will be observed. At No. 224 is the handsome home of the Young Men's Gymnastic Club. Admission is by card. The club possesses very elaborate marble baths and swimming tanks and a magnificent gymnasium.

The quaint little Church of St. Anthony of Padua stands on the corner of Conti and Rampart Streets. This is the ancient

Mortuary Chapel of Old New Orleans.

There is an old Spanish law still observed in the American colonies that once belonged to Spain, that forbade the burial of the dead from the Cathedral churches. When the Episcopal See of New Orleans was founded in 1793, and the beautiful old edifice erected by Don Almonaster facing the Place d'Armes was advanced to the dignity of a cathedral, it became necessary to have a church for the celebration of services over the dead. This chapel, which is a pure type of the old mortuary chapels of Spain, was built, and dedicated to this purpose. After the close of the Civil War the chapel was diverted from its primitive uses and made a parish church, with Father Turgis, the famous Confederate chaplain of the Pointe Coupée Regiment, as its first pastor. In the curious old house around the corner, with the quaint balcony reaching far out on the sidewalk, Father Turgis lived, and here the survivors of the old regiment used to gather evening after evening to share his humble hospitality and talk over the dead days. After Father Turgis' death the Church was used as a special place of worship for Italians. Recently the Dominican Friars were given charge of it, Rev. Thomas Lorente, lately of St. Thomas University, Manila, being the first Dominican Rector. Many of the foreign customs of the churches in Italy prevail here. The shrine of St. Anthony and St. Bartholomew surrounded by lighted tapers and "ex voto" offerings in thanksgiving for favors received, are peculiarly foreign in appearance.

Just over the way from St. Anthony's Church is an old building erected in 1822 as a synagogue for early Jewish emigrants. Upon the consolidation of the congregation in 1878, with that of the "Dispersed of Judah," who worshiped in the building on Carondelet street, near Julia, above Canal Street, the edifice in Rampart Street was put on the market for sale. It is now used as a laundry.

OLD MORTUARY CHAPEL.

The next corner is St. Louis Street, and right here while doing Rampart Street and its vicinity, the tourist will do well to turn into this ancient thoroughfare, which still bears the name given it by the loyal-hearted Bienville, and view the

Old French Cemeteries.

the first of which, lying at the corner of North Basin, is the oldest cemetery in New Orleans. St. Louis Nos. 2 and 3 are in the immediate vicinity. These are the ancient burying grounds of the old "carré." They are very foreign-looking, very quaint and picturesque. A brief history of each is given in the chapter on "Cemeteries," to which the follower of this Guide is directed to turn at this particular point.

Passing from these ancient cemeteries, where have been sleeping these hundred years the old French and Spanish noblesse who gave to New Orleans its history and name, the tourist again enters St. Louis Street, and at the corner the

"Old Basin,"

with its curious freight of oyster luggers and charcoal schooners, discharging their cargoes, bursts upon the view. The Basin is the terminus of the Carondelet Canal, which was the monumental work of the administration of the Spanish Governor of colonial days, Baron de Carondelet. The "Carondelet Canal" extends from the Old Basin southwest to the Bayou St. John, in the Second District. The banks are called the "Carondelet Walk." The canal was dug by orders of Carondelet for the purpose of draining the vast swamps in the rear of the city. He also thought that by bringing the waters of the Bayou St.

A GLIMPSE OF THE OLD FRENCH CEMETERIES.

John into a "basin" close to the city "ramparts" he would greatly facilitate the commerce of New Orleans. In recognition of his work the "Cabildo" bestowed his name upon the canal and its banks. The Old Basin is large and square, and occupies the area between St. Claude and North Franklin Streets, Carondelet Walk and Toulouse. The canal empties at Hagan Avenue into the Bayou St. John, by which access may be had to Lake Pontchartrain at Spanish Fort. The scene along the canal and basin is at all times picturesque, and exceedingly curious and foreign-looking. It furnishes a frequent theme of study for local and visiting artists.

The New Orleans Terminal Railway, organized to build terminal railway accomodations, that will be used by other roads, recently came into possession of an extensive area of ground in the rear of the City along the Old Basin Canal, extending from Basin Street about twelve or fifteen squares along the Canal. The Railway Company expects to erect here its car yards and warehouses; it has agreed to run a track out Basin Street to Canal and at this point will put up a fine union depot. The Railway Company also expects to build a part of the Public Belt Railroad, along the river front, and will have close connections with other railroads. It has bought up an extensive tract in the Parish of St. Bernard, and expects to build wharves for the loading of grain, cotton, etc., with wharf room for about twenty-five vessels.

The scene along the banks from St. Louis Street to Toulouse, where the Dagoes have their "lugger landing," is particularly unique. From Toulouse it is just one square to Rampart Street, and the tourist finds himself again at his point of departure.

At the southwest corner of Rampart and Toulouse stands a high three-storied brick building, with iron verandas. This was known during the period of the early American domination as the "Café des Ameliorations," and was to the old New Orleans of that day what the famous "Café des Exiles" and the "Café des Enfants Fideles" were to French and Spanish New Orleans of a more remote period. At the "Café des Ameliorations" the old Creole gentlemen discontented and alarmed at the growing power of the "Americans," used to meet and discuss questions for the amelioration of their "dear city," and its rescue from the hands of the invaders. Here they used to weekly concoct plans

DAGO LUGGER LANDING—OLD BASIN.

for the overthrow of the government, the arrest of the State officials, and the assertion of the supremacy of the Creoles. All this reads like a romance now, but it was very real to the Creoles of those days, this question of absolute American domination.

And now you are in that section of New Orleans around which cling wild superstitions and legends of fetich worship, echoes of weird music and visions of ghostly figures dancing the wild "Congo" of their native plains; of negroes gathering in the dead hours of the night while the old Faubourg slumbered on, to work their charms and spells and offer tribute to their idol "The Grand Zombi." For the large open area on the west side of Rampart Street, between St. Peter and St. Ann, is the ancient

Congo Square,

the "Place des Negres," or Negro Square, the great holiday place of the slaves in early Creole and later ante-bellum times; the spot, too, in which by night the awful worship of "the serpent" took place. Sunday evening was the great holiday for the negroes in slavery times; for this one evening they enjoyed almost absolute freedom to go and come as they pleased. On Sunday evenings, therefore, decked in their most gorgeous colors and many of them wearing the cast-off finery of their masters and mistresses, the negroes of both sexes used to assemble by the thousands under the shade of the sycamore trees of the "Congo Plains" as they termed the square and the woods beyond, to dance the wild "Bamboula," or the gay "Calinda, Badoum! Badoum!" Every Sunday afternoon the "Bamboula dancers" were summoned to a woodyard on Dumaine Street, by a sort of drum roll effected by rattling the ends of two huge bones on the head of a cask. The male dancers fastened little bits of tin or metal to ribbons tied about their ankles. These rattles were very much like the strings of copper "gris-gris," worn by the native Soudans. After the Congo Plains were built up the dances were restricted to the square. Of a Sunday evening it presented a most picturesque and animated scene with its hundreds of dusky dancers, singing their quaint half-Congo, half-Creole songs. Hundreds of the best whites, lured by the fascinating, curious rhythm, sung to the beating of the "tan-tam," used to promenade in the vicinity of the square to see the negroes dance "Congo." In the center of the square stood a cannon which was fired promptly at 9 o'clock. This was the signal for dispersal and the revelers would troop merrily homeward, singing as they went, "Bon soir, dansé! Soleil Couché," or "Good night dance; the sun is set! But this did not trouble them much, for they knew the sun would rise next Sunday, after their week's labor was over, and they would have another holiday. Such was the happy, joyous life of the slaves in the old days.

But as might have been already inferred, Congo Square did not always present such an innocent scene of merry, careless pastime. Rather does its name suggest to the natives of the present day the memory of ghostly stories of wild revelry of witches and bacchanals, and of a mysterious fetich worship, so strange, so awful, that for upwards of a hundred years it exerted over the minds of the ignorant of both races, a sway as powerful and tragic as that of witchcraft in the medieaval ages. For in Congo Square were held the weird

Voudoo Rites,

or worship of the serpent. This awful fetich worship was brought to New Orleans by the negro slaves who faithfully followed the fortunes of their masters after the San Domingo revolution. The worship was introduced into Hayti and San Domingo by the Congo negroes who dwelt on the western plains of Africa. The term "Voudoo" is a corruption of the Haytien "vaudaux," softened by the Creole lingo and further corrupted by the negroes into "hoodoo." To be a "Voudoo" was an awful term of reproach among the negroes, for a "Voudoo" was supposed to be in direct communication and league with the spirit of darkness for the propagation of evil. The "Grand Zombi," or serpent, was the peculiar object of worship and was guarded as sacred by their queen and high-priestess, Marie Laveau, "in an exquisitely carved box of alabaster in her own bedchamber." The Voudoos first held their orgies in the Congo Plains, which used to embrace Congo Square. They met at the midnight hour to work their spells, while the French Quarter slept; yet many a master and mistress awoke in the morning happily unconscious of the fact that their favorite slave had perhaps danced with the Voudoos that night. The Voudoos believed Congo Square to be a charmed spot, which the Grand Zombi had chosen for his favorite haunt; and though it has been many, many a year since they have dared to hold a dance there, occasionally some fowl or bird finely roasted with needles and pins stuck all over it, and dimes and nickles arranged around the dish is placed in the middle of the square at the midnight hour, as an offering to the voudoo spirit, and miniature coffins and lighted candles are found on the doorsteps of houses, showing that though the once powerful cult has been rigidly suppressed by law, remnants of its followers still exist in New Orleans. St. John's Eve, June 24, was the great Voudoo festival. After the Congo Plains were laid out into streets, and the square itself placed under such strict police surveillance, the Voudoos used to assemble on the banks of the Bayou St. John, just where the waters meet the dreary swamp land. In this wild and dismal spot they used to erect their altars and sing their weird unearthly chants while they danced the wild "Dance of the Serpent" around the boiling pot. This pot contained bits of the skins of alligators, frogs and snakes from the bayou beyond, pieces of human hair, fingernails and toe nails; the higher the flames leaped in the air the wilder the dance, and when the flickering fire began to die out these skins were laid on the altar of the serpent and then distributed among the Voudoos. They became the famous "gris-gris" charms with which they were supposed to work out their evil designs.

Just around the corner there stood until recently, on St. Ann Street, between Rampart and Burgundy Streets, the ancient homestead of

Marie Laveau, the Voudoo Queen.

For upwards of eighty years this woman was the high priestess of the Voudoos and held them at her beck and call. Though the cult was a secret one, she numbered her followers by the thousands, and only a voudoo knew postively who her associates were. Not that the negroes as a body, were members of this particular sect; on the contrary so great was the terror inspired by the name that to be known as a "Voudoo" was to be ostracized from all intercourse with the respectable colored element, whether free or slaves. Marie Laveau was not a quadroon nor yet a mulatto, she was not as fair as the one nor as dark as the other. But in her youth she was said to have been very tall, majestic and beautiful, and easily swayed her subjects by her magnetic eye. Two years ago the old homestead, built 200 years ago and held together by nails that were veritable spikes, was demolished. Seven generations of Laveaus were born and reared within its walls, for Marie Laveau's mother before her had been the Voudoo Queen, and so had her grandmother. In this home was shown for many years by the Voudoo Queen's only surviving daughter, the famous shawl sent to Marie Laveau by the Emperor of China seventy-five years back. It was of softest silk, and it was in this shawl that tradition says she used to dance the wild "Dance of the Serpent." Marie Laveau died within the last two decades. She repented before her death and died a Christian.

Before leaving this romantic section the tourist should cross to Orleans Street, where just behind the square used to stand the old Parish Prison. For sixty-one years it squatted in gray grandeur, gloomy and forbidding in the square bounded by Orleans, Marais, St. Ann and Tremé Streets. In 1895 the city built a new prison and jail house, in Tulane Avenue, and the old structure was torn down. Many associations were linked with the antiquated prison and there was perhaps no building in the United States to which so varied a criminal history was attached. It was utilized in the sixties as a military prison, and was subsequently the scene of many memorable executions, chief among which was the celebrated

Mafia Lynching

On March 14, 1891, when two Italians were hung outside of the prison and nine others were shot to death in various parts of the building. These men and eight others were charged with the assassination of David C. Hennessy, Superintendent of Police, on October 15, 1890. Of the Italians indicted for the crime nine had been placed upon trial on February 16, and of these the jury, which had been corruptly influenced, acquitted six, a mistrial resulting as to the other three. Of the men lynched five were awaiting trial. The lynching led to international complications, and resulted in the payment by the United States of heavy damages to the relatives of the slaughtered men. The Mafia, it should be said, is a secret society of Italians, Corsicans and Sicilians.

Just beyond the site of the ancient prison the towers of the Tremé Market rise in view. The market was built on a portion of the Congo Plains, and named for Mon. Tremé, a wealthy Creole citizen, who purchased much land in that section when the old wilderness was cleared and cut into streets. The market was intended to supplement the French Market in that section.

The ornate, two-storied brick structure between Dumaine and St. Philip is the Hall of the Union Française. The celebrated French Literary Society, "L'Athénée Louisianais," holds its meetings here.

And now you are away from echoes of old superstitions, in the gay, laughing heart of the social life of the French Quarter of to-day. Over the streets float the echoes of piano and guitar, and the rich voice of some beautiful girl singing that favorite chanson of the old "carré," "Zozo Moquer."

The large two-storied structure standing out upon the banquette in the center of the square on the east side of Rampart Street, between Ursulines and St. Philip, is the ancient home of the Lafitte family. The gallery, with its immense fluted columns, is a typical Southern mansion of later Creole days, as may be noticed all along the Rue Esplanade.

At the corner of Rampart and Hospital streets, diverge one square toward the lake side, and at the corner of Hospital and St. Claude Streets, see the old St. Augustine's Church. This site was formerly an open stretch of land, upon which stood the historic Orleans College. One of the first acts of the American reconstruction, in 1804, was to incorporate by act of Legislature an "English College" for the education of the Creole youth, and to obviate the necessity of sending young men to Paris for higher study as heretofore. Latin, Greek and French were fundamental studies in the institution.

A tradition of the Old Quarter is the memory of Monsieur D'Avezac, who was the first President of the College. He was a great classical scholar and was noted for his translation of Sir Walter Scott's "Marmion" into French. Scott wrote back a beautiful autograph letter telling how pleased he was with the "perfect translation." This letter is religiously preserved by the descendants of Monsieur D'Avezac in New Orleans. Monsieur D'Avezac was so polished in Latin and Greek, and so famous for his ponderous quotations from these languages that his young collegians used to call him "Titus." Monsieur Rochefort, another professor, was noted for his graceful translation of Horace into French. It was the boast of the "Faubourg" that his "boys" used to walk the Quarter quoting the odes so faithfully that even the little "niggers" were imbued with Horace, from hearing their young masters descant so much upon him. Racine and Corneille and the Greek tragedies (translated into beautiful French) were served with breakfast in the French Quarter in the first decade and a half of the nineteenth century. The college had a "day school" for children who were unable to pay board, and a "free or charity department," the pupils of which were chosen by the trustees. The Creole mothers of New Orleans broke up the college. In 1818 Joseph Lakanal, a member of the French Institute, whom Napoleon had appointed President of the Bonaparte Lyceum, came as a refugee to New Orleans and was called to fill a vacancy in the college directorate. Lakanal was an atheist and an ex-priest; this fact became known, and the first public

Meeting of Women in New Orleans

resulted. The pious Creole mothers of New Orleans declared that "They would have no anti-Christ teach their boys: that the trustees of an institution who could appoint such a man were unfit to be intrusted with the education of youth." A mass meeting of citizens was held, as a sequel to the meeting of women; and the demand was made that the trustees rescind their action. These gentlemen persisted and the next day the great majority of the best-paying pupils were withdrawn; in fact, as the old Creoles were proud afterwards of declaring, "there were not sufficient pupils left to pay the salary of even one director." The "day school" also was obliged to close its doors, and as for the "charity contingent," the mothers of these boys also met and sent word to the directors "that they might be poor, but that they were too honest to allow their sons to meet on the same ground as Monsieur Lakanal." So perished the old Orleans College, at which the historian Gayarre, and all the most cultured gentlemen of the early American domination were educated. All that remains today is a remnant of the long old-fashioned "dormitory," now used as a tenement row. "Joseph Lakanal, le Canaille Directeur" is a fragment of an old Creole chanson composed in derision of the College d'Orleans at the time it fell into disfavor. Lakanal was given a famous "charavari," and finding his presence so odious to New Orleans, he left the city. Then a new verse commemorating his departure was added to the old song. Upon the site of the college there rose a few years later St. Augustine's Church, the second oldest in the French Quarter. It is very quaint and beautiful and remaining just as when erected, is worth a visit.

Just back of the Church was erected in 1836, Mount Carmel Convent for

The Higher Education of Young Ladies.

The Sisterhood is a local foundation and the school has always enjoyed the patronage of the best Creole families. Almost all the Sisterhood are native Creoles. An interesting bit of history is that the Sisters seeing the demoralization prevailing among the quadroons and octoroons at the time of their foundation, sought to stem the current by establishing a "Pension des Demoiselles de Couleur" as a separate and distinct department. In this colored department the children of the free colored people were taught reading, writing, sewing, embroidery, fancy work and music, along with thorough moral and religious training. They returned to their homes educated, accomplished and filled with the purity and truth of life inculcated in the old convent, and many of these women are most active workers in charity and philanthropic effort among their race in New Orleans to-day. When the war was over the old "Pension des Demoiselles de Couleur" was closed forever.

Returning to Rampart Street, around the corner, near Dauphine Street, is "La Maison Hospitalière," a home founded by Creole ladies after the war, for reduced gentlewomen.

The large brick building passed on the way back to Rampart Street, is McDonogh No. 15 School, formerly the ancient Barracks School.

It is very beautiful with its great galleries, spacious rooms and lofty ceilings. The courtyard is very quaint and pretty. For many years the building stood as a type of the early public school buildings of the city. Some years ago it was renovated and enlarged through the McDonogh Public School Fund, and the new name bestowed upon it. The ancient characteristics of the school were, however, retained in the repairing and enlarging. The school is interesting to the visitor as being patronized solely by the French-speaking children and those of the other Latin races that have poured into New Orleans. In this respect McDonogh No. 15 is unique among the public schools of the city.

And now you are at the end of the old Creole street. It seems a strange coincidence that the old "Ramparts," whose first building was a church over a hundred years ago, should in these later days, harbor at its further end another church or chapel on the grounds of the dim

Cloistered Monastery of Discalced Carmelites.

The Monastery stands at the corner of Barracks and Rampart Streets. There are only four convents of this order in America. The one in New Orleans was founded by two cultured Creole ladies. The nuns lead the most rigorous life, wearing sackcloth next their skin, going barefooted the year round and eating nothing but vegetables and fruit. The order is a strictly cloistered one. From the moment a Carmelite pronounces her vows she never again looks upon the faces of friends. Visitors are only admitted to the chapel, or to the little reception room in the old courtyard. They may speak to the lay or outer sisters, and also to the cloistered ones if they desire prayers for themselves or others; but the cloistered nuns sit behind a grating over which a heavy black veil is nailed, and you only hear their voices, sweet and low, exhorting you to patience in trials and afflictions and greater confidence in the mercy of God.

At the Matin and Vesper Services, which are sung daily, the invisible nuns, within the grating, use the solemn Gregorian chant of ancient Catholic Rome, which is only in one key.

Across Esplanade Avenue, where the great, white building stands, called "St. Aloysius Commercial Institue," begins the new "Rampart" Street, laid out many years after the foundation of New Orleans, by Mandeville de Marigny, when he cut up his old plantation into streets and lots. It was called by him the Rue Amour or Love Street. In recent years by an act of the City Council seeking to reduce order out of the multiplicity of the names of the streets running parallel through the various old "Faubourgs," or "municipalities," and to simplify the arrangement of the city map, Love was made a continuation of Rampart Street. The old name still holds, however, with ancient residents of the "Faubourg Marigny."

CHAPTER VII.

The "New Rampart Street"—The Ursuline Convent—The Barracks, Chalmette Monument and Battlefield.

Though it is called the "New Rampart Street," it is full of historic interest. The Rampart car, which may be taken as the visitor completes the tour of ancient Rampart Street, just at the intersection of the Rue Esplanade, or in Canal Street, if a day is reserved for such important points of interest as the Ursuline Convent, the United States Barracks or the Chalmette Monument and Battle Field, carries the tourist through the heart of the old City of Mandeville de Marigny. The car runs down Dauphine Street and returns by way of Rampart to Canal. At the corner of Esplanade and Dauphine Street is a fine old

ANCIENT SUN DIAL—URSULINE CONVENT.

colonial house which is now occupied by Mr. Charles Claiborne, a grandson of the first American Governor of Louisiana.

Near the corner of Union and Dauphine stands the "Ecole des Orphelins Indigens." This was the first free school ever opened for negro children in the United States. In 1840 an old free colored woman died and left to the Catholic archdiocese a fund in trust, for the establishment of a free school for colored orphan children, and directed that her old home, which stood on the spot, should be used as a schoolhouse. Some years ago the old landmark of ante-bellum days was torn down, but the school, which had a continuous existence since its foundation in 1840, has endured.

Between Frenchman and Elysian Fields Streets lies Washington Square, the first public recognition given in New Orleans to the illustrious Father of His Country. The park is inclosed. Formerly all the parks were similarly inclosed, and at night, promptly at 9 o'clock, the watchmen cleared the park and locked the gates. The custom still maintains at Washington Square.

Just across from the square is a large, brown, two-storied brick building; this was the ancient residence of Governor Claiborne. His descendants still live in this beautiful old home.

At Washington Square the car crosses

¡Elysian Fields Street.

or the "Champs Elysées," as it was called by the old Creoles. What visions of Parisian splendor rise to mind at the mere mention of "Les Champs Elysées." In early days the famous old Marigny Canal ran along the street from the Mississippi River to Lake Pontchartrain. When Marigny decided to build his own city and cut up all his plantation domain into streets, he laid out this wide avenue and called it the "Champs Elysées." Trees were planted all along the canal; beautiful sailing boats were always to be found in the waters. He intended that the New Orleans Champs Elysées should rival its famous Parisian namesake. Seeing the advantages offered by the street, the American Company which contemplated the erection of the old St. Charles Hotel offered to erect the famous hostelry in this street if they could secure the section lying between Dauphine and Burgundy Streets. But Marigny said that the Champs Elysées was for the children of France and asked such a fabulous price for the lot that the Company finding it above all consideration in sheer disgust purchased the square above Canal Street, where after many years was erected the old St. Charles Hotel. Alas! for the dreams of the colonial magnate. The "Champs Elysées" is now a railroad street, frequently used for parking cars, and none of the grandeur that its founder intended for it ever materialized. From the car window may be seen toward the Levee the depot of the Pontchartrain Railroad.

It may interest visitors to know that this is

The Second Oldest Railroad in the United States,

and that along its line, after the canal, which had been drained, was gradually filled in, were erected the first freight platforms ever used. It is a curious fact that in the old days when the engine could not generate sufficient steam, sails were attached to the cars to assist in propelling the train. This may read like a fairy tale, but its veracity was vouched for by such authoritative eye-witnesses as the late historian Gayarre the old Notary Guyol, and others. The Pontchartrain Railroad still bearing its ancient name, though owned by the Louisville and Nashville Company, runs along Elysian Fields to the old town of Milneburg, which stands on the banks of the "Old Lake," which was the only lake resort of early Creole days.

Next the corner of Dauphine and Elysian Fields is an ancient "Calaboose," or prison, which was erected when the Faubourg Marigny was a distinct municipality.

At the corner of Elysian Fields and Burgundy Streets stands the Elysium Theatre, recently erected at a cost of $30,000.

At St. Ferdinand Street the car reaches the terminus of the old French Faubourg, and there begins that thrifty and interesting "German Settlement," which did so much for the building up along industrial lines of this section of New Orleans. The settlement extends far out to the verge of St. Roch Cemetery, and towards the Barracks far into Clouet and Montegut Streets, where another distinct French settlement begins, consisting of later settlers who established here their little farms and truck gardens and supplied the French Quarter with vegetables.

The Holy Trinity Church of which Father Thevis founder of St. Roch's Chapel was for many years pastor is near the corner of St. Ferdinand and Dauphine. The customs of old German Catholic countries still maintain in this church.

At 3029 Dauphine Street is the Benedictine Convent of the Holy Family. The sisterhood was driven out of Germany after the Franco-Prussian war when Bismarck enacted the May laws. New Orleans ever friendly to the exile offered it an asylum and its work has been marked by continuous progress and prosperity.

At Press Street the car crosses the tracks of the Queen and Crescent Railroad. All this section, extending along the road from the river front to Rampart and down Dauphine and Royal for several squares, was once the

Great Cotton Press Section

of New Orleans. Here, the year round, in season and out of season, could be seen thousands of bales of the fleecy staple piled so high one above another along the sidewalks and through the extensive cotton yards that it seemed as though all the world of cotton had come to New Orleans to find a market. These were the busy days when "Cotton was King." It was stored and pressed here in immense quantities until the Queen and Crescent Railroad came and ran its line right through the heart of the old presses and pickeries and in time acquired all this ground; the great brick-walled presses were torn down, and all that remains of the old yards are the long line of sheds under which cotton was formerly stored in the famous Natchez Press. These now serve for car sheds.

The handsome edifice on Dauphine Street, between Clouet and Montegut Streets, is St. Vincent de Paul's Church, which was erected some thirty-five years ago on the site of the little frame chapel that did duty for a church in this section fifty years ago.

On Piety Street, near Dauphine, is the Mount Carmel Female Orphan Asylum, established sixty-three years ago. On the corner of North Peters and Reynes Streets, clearly seen from the car, is St. Isidore's College, a large educational institution under the direction of the Congregation of the Holy Cross. It was opened in 1879 as an industrial school and model farm, and is closely modeled upon the famous school of the Fathers of the Holy Cross, at Notre Dame, Ind.

The ancient

Ursuline Convent

is situated on North Peters, between Manuel and Sister Streets, but the plantation extends from the banks of the Mississippi to the woods. At Manuel Street the Rampart cars cut through the grounds, the sisters having granted the right of way. A neat little waiting place and porter's lodge marks this rear and most convenient entrance to the grounds. A paved walk leads up to St. Ursula's Hall, a modern building, in which the reception rooms of the Convent are located. A few steps further from the river banks, the full beauty of the old historic edifice bursts upon you. The Convent occupies an immense area upon which are several buildings, all communicating with one another, and with a beautiful chapel at the lower end. The main building faces the river. It is very imposing with gables and towers and broad galleries; it is always robed in white and forms a prominent landmark for mariners. The Ursulines nuns were the pioneers of the religious orders of women in the New World and the pioneer educators of women. The sisters were invited to come to New Orleans by Bienville and arrived in 1727. Their school established that same year in Chartres Street, was the oldest institution for the education of young ladies in America. It is with pride that the people of New Orleans point to the old Convent and tell of the work of the Ursulines in Louisiana. For upwards of a hundred years they were the only teachers of girls, the only nurses in hospital and on battlefield, the moulders of the virtues that formed the groundwork of the sacred sanctuary of the home. Our historians are proud to acknowledge that "they were the spiritual mothers of the mothers of Louisiana." Such early Presidents as Thomas Jefferson and Andrew Jackson publicly and in autograph letters preserved in the old Convent told of the debt that the people owed these pioneers. The nuns removed to their present domicile in 1824. Their library contains over 10,000 volumes and the most ancient archives in Louisiana, are the records of their order. They were the first historians of the State, and the daily diary kept by one of their nuns, "Madeleine Hauchard," from the time the sisters set sail from France down through a period of over thirty-eight years, is the only record extant in Louisiana of this early period. It is written in a most vivacious and entertaining style. The grand old halls of the convent are most interesting, and no sight is more picturesque than the old Spanish courtyard, the most beautiful in New Orleans, surrounded by stately arcades and arches and quaint colonnades. The chapel of "Our Lady of Prompt Succor," which is reached from the river entrance to the curious old peaked-roofed building where the chaplain resides, was erected in 1824. The chapel contains handsome altars.

and a statue of "Our Lady of Prompt Succor," which was carved way back in 1700, and brought to New Orleans by the sisters when they came to found their beautiful work. The statue is of wood richly gilded and carved and represents the Virgin and Child. The solemn coronation of this statue took place in 1895. The crowns, which were the gift of the people, are of solid gold, magnificently studded with precious stones and are valued at $20,000. The work of the Ursulines runs as a golden thread throughout the history of Louisiana. For nearly one hundred and fifty years, every incident of note was in some measure connected with their earnest efforts, and their influence has always been exercised for good; so much so, that every report of Governors of early days insists upon the fact that one might "as well try to establish a government without funds as to do without sisters."

Recently the old Convent celebrated its one hundredth and seventy-sixth commencement. Year in and year out, in sunshine and shadow, as the history of the city ran, the Convent has sent out its laurel-wreathed graduates to reflect credit upon its ancient name. Still do the invitations to these exclusive occasions

URSULINE CONVENT.

announce "Le Couronnement de la Sagasse," or the "Crowning of Wisdom," This simple term, so beautiful and expressive, as compared to the somewhat dubious word "Commencement," so commonly in vogue, illustrates perhaps, in a forcible manner, the reason why, throughout New Orleans, there is so much significance in the names of places, streets, objects, as applied by the early colonists and retained to this day. The Ursulines were the teachers of the women of Louisiana, and the women made the homes; here the sure foundations laid by the nuns, bore fruit and later found expression in the life and thought of the people.

A few squares further on is the old Church of St. Maurice, lying over towards the woods. It is the parish church of upper St. Bernard Parish.

The next point of interest below the city is the Slaughter House. It is just across the lower boundary line of Orleans Parish, in St. Bernard. The slaughtering pens, or abattoirs, are in full operation about 3 o'clock p. m., and are usually interesting to visitors. Adjacent to the abattoirs are the pens where the cattle are confined pending execution. Most of the cattle received and butchered here come from Texas. The butchers are, for the most part, Gascons, who speak the language of the Lower Pyrenees.

The United States Barracks,

officially known as the Jackson Barracks, are at the terminus of the Rampart cars. The entrance, which is in a sort of network in the river front, is between two heavy brick towers over fifty years old. The Barracks buildings are disposed around the parade ground, and the whole is inclosed in thick brick walls. The corners of the walls are defended by towers pierced for musketry. Every evening the twilight gun is fired, the soldiers salute the flag in the center of the grass plot, and the nation's symbol is then hauled down for the night.

The Battle Field of Chalmette,

where General Jackson on January 8, 1815, won his famous victory over the British, is about a mile and a half from the Barracks. It may be reached by a carriage drive along the river front; but on a pleasant day the walk is enjoyable. Intelligence that the British Government had fitted out an expedition which was intended for the capture of New Orleans and Mobile reached the authorities at Washington, December 9, 1814, and the President directed the Governors of Kentucky, Tennessee and Georgia to dispatch their militia to New Orleans. General Andrew Jackson went to the city to take charge of the defense. He promptly organized his forces. The Creoles gallantly enlisted. Jackson also enrolled convicts and free men of color. With the volunteers from other neighboring States, his force was speedily swelled to 5,000 men, of whom less than 1,000 were regulars. The British Army was in command of General Pakenham. It was composed of 7,000 picked soldiers, including veterans who had served under Wellington, and a portion of the British Chesapeake force under Admiral Cochrane. They were transported in fifty large vessels, and anchored off the entrance to Lake Borgne in the latter part of December. A meager flotilla of American gunboats opposed their landing, but it was speedily and effectually dispersed. The enemy took full possession of Lake Borgne, and effecting a landing an Ship Island crossed to the Northwestern end of Lake Borgne, and on Dec. 25 struck the Mississippi about nine miles below New Orleans. The British believed that their near approach was unsuspected, but Major Villere, who resided at Corinne Plantation warned General Jackson. The latter, supported by two armed vessels, took a small portion of his force and boldly attacked the enemy on the evening of Dec. 24. He succeeded in doing little else than showing the British that he was prepared to make a gallant defense. On December 28 Pakenham returned General Jackson's attack, but being unable to break the American lines recoiled before the effective artillery fire of the Americans. Nothing was then done for nearly two weeks. In that interval General Jackson was reinforced by 2,000 Kentuckians under General Adair. Of this number 700 were marched to the front. The British also were reinforced by a detachment under General Lambert, one of Wellington's officers. This brought up their number to 10,000. On the morning of January 8, 1815, the battle of New Orleans was fought. General Pakenham made a desperate effort to carry the American position. The Americans were drawn up within five miles of the city, along the banks of Rodriguez Canal and the Chalmette Plantation. The defense extended from the river back to the swamps. The British occupied a position between the Chalmette and Villere Plantations, and their field works extended to the old Bienville Plantation. The attack began at dawn and lasted till 8 o'clock. It began with artillery fire under cover of which Pakenham advanced with the main body of his troops. The Americans withheld their fire till the enemy was within 200 yards. Then volley after volley was fired with marvellous precision. The slaughter was tremendous. The attack was renewed repeatedly, but with no better results. General Pakenham was mortally wounded and was borne off the field to the plantation of Major Villere, where he died. General Gibbs, the second in command, was also mortally wounded, and General Keane upon whom the command then devolved was disabled by a shot in the neck. General Lambert then assumed command. He abandoned the attack, withdrew to the ships, and on the following day retreated to Lake Borgne. The British loss has been conservatively estimated at

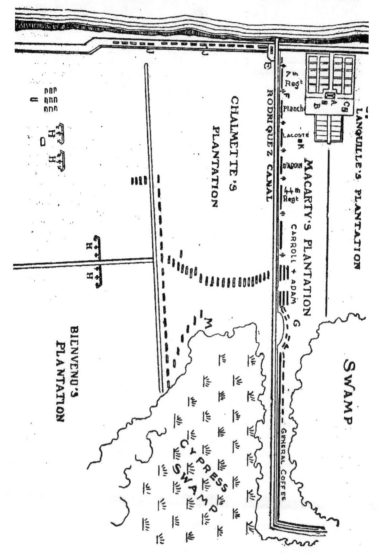

MISSISSIPPI RIVER

MAP OF BATTLE FIELD OF NEW ORLEANS, JAN. 8, 1815.

A—Jackson's Headquarters. B, C, D—American Cavalry. E—American Redoubt. F—Laffite's Pirates. G—Adair's Position. H—British Batteries. J—Part of British Attack. K—Monument. M—Pakenham killed.

2,000, of whom less than 500 were taken prisoners. The American loss was 8 killed and 13 wounded.

The Chalmette Monument

marks the place where the battle was fought. It stands on the grounds of the ancient Chalmette Plantation, which was laid out by M. Chalmette de Ligny, the ancestor of one of the oldest families in Louisiana. The erection of the monument was begun between 1830 and 1840, under an appropriation from the State. When the shaft reached the height of 60 feet the money was exhausted and the work abandoned. The monument has been placed by a State enactment under the care of the Daughters of 1776-1812. The Association intends to petition Congress for funds to complete the monument as the victory of the Battle of New Orleans was a national one.

CHALMETTE MONUMENT.

Adjoining the monument site, is a fine old colonial building. In the year 1815 it was the residence of Mr. Montgomery, a wealthy merchant. It was here that General Jackson made his headquarters during the battle. This historic house, lately owned and occupied by Judge René Beauregard, son of the famous Confederate General, has lately come into possession of the New Orleans Terminal Railway Company, which has bought up extensive tracts for terminal facilities in the Parish. The old mansion is now unoccupied.

It was here that the Marquis de Lafayette was first received when he visited New Orleans early in the century. He landed in a small boat immediately in front of the house, and was received in a room on the second floor by the then Governor, Mayor and principal officials.

Further on is the old Villere plantation, where General Pakenham breathed his last.

The property now called the Corinne Plantation is owned by The New Orleans Railway Company. General Pakenham was buried beneath an immense pecan tree near the old mansion house. At his side was laid Colonel Dale of the Ninety-third Highlanders. The pecan tree still bears fruit, and curiously enough, while the meat of all the pecans on the plantation is the usual white and brown, the fruit of this particular tree is a deep red. The negroes have an old tradition that the blood of Pakenham saturated the soil of the tree under which he was buried, and this percolating through the roots of the tree, caused the fruit to be dyed with his blood. You could not persuade one of the negro slaves for miles around to eat one of the pecans from that tree. A short distance further down will be found the beautiful

Chalmette Cemetery.

The United States purchased, in 1865, a portion of the old battle field and converted it into this lovely burial place. The grounds, covered with hundreds of little white marble headstones, each marking the grave of some unknown

JACKSON'S HEADQUARTERS DURING THE BATTLE OF NEW ORLEANS.

soldier killed in the Civil War, are laid out in a tasteful manner, with shelled walks and avenues of trees. The earthworks outside the walls of the cemetery were erected by the Confederates during the Civil War as part of the defenses of the city.

A mile below the cemetery is the terminal of the New Orleans and Western Railway, known as Port Chalmette. It is owned by an English syndicate and represents an investment of $2,000,000. Port Chalmette may be reached by the Shellbeach train, whose depot is at the corner of St. Claude and Elysian Fields Streets.

Returning from the battle grounds of Chalmette by the Rampart and Dauphine car, just after the curve in Poland Street, where the car station stands, are the old grounds of the "Macarty Square." The grounds are named for an ancient Franco-Irish family that followed the fortunes of the Bourbons, and came as exiles to New Orleans.

Overlooking the square is the handsome McDonogh No. 12 public school.

At the corner of Independence and Rampart Streets is the Convent of the Marianites of the Holy Cross, a sisterhood which, having its mother house in France, was called to New Orleans some sixty-eight years ago to assist in the education of youth.

Two squares from Rampart Street, and easily seen from the cars, there stands at the corner of Marais and Mandeville Streets the little old French Church of the Annunciation, erected over fifty years ago for the French-speaking people of the Faubourg Marigny. It is in the old French style of architecture, as also the portion of the quaint presbytery, now the residence of Rt. Rev. Gustave A. Rouxel, auxiliary bishop of New Orleans. The beautiful old-fashioned garden, with its little shrine of Our Lady of Lourdes, is well worth a visit.

Adjoining are the handsome convent building, school and chapel of the Sisters of Perpetual Adoration, an exiled order of nuns from Alsace and Lorraine, who came to New Orleans after the German occupation. The chapel is very beautiful. Night and day, at all hours, there are always two sisters kneeling and keeping watch before the "Blessed Sacrament;" hence the name, "Perpetual Adoration," which distinguishes the community.

At the corner of Rampart and Kerlerec Streets is the hall of the "Etoile Polaire," or Polar Star, the home of a Masonic Lodge, which existed in New Orleans in Père Antoine's day, and which celebrated the one hundredth anniversary of its organization several years ago. Riding thence to Canal Street, the circuit of the French Quarter is completed,

<hr>

CHAPTER VIII.

Front, Lower Chartres and Esplanade.

The Levee and Barracks car, which may be taken just before the Custom-house, on Canal Street, will afford a fine view of the entire Lower Levee front, the shipping in port as far as the rue d'Enghien, when the car curves around into the ancient Moreau (now Chartres) Street of the old Faubourg Marigny. Between Port and St. Ferdinand, the car passes a long row of fine old brick buildings, now, for the most part, alas! degenerated in the social scale to the rank of cheap lodging-houses and Italian fruit vendors' establishments. But this square was, in its day, the most aristocratic of the old Faubourg Marigny; each house was a mansion in itself, and the tall, brick buildings annexed in the long rows in the rear were quarters of the household slaves that served in the exclusive families of the Notts, Kennedys, Dolhondes and others, who were the owners of the soil. Receptions seeking to rival the palmiest days of the "Vieux Carré" were given in these homes. At the corner of St. Ferdinand and Chartres stand the old Kennedy and Nott mansions. Adjoining was a famous and exclusive "Creole Pension." It was here that General Joseph Wheeler, the "Fighting Joe of the Confederacy," and his beautiful wife stopped when they visited New Orleans in 1866, immediately after the war.

Just around the corner, in the ancient rue Casa Calvo, now a continuation of Royal Street, is another fine row of old houses, three stories in height; in one of these, 2712, Mme. Beauregard, mother of the famous Louisiana hero, lived when she was a young girl. One of the most beautiful old courtyards in New Orleans lies hidden from the street, in the rear of this ancient home.

At the corner of Chartres and Mazant streets, St. Mary's Orphan Boys' Asylum, an immense brick pile erected nearly sixty years ago for the accommodation of the orphan boys of the city, stands. This institution is in charge of the Sisters Marianites of the Holy Cross. Since the first days of its erection it has seldom harbored less than 400 boys at a time, ranging in all ages from babyhood to fifteen and over. Some of the best citizens of New Orleans have been reared in this asylum.

At Poland Street the car diverges to the station.

The Esplanade and French Market Line may be taken in front of the Custom-house, at the corner of Canal Street; at Villere Street a transfer is given to the Esplanade Avenue car.

At the intersection of Esplanade and the Levee the car turns into the fine old avenue, the historic residence portion of the city in later Creole days. It is one of the most beautiful streets in New Orleans, and is to the Creoles what St. Charles Avenue is to the Americans—the aristocratic residence street. The avenue, through its entire length, from the river to the Bayou St. John, is lined on either side of the car tracks with a continuous row of shade trees, which makes the street very pretty and attractive. The homes in the avenue are the center of Creole culture and refinement; fine old furnishings of the Louis Quatorze style adorn the interiors. Many romantic stories cluster about these homes, and it is here, if you are so fortunate as to have a friend who can gain you admittance to the exclusive society of the old French Quarter, that you will see Creole beauty and society at its best.

At 704 Esplanade Avenue, corner of Royal Street, is a fine old brick mansion; this is the home of Mr. R. M. O'Brien, brother of the late Colonel Patrick O'Brien, who recently left a legacy of $150,000 to the Catholic University of America, and erected, at a cost of $45,000, the beautiful new Church of the

HOME FOR THE AGED—LITTLE SISTERS OF THE POOR—WOMAN'S DEPARTMENT.

Sacred Heart, in Canal Street, New Orleans, and, besides, left numerous benefactions to charity, irrespective of creed.

The large, three-storied brick building at the corner of Esplanade Avenue and North Rampart Street, is St. Aloysius Commercial College. The building was erected by the Ursuline Nuns some twenty-five years ago at a cost of $75,000, and subsequently sold to the Brothers of the Sacred Heart for school purposes.

At the corner of St. Claude and Esplanade, just one square further on, is another beautiful and imposing brick structure, with an old Roman portico. This is the residence recently purchased by the Catholics of New Orleans for the Archbishops of the diocese. The hall, laid in marble mosaic, is an exact reproduction of the famous Pompeiian Hall in Rome. The house was built by a wealthy merchant some fifty years ago, at a cost of $175,000, and was the home of Captain Cuthbert Slocomb, of the famous Washington Artillery, who served nobly in the Civil War.

The handsome brick church on the lower side of Esplanade Avenue, between Marais and Villere, is

St. Anna's Episcopal Church.

It occupies the site of a frame church which was erected in 1869 at a cost of $10,000, by Dr. Mercer, in memory of his only child, Anna. This building was destroyed by fire in 1876. Through the insurance and subscriptions which he obtained from friends, Dr. Girault, who was then rector, began the erection of the present edifice, the cornerstone of which was laid in March, 1877. The church freed from debt, was consecrated in 1886. The total cost was $15,000. Dr. Girault died in 1889, and was succeeded by the present rector, Dr. E. W. Hunter. Dr. Hunter is a Prayer Book Churchman, and, while the services at St. Anna's are, by no means, ritualistic, the Church stands in the City as the representative of the High Church School of Thought. The parish is one of the oldest in the diocese, having resulted from a mission begun in 1846. In this parish was begun the first organized effort to provide seamen with religious worship, it having been originally called St. Peter's Church for Seamen. Since 1890, many improvements have been made, among them the purchase of a handsome rectory in Esplanade Avenue and the erection of a Chapel, in memory of the Right Rev. John Nicholas Gallegher, S. T. D.

At 1631 Esplanade Avenue is the residence in which General P. G. T. Beauregard died.

Within sight of the Esplanade Avenue car, as it reaches the corner of Johnson Street, is the "Home for the Aged and Infirm," conducted by the Little Sisters of the Poor. The building, a large, three-storied brick structure, stands within beautiful grounds at the corner of Laharpe and Johnson streets, within two squares of Esplanade. Nearly three hundred old men and women, all over sixty, and many reaching far into the nineties, are cared for here by this

HOME FOR THE AGED—LITTLE SISTERS OF THE POOR— MEN'S DEPARTMENT.

gentle sisterhood. Everyone in New Orleans knows the "Little Sisters" as they go about, from day to day, in their great black capes and hoods, begging food and clothing for their helpless old charges. A visit to the institution is both interesting and instructive. The home is the old down-town counterpart of the great building on Prytania Street, in the up-town section of the city. At this latter institution 200 old men and women are the wards of these faithful nuns. Both of these magnificent "Homes for the Aged" were erected through the tireless efforts of the "Little Sisters."

BAYOU ST. JOHN.

The small triangle, containing a beautiful fountain in terra cotta, on the avenue, between Miro and Tonti Streets, is the Gayarre Place, so named for Louisiana's illustrious historian.

At 2410 Esplanade Avenue, in a square of ground exquisitely laid out in flowers and tropical palms is the home of Hon. Paul Capdevielle, the

Present Mayor of New Orleans.

This fine old mansion with its stately porticoes, broad galleries and spacious surroundings, is a fine type of the later Creole style of architecture. It was built in 1857 by Pierre Soulé, United States Senator and American Ambassador to Spain. Mr. Soulé occupied it from January to June of that year. Mr. Capdevielle, who sbsequently purchased the place, has greatly beautified it. His home is the center of the culture and hospitality that made old New Orleans distinctive among the cities of the South and of the Union. The home is easily recognized by the beautiful fountain playing in the avenue that leads up to the main entrance, and by the stately magnolia trees, twined with ivy, which surround the garden on all sides. A little further on, between Crete and Bell Streets, is a beautiful little garden plot called Capdevielle Park, in honor of the Mayor.

The Greek Church of the Holy Trinity is on a street known both as Dolhonde and Dorgenois, within view of Esplanade Avenue. Services are not held regularly. The ornaments on the altar were presented by the late Empress of Russia.

The Jockey Club is on Esplanade Avenue, near Bayou Bridge. It was a private residence and occupies a whole square of ground on the lower side of the street. It is one of the most attractive spots in New Orleans. The house is of the French style of architecture and opens upon a beautiful terrace. In one of the wings is a bowling alley. The mansion stands in the midst of a garden. On gala occasions these gardens used to be illuminated with Chinese lanterns and electric lights, presenting a scene of enchanting beauty. Admission is by card from members.

In the rear, and a little to one side of the Jockey Club, are the Fair Grounds. These contain a race course, and grandstand capable of seating 8,000 people. Horse racing takes place here annually, there being a winter meeting of over 100 days, conducted by the Crescent City Jockey Club, followed by a spring meeting of six days under the auspices of the New Louisiana Jockey Club, in which the best horses and most famous jockeys participate. The

VIEW IN CITY PARK.

course was formerly called the Gentilly Race Course. During the season the cars run directly to the course, depositing passengers at the entrance. The race track is esteemed one of the best and fastest in the United States. As the name implies, the Fair Grounds were laid out and devoted for many years to the annual exposition of Louisiana industries in the form of a State Fair. For some years, however, the State Fairs have been discontinued. The reunión of United Confederate Veterans will be held at the Fair Grounds May 19, 1902. The acceptance of the invitation to come to New Orleans necessitated the immediate erection of an immense Auditorium, which will be located near the center of the grounds, just beyond the grand stand. It will cost from $12.000 to $15,000, and will have a seating capacity of about 15,000, while the spacious grounds and other buildings will afford ample room for entertainment.

Adjoining the Jockey Club Grounds is the new St. Louis Cemetery. Some of the tombs are very handsome.

On Bayou St. John, 300 yards from Esplanade, will be found the Soldiers' Home, or Camp Nicholls, as it is sometimes called. It derives the latter apcellation from Ex-Governor F. T. Nicholls, under whose administration it was founded as a retreat for maimed and disabled Confederates. The place is noted for the beauty of its gardens.

Crossing Bayou Bridge, it may interest the tourist to know that he is in the immediate vicinity of the spot where Bienville effected his first landing on Louisiana soil, when he came across Lake Pontchartrain and down the Bayou in 1718. It is not possible to identify the exact spot now. Some curious old shipyards lie along the Bayou, one of which, at least, dates from Spanish days.

The Louisiana Boat Club and the Crescent Boat Club have quarters on the bank, and hold an annual regatta here.

During the year 1904, a Country Club House, to cost approximately $15,000, is to be erected by the St. John Land Company on Bayou St. John near the Esplanade Avenue Bridge.

The handsome oaks of Southern Park, a picnic resort, will be noticed along the route.

LAKE—CITY PARK.

Bayou St. John,

named for Bienville's patron saint, is one of the most picturesque and historic spots in the city. It was on the banks of this bayou that Le Page du Pratz, the first Louisiana historian, built his pretty villa. He came to New Orleans in 1718 to cast his fortune with the infant colony. It was on this Bayou that his life was miraculously saved by a beautiful Indian girl, who became devotedly attached to his service and who gave him the thread of the wonderful traditions and songs of Louisiana that he has so beautifully woven into fact and fiction. As the colony grew, the most aristocratic families of the ancient colony had their summer villas on the Bayou St. John, and here and there, nestling amid the tropical palms and foliage, one still catches a glimpse of these olden villas, alas! falling into decay. The banks of the Bayou are fringed with palmettos and plantain trees, and the tall "Spanish Dagger," whose beautiful white blossoms, rising in pyramidal clusters, are the wonder and delight of the tourist

CITY PARK—ALONG THE BRIDGEWAY.

in the early summer and late spring. The Bayou is very mysterious and is crowded with a dense growth as it merges into the lake. It was in these sylvan solitudes that the "Voudoos" used to hold their bacchanalian festivals on the night of St. John's Eve.

City Park.

The park was once a wooded plantation, and contains 216.60 acres, only a portion of which, however, has been improved. The grove of live oaks are the wonder and admiration of botanists and scientists. These live oaks are said to be the finest in the world. The trees are draped in the ghostly gray Spanish moss, to which allusion is so frequently made by Louisiana poets. The lake was formed artificially by enlarging Bayou Sauvage, which formerly ran through the park. Under one of the oak trees stands a tomb in saddest decay. It is the last resting place of Louis Allard, a man of letters and a poet, who owned all that tract of land extending from the Bayou St. John to the Orleans Canal, and from the Metairie Road to the old toll-gate. The portion which is called the "Lower City Park," was sold by Allard, previous to his death, to John McDonogh, the millionaire miser-philanthropist, of old New Orleans. At his death, McDonogh left it by will to the cities of New Orleans and Baltimore; the City of New Orleans acquired it in full ownership at the partition sale, and decided to devote it to park purposes. Allard, who was then very poor, was

ANOTHER VIEW OF THE LAKE CITY PARK.

permitted, by special agreement, after the mortgage sale to continue to live at the place. He spent his declining days under his beloved oaks, dreaming of the past and reading his favorite authors. In compliance with his dying wish he was buried in this quiet spot under his favorite oak. The tomb is in full view coming from the Metairie Road. Glance obliquely to the left and the legendary oaks on the

Famous Dueling Ground

of old New Orleans rise in solemn grandeur.

Their green boughs throw back the sunlight with all the brightness and elasticity of everlasting youth, and the whispering leaves tell of a time, scarcely fifty years remote, when tragedy and gayety walked side by side in New Orleans, and it was an every day occurrence to see under those very branches a meeting of adversaries in mortal combat, with pistol, saber or shotgun, or "colichemard."

A thousand stories are told of the bloody encounters which took place in the early morning under the "Oaks." There was no compromise with honor in those days; society did not permit it. With the advent of Napoleon's disbanded legions and noble "emigrés" from France, there was a great renaissance in duels, and fencing masters were kept busy teaching the "jeunesse doré" in the ancient "Salle de St. Philippe." Among the most famous masters were Marcel Dauphin, who was killed in a duel by another master, Bonneval, who was wounded by the professional swordsman, Reynard; L'Alouette, who killed Shubra, another professor; Thimecourt, who killed the famous Italian fencing master, Poulaga, and Gilbert Rosiere, called by his pupils " 'Tit Rosiere," the most popular of all the fencing masters who ever came to New Orleans. But the most famous of all was Pepe Llula; of him the most wonderful stories were told, but the following will suffice:

It happened that New Orleans was all aflame with sympathy for the filibusters who had made an unsuccessful attempt to free Cuba from the control of Spain. Pepe was an ardent Spanish partisan, and issued a manifesto, challenging all the Cuban sympathizers. Many of them took up the glove. Pepe met them, and, making use of a thrust for which he was famous—driving his

PATHWAY ALONG THE LAKE —CITY PARK.

colichemard into the lung and giving it a vicious twist there—killed each of his antagonists. The result was that after a while the Cubans refused to meet him.

What a troop of ghostly stories come up under the "Oaks!" Every imaginable cause of quarrel was settled under these ancient trees. Some slight infringement of ballroom etiquette, a quarrel with a rival lover, a difference of opinion in politics, the last opera, the ability of the famous "falcon" to reach a certain note, legal points, scientific questions—all came to a direct issue under these "Oaks." It was at a famous ball at Mme. ———'s, in the Rue Royale, that a gallant cavalier approached a beautiful belle as she was promenading. The dance was given for charity's sake. The girl held a little book of "raffles" in her hand. "Allow me, mademoiselle, to take some chances," asked the cavalier. Before she could reply, her companion replied grimly: "The chances are all taken, sir." "I will meet you later," said the cavalier, under breath. They met in the morning with broadswords under the oaks. An hour later the gallant cavalier breathed his last, just on the spot where Louis Allard is buried. A celebrated European scientist, who was visiting New Orleans, laughed at the

Mississippi River in the presence of a Creole, saying that it was nothing but a tiny rill compared to the great rivers of Europe. "Sir," answered the Creole, "I will never permit anyone to disparage the Mississippi River in my presence." The result was a duel under the oaks at sunrise, and the scientist received a severe wound in his cheek. Oh! there are legends enough and true stories, too, of those who fought and died in this spot, and of beautiful maidens rushing between the combatants just as the fatal lunge was given. There were the famous series of duels with broadswords in the year 1840, when the fencing masters themselves fought and killed one another, just to "show their art." And there was the famous duel on horseback between a French cavalry officer and a young Creole, when the Creole, by a peculiar half-circle stroke which he he had learned from his master, Pepe Llula, plunged his sword through the French officer's body.

All these, and a thousand others, are the stories inseparably connected with the "Oaks." The code was very strict. A gentleman could not fight anyone whom he could not ask to his house. Dueling is a thing of the long, dead past in New Orleans to-day. It does not matter much whether a man fights or not: men have other ways of showing themselves gentlemen. But "Killed on the Field of Honor" is a common enough legend in the old St. Louis cemeteries.

Leaving the ancient "Oaks" the tourist may see another very interesting section of "Old New Orleans" after it had spread beyond the Rampart Street limits, by taking the "Bayou Road" cars, near the Grande Route St. John.

OLD DUELING OAKS—CITY PARK.

This line passes through the old street that was the fashionable drive of New Orleans in early days. The beautiful trees and gardens all along the Rues Ursulines and Bayou Road show the interest which the ancient Creoles took in this "grand promenade."

On Bayou Road, between North Dorgenois and North Broad, is the beautiful little church of St. Rose de Lima. The congregation is exclusively French.

At the corner of North Tonti and Hospital Streets stands the Thomy Lafon Home for the Aged and Infirm of the colored race. The site is that of the old "St. Bernard's Home for Aged Colored Women," founded by the Sisterhood of the Holy Family, in 1842.

At the corner of St. Philip and Galvez Street, is St. Joseph's Convent, for the education of young ladies. The beautiful old grounds and quaint building are deserving of a visit. Within the grounds is a handsome fac simile of the famous Grotto of Lourdes. Thence the car passes through Ursulines and Burgundy Street, curious even in its decay, to Canal Street.

A good view of this rear portion of New Orleans may also be had by taking the Broad Street car, some fine morning, in Canal Street, and riding through old Dauphine Street, now, alas! also in decay, to Dumaine, Broad, Laharpe and Gentilly Road. Quaint old Creole houses line the route, and occasionally one comes across an entire square in the rue Dumaine of almost primitive Spanish architecture. The people in this rear section of the olden city are all French-speaking, and, at times one comes across a family speaking nothing but the Spanish of colonial New Orleans.

At the corner of Dumaine and Dauphine Streets is the old French Convent of "Les Dames du Sacré Coeur," or the Ladies of the Sacred Heart. It is a French order, founded a little over a century ago in France by Mme. Barat, for the education and religious training of the daughters of the French nobility. At the request of the "exclusive" old French Quarter, a branch of the order came and located in New Orleans. To have attended the school of "Les Dames du Sacré Coeur" is considered "tout ce qu'il y a de parfait" among the ancient families. There is a magnificent old courtyard within the convent, and one is immediately impressed with the dignity, refinement and culture of the nuns. The handsome brick edifice in the rear of the Convent was erected some years ago by the Sisterhood at a cost of $20,000 as a free school for poor children.

The old French Church of St. Anne is in St. Philip Street, near N. Prieur. As in St. Rose de Lima, the congregation is exclusively French; indeed, one may go for squares and squares in this rear portion of New Orleans and hear nothing but French in all its original purity.

TOMB OF LOUIS ALLARD.

The "French Benevolent Association" has its asylum on St. Ann Street, between Derbigny and North Roman. Returning by Bayou Road to Broad Street, the car passes into the old French Street of "St. Pierre," or St. Peter famous as the street in which the opera, drama and comedy, had birth in New Orleans.

At the corner of this street and Dorgenois will be seen a beautiful old-fashioned building bearing the inscription, "Asile Thomy Lafon Pour Garçons Orphelins," or the Thomy Lafon Asylum for Orphan Boys. Mr. Lafon purchased and donated this building to the Sisters of the Holy Family as an orphanage for colored boys. The house is built with great brick columns and broad galleries, after the manner of the ancient plantation homes. It was formerly two-storied; but, after the purchase, Mr. Lafon added a third story, which consists of one immense dormitory, containing fifteen or eighteen windows and commanding a pleasant view of the entire grounds. One spacious apartment has been fitted up as a chapel, and within is a marble tablet to the memory of Mr. Lafon, the noted colored philanthropist of New Orleans. The Sisterhood found in him the type of a noble Catholic gentleman and true benefactor. Mr. Lafon continued his great benefactions, donating to the Sisterhood the money to erecte and establish a "Home for Aged Colored Men," adjoining the ancient "St. Bernard's Home for Aged Colored Women" in Tonti and Hospital Streets. He put the latter home in perfect repair, renovating and enlarging it on the same plan as the home for old men.

The colored people of New Orleans owe much to Thomy Lafon. No man ever did as much for the elevation of the race. At his death he left thousands of dollars to charity, irrespective of race or creed. Conspicuous among his charities was a bequest of some $30,000 for the establishment of a home, under the auspices of the Sisters of the House of the Good Shepherd, for the reclaiming of fallen colored women.

CHAPTER IX.

The Old French Parish of St. Bernard—Algiers.

Before leaving the lower section of the city and while its songs and stories still linger in the mind the tourist will do well to visit the old French Parish of St. Bernard, with which the "Vieux Carré," in its families and histories is inseparably connected. as also to cross over the river to Algiers, where Bienville located the "Plantations of the King."

St. Bernard's Parish extends southeast of New Orleans, from the Barracks to the English Turn, for a distance of twelve miles along the left bank of the Mississippi River, and thence obliquely to the south, following Bayou Terre-aux-Boeufs and Lake Lery till it touches the sea.

It was way back in 1778 that a colony was founded in this section by Governor Bernardo Galvez. He called the spot New Galvez; but the colony insisted that the entire parish be called St. Bernard, after its founder's patron saint. Afterward, the Creoles nick-named it "Terre-aux Boeufs," or "Oxen Land," because the colonists used oxen in working the soil. Even to this day the village next to St. Bernard, as also the Bayou that skirts it, carry the name of Terre-aux-Boeufs.

Properly speaking, St. Bernard cannot be classed among the rural parishes of Louisiana; by its contiguity to New Orleans, many hold it as a sort of prolongation or suburb of the great metropolis, and even before the advent of electricity one could mount a horse or take a carriage, or even the bobtail car, and before breakfast have a pleasant stroll under the oaks of St. Bernard, where many of the wealthy residents of the city had their country homes. Driving through the parish, along the river bank, one sees on all sides magnificent sites for parks and homes, and fine old colonial houses nestling among the trees.

"Saxenholm," is the ancient home of Colonel B. S. Story, who married Miss Jennie Washington, great-great-grand-daughter of Colonel Lawrence Washington, the older half-brother of the illustrious "Father of the Country." No home in the entire South is more interesting than this old mansion, which is a type of Louisiana's earliest colonial homes. The house is upward of one hundred and twenty-five years old, and is one of the most magnificently furnished in the South; grand old pieces of black carved oak, rarely seen in these days; ancient tapestries and paintings; and, above all, relics innumerable of our own Washington, Martha Washington and Nellie Custis, make it a place of historic interest. Many of the most valuable souvenirs and relics at Mount Vernon have been furnished by Mrs. Story.

A mile northwest of Saxenholm is an old ruined brick pile, around which clings the wildest and most romantic story in Louisiana. It was the home of no less a person than Alexandra Petrovitz, the morganatic wife of the Czarowitz, Alexis Petrowitz, who married her without the consent of his royal father in 1722. The stern, uncompromising Russia of that day banished her from its borders, and forced her to take passage on a German emigrant vessel, bound for John Law's concession in the Arkansas District. The fact that the distinguished and unfortunate lady was really on this vessel is vouched for by Voltaire in his "History of the French Revolution." The vessel, tossed by winds and storms, finally made its way to Louisiana and the emigrants landed in St. Charles Parish just above New Orleans, on a strip of land that is called "The German Coast." Torn to the heart by the brutal treatment that she had received, the Russian Princess sought a home far from the settlement at New Orleans, and had this old brick pile erected in the fastnesses of primitive St. Bernard's Parish. It was here that the Chevalier d'Aubant, who had never forgotten the beautiful Princess who had won his heart at the royal festivities in St. Petersburg years before, found her at last. He had sailed the world over trying to locate her, after hearing of the brutal treatment that she had received from the monarch whom she loved. Determined to be near her to watch over and protect her, if he could not marry her, the Chevalier d'Aubant took up his residence in the New Orleans colony, and it was here that many years after the death of Alexis Petrowitz, he at length persuaded her to forget the past and marry him. She returned with him to Paris, and afterward accompanied him to the Ile de Bourbon, when he was sent into banishment. After his death she returned to this old spot, where she died in great poverty and misery. She was buried near the ruins.

TYPICAL PLANTATION HOME.

It is the pride and glory of the ancient Parish of St. Bernard that it was the

Cradle of the Sugar Industry.

It was on the old plantation home of Don Antonio Mendes, now known as the Réaud Place, that the historic word "Ça Granule" (it granulates) were heard for the first time as in 1791 a small group of planters interested in Don Antonio's experiments gathered around an old wooden mill, while Morin, a sugar-maker from Cuba, whose services Mendes had secured, sought to teach them the fabrication of sugar from the cane. This was the first sugar ever made in Louisiana. Mendes also succeeded in refining sugar; at a dinner given to the Spanish authorities he presented them with several loafs of the sugar he had refined. At dessert Don Rendon, the Spanish Intendant, toasted the sugar and held it up to the assembled guests as a "Louisiana Product." Mendes continued the culture of cane, but on a very small scale. In 1794 he sold his plant to another planter named Etienne de Boré, who succeeded in producing a crop that was the death blow to the ancient indigo industry of Louisiana, and placed sugar forever at the head of its great staples. But the Mendes family clung to the fact that Don Antonio had produced the first sugar, and it is pathetically told how on her dying bed his daughter repeated again and again till her breath failed, "Dire que c'est mon père qui a fait le premier sucre dans la Louisiane." (Say that it was my father who made the first sugar in Louisiana.) Near by this historic site is the ancient estate of Mr. Joseph Coiron, now known as the Millaudon and Lesseps Plantations. In 1818 Mr. Coiron put up on this site the first steam engine ever used to grind sugar cane. Two years later he introduced the first red ribbon cane from Georgiga and used it instead of the tender Creole variety. These improvements operated most advantageously to the success of the industry and Coiron's name lives in the history of sugar in this section. The fine plantations of Marcel Ducros, Story, Claverie and Reggio follow. It was on the Reggio place that a Spaniard named Solis, who then owned all this tract, essayed in 1785 to manufacture sugar from the cane and continued his operations until 1790, using a little wooden mill that he had

LAFITTE'S TRYSTING PLACE—ALONG BARATARIA BAY.

brought from Cuba. He succeeded only in making syrup and an indifferent quality of rum called "tafia."

Large tracts of land along this route are owned now by an English syndicate, which has erected an immense plant on the "Kenilworth" estate.

The New Orleans Railway Company has also bought up extensive tracts, comprising ten or twelve of the old historic plantations, running from Port Chalmette to the verge almost of the St. Bernard and Orleans Parish lines, for the purpose of establishing terminal accomodations for other roads.

The most romantic memories of St. Bernard are connected with stories of

Lafitte and His Barataria Pirates.

The word "Barataria" is an adaptation of a curious old Creole word, "Barateur," or "Barato," signifying "cheap," for the smuggled goods, rare and beautiful that were sold by the pirates were "very cheap." It has already been told how Lafitte had his famous smithy in Bourbon and St. Philip Street. But he had his trysting place on the Island of Grande Terre, in Barataria Bay.

His smugglers were composed of desperate men of all nations, contrabands, pirates and what not. They were the "wild men of the Spanish Main," and it was said that they carried the black flag and attacked vessels of all nations and did not hesitate to make their prisoners "walk the plank," that terror of old pirate stories of the deep. "Nez Coupé," so called because his nose was cut off, and who lived at Grande Terre many years after the pirates ceased their depredations, used to declare that the beautiful daughter of Aaron Burr, who was supposed to have been lost at sea, was made "to walk the plank" by command of Lafitte. Lafitte used to deny that he was a pirate and dignified his calling by the name of "privateer." Whenever he was apprehended he said that he and his men were cruising with the permission of France. He carried the flag of the Republic of Carthagena, a province of New Grenada, that had rebelled against Spain, and said that he attacked the vessels of Spain, which was then at war with Carthagena and France. "Nez Coupé" used to tell how one of the boldest of Lafitte's men laughed in the face of his commander one day at the mere idea of being a "privateer," and said that he was "a pirate and was proud of it." Lafitte drew his pistol and shot him through the heart in the presence of his companions. A tradition of the parish is that when Claiborne, the first American Governor,

A TOUCH OF SOUTHERN JUNGLE.

indicted the Baratarians and arrested the two brothers, Jean and Pierre Lafitte, at their smithy and lodged them in the "calaboose," without the privilege of bail, the brothers engaged at a fee of twenty thousand dollars each the services of the celebrated lawyers, Edward R. Livingston and John R. Grymes, the most distinguished members of the bar of Louisiana. Of course, with such advocates, the Lafittes were acquitted; the fee was instantly paid, and John Lafitte, after giving warning to his men, invited Messrs. Livingston and Grymes to spend a week with him at Barataria and see for themselves if the verdict were not just. Mr. Livingston politely declined, but Mr. Grymes accepted. It was impossible to discover a trace of smuggled goods or illicit trade. Lafitte entertained him royally, but it is also told that before Mr. Grymes had finished accepting his hospitality or that of Lafitte's "planter friends" along the coast, that he lost every "picayune" of his immense fee playing cards.

A pleasant day may be spent by taking the

Shell Beach Railroad,

at the head of Elysian Fields Street, and enjoying the run of an hour and a half down to the Gulf. The trip takes the tourist through beautiful plantations, a touch of southern jungle, and finally brings one out on the shelving, shelly beach, with the gray waters of the Gulf of Mexico lashing and lapping at one's feet.

At the terminus of the Shell Beach Road is the old town of Proctorville, which was destroyed by a storm in 1860. It was then the terminus of the ancient Mexican Gulf Road, which has been replaced by the Shell Beach.

The little village of Ste. Croix, situated on both sides of Bayou Terre-aux-Boeufs, is very picturesque. The village is still the property of Mme. La Comtesse de Livaudais du Sivan de la Croix, who belongs to one of the most distinguished families of France and who now resides in Paris.

The village came down to her as an inheritance from her ancestors, who came as exiles to Louisiana, and her interest in the simple "fisher folk" who inhabit it, and whom she calls "her children," is very pretty. She also owns a large plantation extending miles along the bayou, and has lately given, at a central point on her plantation, a beautiful site for the erection of a church, and school, on the exact spot where died, in 1814, M. le Compte de Livaudais de la Croix.

The quaint old church on Lake Lery, which runs through the settlement, is also worth a visit. This church was erected in 1778 by Galvez. It contains in its ancient register the baptismal certificates of General P. G. T. Beauregard, and his father and mother; of Mendes, Coiron, Livaudais and other founders of St. Bernard's Parish.

Algiers

is located on the right banks of the river and is best seen by taking the ferry at the foot of Canal Street or Esplanade Avenue. Algiers has a population of about 13,000. The principal points along the river front are the dry docks, of which there are three. There are several coal yards along the river, at one of which is a modern iron and steel coal elevator, with a bucket capable of lifting over a ton of coal at a time. In the lower part of the town is located the great plant of the Southern Pacific Railroad and Steamship Company. Its extensive system of wharves, over 2,500 feet long, all covered with substantial roof, furnish a landing for the Company's fleet of magnificent steamers running to New York and Havana. Just back of these is a series of buildings—workshops, foundries, storehouses, etc. The machinery plant is so complete that a perfect locomotive can be turned out. The Company builds freight cars here, and makes all necessary repairs to passenger and freight cars. When all departments are at work it is estimated that as many as 1,500 men are employed there at one time.

Algiers has its own ice and electric plant.

Just below the Southern Pacific landing is situated the New Naval Station, with its immense floating dry dock, which is among the largest of its kind in the world.

=====▶◆=====

CHAPTER X.

Peculiar Street Scenes—Vendors—Customs—The "Creoles."

Having completed the circuit of the old French section of New Orleans before leading the visitor through the ever changing panorama of Canal Street, and across into the "American Quarter," attention is called to peculiar street pictures that are nowhere else to be seen except in this unique old city.

A vivid and charisteristic street life lends animation to the curious thoroughfare.

Of a morning the French Quarter is alive with the cries of the vendors, "Belle Calas! Tout chauds! tout chauds! "Belle Fromage," "Belle Chaurice," indicating, first, a species of coffee cake called calas, which are "hot! hot!" and again "Cream cheese," and still again, a species of sausage very much liked by the children and called by the old Creole negresses, "Chaurice." Of an evening the old women pass with their baskets of "Comfitures Coco," and "Pralines," "Pistaches," "Pacanes," etc. Jackson and Washington Squares, where the children gather for an airing, are great resorts for these old vendors. A most welcome cry in the heat of summer is to hear "Belle des Figues! Belle des Figues!" (Beautiful figs! Beautiful figs!")

Everything sold by these old negresses is either

"Belle" or "Bon,"

("Beautiful" or "Good.") and to their credit, be it said, one can always rely upon their veracity.

The fruit and vegetable vendors are for the most part Italian emigrant men and women. Negresses, bearing vegetables in large, shallow baskets poised upon their heads, also go by, calling their wares "fresh and fine;" many housekeepers purchase their supplies from these itinerant vendors, the prices being exceedingly small, and usually scaled with the "Picayune" as a unit.

A "Picayune" is equivalent to five cents, and is a corruption of the Spanish term "Picayon," applied to a coin in use in colonial days.

"BELLE CALAS! TOUT CHAUDS!"   "TIN-A-FEEXY, MADAME!"

The milk carts are strictly indigenous. They are formed of a tall, green box, set between high wheels, and are driven almost invariably by Gascons. The two large, bright, brass-bound metal cans that ornament the front of the wagon compel the driver to stand up much of the time when driving, in order to see clearly the road before him. The milkman carries a bell, which he rings before the gates of patrons.

Every retail grocer or street vendor or bakerman or cake-woman who sells in the old French Quarter is expected to give

"Lagniappe."

"Lagniappe" is a Spanish word, and in this connection means a certain bonus in kind, that is given with every purchase. But the children always expect "lagniappe candy" or "cake" or "fruit." Some years ago an effort was made by certain progressive shopkeepers to abolish "lagniappe." There was a hue and cry and the old custom remained. It is a sweet and gracious one that the people like, and dealers who seek to ignore it soon find to their cost that their sales are less. "Quartie" is another helpful custom for the poor, by means of which a nickel or five cents is divided, and a purchase made half of one kind and half of another; for instance, half sugar and half coffee, etc. Negroes, especially, like "quartie." Some of them buy half bread (and they get a half loaf) and half coffee, and then ask for "lagniappe" sugar. So what is there lacking for the morning meal? "Quartie" and "lagniappe" help many an humble home, for the grocer is expected to give as "lagniappe," whatever is asked for, whether flour, salt, black pepper, spice, etc. In the neighborhood of the French Market, and down in the Faubourg Marigny, shopkeepers still adhere to the customs of the French merchants of a hundred years ago, and arrange their wares along the banquette to attract the attention of the passers-by.

"Bon Marché, Madame, Bon Marché!" they cry, just as in the olden days, and thrust their goods into your face, especially in the French Market vicinity, while the dark Italian emigrants, apt imitators, spread out their little hoard of bananas, potatoes and cabbages upon rough sacks on the banquette, all along the rues Hospital and Ursulines, and sing out in broken English, "Freshee banana, Madame! Cheapee! Madame, five centee, Madame!" You meet a curiou. old peddler with a little wagon on wheels. He is one of the last of the famous old "Marchand Rabais," for which the quarter was noted in the days

THE RABAIS MAN.   THE BOTTLE MAN.

gone by. Each "marchand" had his own list of regular customers, and what you could not get in the way of small fancy trimmings in the big stores up-town, you were sure to find in his "little store on wheels." But the "Marchand Rabais," as a distinct business, is passing out of the life of the Faubourg, and the faces of the few you meet are very sad and pathetic.

"Tin-a-feexy, Madame, tin-a-feexy!" and you turn to see a curious old man carrying a lighted furnace and a soldering iron. He is the "tin-a-feexy" man, and you catch an idea of his occupation, as some housekeeper rushes breathlessly to the door with a broken pot or tin vessel to be mended. The old man sets down his furnace, arranges his little workshop and begins to ply his trade. And here is the "shaving cake man," with a huge tin box strapped over his bent shoulders. He carries in his hand a small steel triangle, which he constantly strikes with a steel bar. All the "Carré" then knows that the shaving cake man is near, and the children beg for a "Picayune" to purchase the queer little rolls of cakes that he sells and which are very much like shavings.

The "bottle man" passes, buying up all the old wine bottles, or exchanging bits of trimming for them, etc. A peculiar little whistle breaks on the stillness; and a man stops his little "push cart" at the corner. He is the "ring man," the delight of every child in the quarter; in another instant from almost every

THE MILK MAN.

house in the square, little tots are rushing breathlessly toward the quaint little "push store," bottle in hand, to exchange for some gaudy brass trinket, toy or flag, and then the "ring man" goes on his way to the next corner and childhood

LA BONNE VIELLE GARDIENNE.

OLD PRALINE WOMAN.

in that square is made happy. Another unique character is the "clothes pole man." Of an evening, especially in summer, the organ-grinder goes his rounds. The organ-grinder is generally an Italian or negro. He is the last relic of minstrelsy, and the old "Carré" has a tender place in its heart for him. He stops at every corner and plays a tune or two, while the children gaily dance on the sidewalks. He makes many a nickel as he continues his rounds till far into the evening.

The Flower Girls and Praline Women,

are generally to be found in the vicinity of Canal Street. The old "pralinière" looks very quaint with guinea blue dress and bandana "tignon," as she shows the dainty stock of pink and white pecan "pralines." She has others in a basket tucked away in a cozy corner formed by two show windows. Neither the flower women nor the pralinières cry their wares, but sit patiently waiting for

OLD SPANISH COURTYARD—CHARTRES NEAR CANAL.

customers, meantime brushing the flies away with palmetto fans or mops of brown paper. In the "Vieux Carré," you see "Ma Belle Creole," every morning going to early mass, at the Cathedral, and of an evening dancing her pretty feet off at the gracious old time "soirées," so beautiful, so exclusively Creole, and where the olden "eau sucré," or "orangeade," and "orgeat," are often the only refreshments served, as in the parties of the old regime. Here Monsieur must have his good "French wine" for dinner, and his morning cup of "café noir," and dining well is as much a duty for him as going to church. Here are the old Creole restaurants, where Creole viands are a specialty. Here the brazier and the candlestick are still household appointments; old brass knockers are still found on the doors and the keys and locks are big enough for a Cathedral. There the shopman as of old encases his windows with almost impregnable shutters and bars. And sweetest of all, the daily, familiar sights of the "Viex Carré," is the good old mammy, "la bonne vielle gardienne," taking the children for an airing of an evening, and crooning to them, as they fall asleep in her arms, on the granite steps of Jackson Square, the familiar old songs which have been handed down by the Creole nurses to the children from generation to generation.

It is a custom in New Orleans to announce deaths by printing a notice on a double sheet of paper, bordered with black, and to nail these on telegraph poles in the more frequented parts of the town. This practice is confined to the city. It is also a custom to drape the door or gate of the stricken household with crepe, white for the young dead, black for the elderly, and to fasten here also one of the printed notices.

Gentlemen always lift their hats and remain uncovered while a funeral goes by, as a mark of respect for the dead. And this gracious custom is observed in the most crowded marts in the heart of the business day. Catholics invariably lift their hats when passing a church of their faith, and the stranger will observe this done even in the street cars.

DEATH NOTICES.

Creole.

Everything "that is good" in New Orleans is "Creole." The highest praise that can be bestowed upon any article for sale along the streets and in the country is to declare that it is "Creole." Hence in trade one hears continually the application, "Creole chickens," "Creole eggs," "Creole ponies," "Creole vegetables," etc. The term is used to distinguish the commercial produce of New Orleans and of Louisiana Parishes as infinitely superior to those brought in from the North and West.

One hears, too, the term, "Creole negroes," but it must be remembered always that this is a fine distinction, meaning the blacks and colored people that are Louisiana bred and born and French-speaking as distinguished from the negroes of other States. "Creole" means white, though, as already seen, it has been given many shades of signification—shades which have been taken up by ignorant scribblers and gradually accepted by many Northerners as meaning Louisianians of mixed blood. Nothing is more erroneous. The term "Creole," according to such standards as Webster and Worcester, signifies "a native of Spanish America or the West Indies, descended from European ancestors." There never was a nobler or more pure-blooded race than the Creoles of Louisiana, who are proud of their descent from the best families of France and Spain, and who applied to themselves the term "Creole" to distinguish the "old families" of the State from the families of emigrants of other nationalities.

It is very difficult for the stranger to gain access to the ancient Creole homes; he must come with letters of "introduction," or be introduced by a native "to the manor born." And then, as Marion Crawford said when he visited New Orleans: "You will find in little old French houses old-fashioned and tumbling in ruins—houses that must have been built in the last century, with their long hallways opening upon queer, little courtyards, and all suggesting another age and civilization—a people the most charming and cultured that I have ever met, with all the grace and dignity of manners and the equal in birth and bearing of the most distinguished in European centers."

With this beautiful and true tribute from one who knew whereof he spoke, the Guide will lead the tourist from the French Quarter into the brilliant light of Canal Street and the "Uptown Section."

═══◆◆═══

CHAPTER XI.

Canal Street.

Canal Street is the main, central throughfare of New Orleans, the line of demarkation between the French and American sections. It is the most ancient landmark in the city, for it was the point marked out by Bienville as the extreme southern limits of the metropolis which he founded.

In old times a deep "fossé" ran through the street, but when the town spread beyond the limits of the "Vieux Carré," this canal or ditch was filled up, and the "esplanade" or "neutral ground" along which so many car lines now center, was raised. The street bisects the city from the river northwest to the New Basin Canal. It is 170 feet wide, and is beautifully paved with asphalt throughout a great portion of its length.

Canal Street is, indeed, one of the most characteristic streets in the world. It divides New Orleans into two separate and distinct phases of life, two epochs of history, two styles of architecture, two modes of thought and two distinct forms of civilization.

It is the principal business thoroughfare of the city for a distance of about twelve squares, and thence becomes one of the handsomest residence streets and a delightful drive for both sections.

It is the common ground on which "Creoles" and "Americans" meet to shop, to promenade, to see the grand civic and carnival parades, and often as not, when questions affecting the vital interests of the community at large agitate the city, to gather "en masse" and express their opinions as citizens of one commonwealth.

A majority of the fine retail stores are on the lower side of the street. This side is a favorite promenade, and, on a sunshiny day, is usually crowded with well-dressed people. In Carnival time the street is almost impassable.

One cannnot walk along Canal Street without being impressed with the peculiar cosmopolitan character of the New Orleans of to-day. It is a fascinating study with its thousands of faces, for even the faces of a great city, and the composite faces of its floating population grow familiar in time to the stranger who tarries awhile; the jostle of the people, the beautiful street man-

VIEW IN CANAL STREET FROM THE CUSTOMHOUSE

ners of our public, the courtesy, the good humor especially in Carnival times, when the crush is so great, the brilliant dressing of the women, the everlasting blare of music, the constant processions and celebrations, the peddlers, the loafers, the vendors of roasted chestnuts and peanuts, the flower women, the pralinières, the ginger-bread sellers, the wheezing hand-organs, all make up a scene to be nowhere found in this American Continent except in this delightful old French city.

From Canal Street you become acquainted with the city; you learn the names of the old streets, the haunts of the earnest working folks who give life and strength to the town; you find out where the best "Macaroni à l'Italienne" is made, where you can eat the finest "Creole courtbouillon" or the best "omelette soufflé;" you learn the road to rose gardens and orange groves, and return to find yourself in the heart of an old town with a street more beautiful, more picturesque than any other of this American Union—a street whose great stores resemble the famous "Bon Marché" or "Louvre" of Paris, whose counters and shelves teem with the finest imported goods, laces and silks and Parisian novelties, directly imported, and which may be purchased cheaper here than in New York or any other Northern city.

Such is our great boulevard. From "Liberty Place" to Baronne Street, the crowd is continuous, and the varied and cosmopolitan street life lends a charm that makes this street one of the most remarkable places in the Continent.

The celebrated Levees, with their vast stores of cotton, sugar and other products, lie at the head of Canal Street, and there is the landing for the great coast steamboats laden with rice from the golden fields of Louisiana. Near this spot was situated in Spanish days St. Louis Fort, the guns of which commanded the approach to the river. All traces have long since disappeared.

The Algiers Ferry House is the small ornate wooden building that stands on the river bank. At this point the river is about 2,000 feet wide. The ferries cross and recross at short intervals. The fare is five cents each way. The ferry-house contains also the Harbor Police Station. The visitor will notice nearby the huge sugar refineries, that run day and night during the sugar season.

A bright bit of green grass in the small triangular square at the intersection of Canal, North Peters and Tchoupitoulas Streets, upon which rises a granite shaft, attracts attention. This is

Liberty Place,

which has been aptly called the "Bunker Hill of New Orleans," for it was here that, on September 14, 1874, a battle was fought between the armed citizens of this glorious commonwealth and the Metropolitan Police, under command of the Radical Government, which eventually led to the downfall of "carpet-bagism" and "scalawagism" in Louisiana, and the freedom of the State from their corrupt administration. The causes which led up to the battle are traced to the hordes of penniless adventurers who swooped down upon Louisiana like flocks of hungry wolves immediately after the close of the Civil War. They were called "carpet-baggers," and the term "scalawag" was applied to those of the native population who went over to them. These two disreputable elements were perpetuated in office by a "Returning Board," which scrutinized the election returns and threw out sufficient votes to accomplish their nefarious purpose. In 1873 the State elections actually resulted in the election of John McEnery, but the Returning Board secured the inauguration of W. P. Kellogg, a representative carpet-bagger. McEnery went to Washington to appeal to Congress to recognize his rights and the Government de jure was represented in New Orleans by Lieutenant Governor D. B. Penn, lately deceased. Matters remained in this state till August 31, when the registration began for the Presidential election of the following November. Every impediment was thrown in the way of the white voters to deter them from taking advantage of their privileges. Appeal was made to Governor Kellogg for equal share in the election supervision and a curt refusal followed. It was clear that the citizens would have little or no voice in the election. In addition to these grievances, the conduct of the Metropolitan Police, numbering 800 men, and the uniformed and well-armed colored militia numbering 3,000, had become unbearable. The Metropolitans were armed with modern rifles and supplied with artillery. They were under command of General Badger, and the military under command of the Ex-Confederate General James Longstreet. The conduct of the police in making unwarranted arrests, heaping abuse upon reputable citizens and breaking into houses and searching for arms, was resented by the citizens, who organized under the name of the "White League" for the protection of life and property and the reorganization of the State Government. The gallant General Fred N. Ogden was at the head of the White League. The League had decided upon no definite plan of resistance, when the issue was precipitated by an act of outrageous tyranny on the part of the Kellogg Government. As a result, on September 14, the citizens determined to make a brave stroke for the assertion of their constitutional rights. Governor Penn issued a proclamation declaring the existence of the McEnery Government, and appointing General Ogden to the command of the troops. A deputation was sent to Kel-

MONUMENT IN LIBERTY PLACE.

logg at the State House (now the Hotel Royal) demanding his immediate abdication. The committee was met by a member of the staff, who informed it that no communication whatsoever would be received from the citizens. It had become known that a cargo of arms consigned to private parties in New Orleans would arrive on the morning of the 14th of September; Kellogg sent a detachment of Metropolitans, who forbade the removal of the cargo. That morning the Picayune published an address to the citizens, signed by leading men, calling upon friends of Louisiana and of good, pure government to meet at Clay Statue (then in Canal Street) at 11 o'clock. The result of this meeting was the sending of the Committee to Kellogg to demand his abdication. Ou its return the meeting dissolved like magic, and in a few minutes a large organized force, the "White League," assembled, and, throwing up barricades in Poydras Street, the line of men formed extending from the river to Carondelet

Street. Meanwhile the enemy was not idle. General Badger had formed a force of 200 Metropolitan Police on the north side of the Customhouse with one piece of artillery. On the south side was General Badger himself, the left wing of the forces, and four cannon. Badger opened fire on the citizen forces, the Metropolitans marched out to the Levee and confronted the citizens, and were immediately charged by the White League. General Badger fell severely wounded, and Longstreet vainly endeavored to rally the retreating Metropolitans. But they fled in disorder, taking refuge in the Customhouse and the Supreme Court. The League remained in position till the next day and then marched and took possession of the State House in Royal Street, whence Kellogg had fled, taking refuge in the Customhouse, with his negro troops during the night. On the morning of the 15th an immense concourse of citizens met Governor McEnery, who had opportunely returned, and marching from Lee Place to the State House, the rightful administration was inaugurated. A week later Governor McEnery was compelled to yield to the Federal forces, which had hastened to New Orleans in response to the telegram of Kellogg asking for troops. He was re-established in power at the point of the bayonet, but the Republican power in the State was permanently broken. At the following election Governor F. T. Nicholls was chosen Governor of Louisiana and the Democrats for the first time since the war obtained a majority in the Lower House of Congress. The Returning Board was abolished and Louisiana was again free. The monument at the foot of Canal Street was erected in 1891, and the spot called Liberty Place. The names of

MARBLE HALL—CUSTOMHOUSE.

the citizen heroes who fell are inscribed on the monument. Each anniversary the place is decorated with flowers by a grateful people.

The Fruit Exchange is at the corner of Canal and Tchoupitoulas Streets. The long, low building just beyond the square is the passenger station of the Louisville and Nashville Railroad.

The huge granite building which fronts on Canal Street and occupies a whole square between North Peters and Decatur Streets, is the

Customhouse.

It occupies a portion of the site of Bienville's "country house." In old Creole days a small wooden customhouse occupied the corner toward the Levee. It then stood on the river bank just inside of the country road. Constant addi-

UNITED STATES CUSTOMHOUSE.

PHOTO BY RIVOIRE

tions to the soil have extended the batture and pushed the mighty stream further to the southeast. After the great fire of 1788 a larger building was erected by Governor Miro, which covered a great portion of the present site. This ancient "Aduana," as the Spanish called it, did duty for many, many years, till the growing needs of New Orleans demanded a new one. The present building was begun in 1848. The material is granite and the architecture is modified Egyptian. Over $4,000,000 have been expended on it, and it is not yet entirely completed. In 1874 it was the headquarters of the Metropolitan Police, who were here besieged by the citizen "White League." The magnificent entrance staircase of white marble is an imitation of that of the famous Castle of Kenilworth. On the second floor is the "Marble Hall," each of the fourteen marble Corinthian pillars of which cost $23,000. It is said to be the finest business hall in the world. The United States courtrooms are on the second floor. Those of the United States District Court were used during the Civil War as a prison for captured Confederate soldiers. The visitor should not fail to see the memorial to Bienville over one of the entrances to the "Marble Hall." This is the only memorial in the United States to the founder of New Orleans. The cornerstone of the Customhose was laid in 1847 by Henry Clay. In erecting the building great difficulty was experienced in making the foundations secure. They were made of layers of cypress timber and concrete.

Exchange Alley, full of queer, old-fashioned houses, is in this section of Canal Street, just between Royal and Chartres on the north side. It extends from Canal Street back to St. Louis, where it terminates immediately in front of the now disused main entrance to the Hotel Royal. At the corner of Exchange Alley and Customhouse Street is an ancient mansion with a belvidere of wrought iron on the roof. It is often called

The Napoleon House,

and is so designated, because it was erected by Mr. Nicholas Girod, as a residence for the Emperor Napoleon. Mr. Girod was the Mayor of New Orleans in 1814. He was an ardent admirer of Napoleon Bonaparte, and engaged in a plot with a number of enthusiastic Frenchmen to liberate the Emperor from his confinement in St. Helena. The conspirators built a wonderfully fast clipper yacht, and called it the "Seraphine." Their plan was to bring the yacht near the island some dark night and spirit the Emperor aboard. They were going to surprise the garrison, overpower it, and letting the emperor down by means of a chair into the yacht, sail away and bring the hero of Austerlitz to New Orleans. They depended upon the marvelous sailing qualities of the little ship to enable them to distance all pursuit. There is every reason to believe that their plan was directed and approved by the captive of Longwood, and might have succeeded had not the Emperor's death prevented its consummation. Mr. Girod intended to present this house to the Emperor on his arrival in New Orleans. He subsequently occupied it himself. The Napoleon House was recently sold, and it is probable that before the close of 1904, the historic edifice will be demolished to make way for a modern office building.

All along Canal Street in this business section are a number of handsome buildings, the majority being great dry goods emporiums, where the most beautiful effects are offered for sale, rivalling Paris and London, as far as native hand-work is concerned. The show windows are unfailingly attractive. Lady visitors will find every article that they may need in these stores, from a package of hairpins, needle and thread, to the most beautiful silk lace and millinery importations.

Clay Statue, which was for so many years a landmark to visitors, stood at the intersection of Canal, St. Charles and Royal Streets. It was removed to the center of Lafayette Square in Camp Street, owing to the necessity that arose for protecting life by a better arrangement of the network of railway tracks that traverse Canal Street.

The Morris Building, at the corner of Camp and Canal, was one of the first of the modern office buildings to be erected in New Orleans. It contains the offices of the New Orleans Clearing House.

The handsome new building corner of Canal and Chartres street is known as the "Godchaux Building."

Between Royal and Bourbon, on the downtown side of the street, are the Touro Buildings. They were built in the second quarter of the last century and formed part of the estate of the celebrated philanthropist, Judah P. Touro.

The Boston Club,

the oldest institution of its kind in New Orleans, occupies the building at No. 824 Canal, formerly owned by Dr. W. Newton Mercer. The club was organized in 1834 and named in honor of an old-fashioned game of cards erstwhile very popular among the solid business men of the community. During the Civil War some of the members incurred the animosity of General B. F. Butler, and his provost marshal seized its quarters and disbanded the organization. It was reorganized in 1867. It has entertained many distinguished guests, among them General Ulysses S. Grant, Jefferson Davis, and among its presidents was General Dick Taylor, a distinguished Confederate general and son of President Zachary Taylor.

The Chess, Checkers and Whist Club occupies a handsome four-story building at the corner of Canal and Baronne Streets. The entrance is on Baronne Street. It was organized in 1880, and among the celebrities who have played the king of games within its hospitable walls may be mentioned Captain Mackenzie, Steinitz, Zukertort, Lasker and Pillsbury.

Between Dauphine and Burgundy streets is the Grand Opera House, formerly known as the Varieties Theatre. It was opened about 1871 by the late Lawrence Barrett. Barrett remained in charge of the theatre for a number of years, appearing for the first time in that classical repertoire which he afterward made famous. It is a famous old playhouse, and many a name immortal in dramatic literature has appeared on the bill boards in front of it. The staircase, which occupies a space of about 100 feet, is one of the most beautiful in any American theatre. The house belongs to La Variété Association. It is now a popular-priced theatre. The Pickwick Club is located in a handsome three-storied structure of light-colored brick and stone on the upper side of Canal Street, between Dryades and Rampart. To this home the club removed in 1896. This club dates from 1857. Its first president was General A. H. Gladden, of South Carolina, a veteran of the Mexican War, who fell at Shiloh while in command of the First Confederate Regulars.

At Basin and Canal Streets is the Spanish Fort Railroad Depot.

The New Orleans branch of the famous organization known throughout the United States as "The Elks" has its "home" at 121 South Basin Street, within sight of Canal Street, and the Square in front has been called "Elks Place," in honor of the order.

On Canal, between Villere and Robertson, stands the

Richardson Memorial

Medical School, built in 1894, and presented to the Tulane University by Mrs. Ida Slocomb Richardson, widow of the late Dr. Tobias G. Richardson. It is a handsome building of white stone, equipped with every modern appliance for the prosecution of medical investigation. It cost upwards of $100,000. A bronze tablet bearing a profile of Dr. Richardson ornaments the wall of the entrance hall. The museum is remarkably rich in medical curiosities. The Medical School is famous throughout the Union. It constitutes a part of the Tulane University. It was organized in 1834. The students have access to the Charity Hospital.

On the corner of Robertson, diagonally opposite the Richardson Memorial, is the colored medical school conducted under the auspices of the New Orleans University, colored.

The Phyllis Wheatley Training School for Colored Nurses is located in this building.

After crossing Claiborne Avenue, Canal Street thence on to the Cemeteries is lined with beautiful residences, many of them embowered among trees and vines. At No. 2036 Canal is the residence of Mr. John T. Gibbons, brother of the great American Cardinal.

RICHARDSON MEMORIAL MEDICAL COLLEGE.

The Canal Street Presbyterian Church is at the corner of Canal and Derbigny Street.

Straight University (colored) occupies a whole square on Canal Street, between Tonti and Rocheblave. It is fully equipped for the higher education of its matriculants.

The beautiful Church of the Sacred Heart of Jesus stands at the corner of South Lopez and Canal Streets. It was erected entirely at the expense of one of New Orleans' philanthropic citizens, the late Colonel P. A. O'Brien. The cost was $50,000. Mr. O'Brien, at his death, left a handsome sum for the erection of the School of the Sacred Heart, which adjoins the Church.

Just back of these edifices, plainly seen from the car, is the Frank T. Howard School No. 1, erected at a cost of over $40,000 by the public-spirited citizen whose name it bears.

As the car nears the corner of Broad and Canal an imposing and beautiful edifice known as the House of

The Good Shepherd

rises in view. It stands at the corner of Bienville and Broad Streets, just two squares from Canal, and is one of the noblest and most interesting of the many charitable and religious institutions for which the old city is famous.

The House of the Good Shepherd is a reformatory institution for the reclaiming of fallen women. The extensive buildings were erected from the fortune of a philanthropic New Orleans lady, who nearly forty years ago determined to devote her pure life to the calling of a Sister of the Good Shepherd. But long before that time the Sisters of the Good Shepherd were in New Orleans devoting themselves to their God-given mission of bringing back to the path of virtue those of their sex who had fallen away. In this reformatory the girls are trained to habits of industry and order and assist in their self-maintenance by performing various household duties. They also sew for private individuals and stores. The sisters also conduct a large laundry, in which washing is done for public institutions, hotels, private homes, etc. Visitors are admitted on application to the Superioress or to the janitress at the Bienville Street entrance. Attached to the institution is a home for the "Order of Magdalens" or fallen women who desire to enter the religious life. After a period of probation, if they show themselves properly disposed and qualified, they receive the brown habit of the order, in distinction from the spotless white-robed women—Sisters of the Good Shepherd—who have entered the order to devote themselves to the reformation of the outcast. In the "work room" where the probationists sit doing that beautiful hand embroidery which is the wonder of the artist, is a handsome altar of the Blessed Virgin, to which a most pathetic story is attached. Over thirty years ago, during a terrible snow storm, that surprised New Orleans, the convent bell rang after midnight and a magnificently dressed and jewel-decked woman alighted from a carriage, and entering threw herself at the feet of the Superioress and asked to be admitted. The next day she donned the humble garb of the "penitents." For nine years she labored faithfully and one spring day asked to be received among the Magdalens. She wished to remain in that sweet haven forever and help to bring other sinners like herself to God. Two years later, on the morning that she received the veil, she came to the Superioress with all the jewels that she had worn that night when she came in tears and sorrow so many years before, and laying them at her feet, she begged that they might be sold and with the proceeds an altar be erected to the Blessed Mother of God in the room where the "penitents" sit daily at work. "For," said she, "it was the picture of that sweet face of pure womanhood looking down upon me daily from that humble altar that so touched my heart with the divinity and priceless truth of the heritage that I had lost, and I wish that out of my sins and tears a more beautiful altar may arise to the Mother of Him who did not disdain the Magdalen, but said to her, 'Go, and sin no more.'" And so this beautiful shrine was erected, and from its shadow hundreds of girls who have entered the reformatory since then, have passed from the humble workroom where industry is the watchword, to the eternally safe harbor of the "Magdalen's Home," or back into the world to lead others to the practice of the God-like purity that they have here learned to love and reverence.

In the rear portion of the grounds is a fine two-story brick building, erected some years ago at a cost of $30,000 through the philanthropy of Mr. Thomy Lafon, for the reclaiming of colored girls. It is also under the charge of the Sisters of the Good Shepherd.

As the car nears its terminus it passes the Beauregard Public School, which was once a fine old Southern mansion.

Canal Street terminates at the

Half-way House,

on the New Basin Canal. Half-Way House is so called because it is very nearly half-way between the river and the Lake. This is Metairie Ridge, one of the highest parts of the city. Just around from the turn along the Bayou St. John was the ancient "Terre des Lèpreux," or Leper Land of early Creole days. The Hospital of St. Lazarre stood here. It was erected in the early French domination, but all traces of it have long since disappeared.

The terminus of Canal Street marks also the cities of the dead. All around the visitor will notice beautiful and picturesque surroundings. The handsome cemeteries of the American section are in the vicinity of the Canal Street terminus, and while exploring this neighborhood the visitor will do well to visit them. In the chapter devoted to "Cemeteries" will be found short sketches of these beautiful resting places of the dead.

The Sportsman's Park, where baseball games take place in summer time and football in winter, adjoins the Firemen's Cemetery.

The scene on the Bayou here is very picturesque. The New Canal was constructed to facilitate the commerce of the city through more direct communication with Lake Pontchartrain, and is navigable for schooners, launches and other small craft. The celebrated Simon Cameron, later United States Senator for Pennsylvania and a member of Lincoln's Cabinet, was the first contractor for the digging of the canal.

The old Oakland Driving Park is on the shellroad adjoining the Metairie Cemetery. The shellroad is a toll road, and leads to West End.

Athletic Park is located on Tulane Avenue, between South Carrollton Avenue and Pierce Street. It has recently become a very popular resort. It is handsomely laid out, and during the summer months music and other forms of entertainment make the spot one of continual delight. It may be reached by means of the Tulane and St. Charles Belt cars.

The tourist may return to the business section of Canal Street by the same route, the "Canal Belt" or "Esplanade Belt."

═══◆◆═══

CHAPTER XII.

The Up-town Section, or American Quarter—Historical Baronne Street, St. Charles, Jackson and Napoleon Avenues.

The growth of the New Orleans above Canal Street took place within the last century. This is the American city founded by the sturdy band of Westerners who, as early as 1772, saw the commercial advantages to be secured by a union of Southern and Western forces. Following the daring adventurers, notwithstanding the coldness with which they were received, there came into the French Quarter, rich traders from Baltimore, Philadelphia and Boston, who established branch houses in New Orleans, and their success led other Americans, young and energetic, to come and locate in the city, and seek the Aladdin's lamp that was said to be everywhere hidden in the rubbish of the old French town. The Creoles, with their easy, elegant manners and luxurious homes had little use for these pioneer American invaders. But the sturdy flow of emigration was not to be deterred, to the utter dismay of the Creoles. National feeling ran high and especially did the bitter sentiment grow after the cession of Louisiana to the United States in 1803. Finally, as has already been stated, the Americans moved in large numbers across Canal Street and built their own city.

Such was the enterprise of the people that in 1830 New Orleans ranked after New York, Philadelphia and Boston, in the order of the great cities of

VIEW OF CARONDELET STREET FROM CANAL.

the Union, and travelers came from all parts to see the "Queen City of the South," so wealthy, so gracious, so cultured, and the greatest cotton and sugar market in the world.

Nevertheless, with all its enterprise the Faubourg Ste. Marie was constantly out-voted by the French city below Canal Street.

The Mayor and a majority of the Councilmen were elected by the French Quarter. As a consequence almost all the city revenues were expended on improvements below Canal Street. The Pontchartrain Railroad, built in 1825, and

VIEW OF ST. CHARLES STREET FROM CANAL.

the Carondelet Canal were voted to the down-town section. The citizens of the American Quarter, incensed at this, built their own Canal, which brought the traffic of the lakes to the foot of Julia Street, and in the excitement of rivalry and antagonism, with the aid of the country members of the Legislature, they forced through that body in 1831 a bill which was an amendment to the city charter, and which divided New Orleans into three distinct municipalities, each with its own City Council. The Faubourg Ste. Marie thus became the controller of its own finances; it built its own Levees, paved its own streets, erected new stores and warehouses and blocks and blocks of residences.

An old quagmire on St. Charles Street was filled in, and upon its site rose the old St. Charles Hotel, with its beautiful porticoes and stately columns. The miserable waste along Camp and Lafayette Streets was converted into Lafayette Square, and around it were grouped picturesquely the present City Hall, Odd Fellows' Hall and the First Presbyterian Church. Newspaper companies, and railroad companies, banks and exchanges, and cotton presses sprang up, and property enhanced fourfold in value. It soon became evident, even to the proud-spirited Creoles, that the "little upstart city above Canal Street," as they contemptuously called the new establishment, had left its French mother in the rear.

In 1852, the three municipalities came together again as one city. The Americans had gained their point; the Creoles gracefully yielded, and the old Cabildo surrendered its ancient rights to the new City Hall. Since then, side by side with the old city, the new one has continued to grow, radically distinct in language and sentiment, customs and manners, yet strangely bound to the olden city by a thousand dear and tender ties, and gracefully accepting many of its most ancient and charming customs as its own.

As remarked in the beginning of this Guide, the best way to see the American section of the city is from the street cars, alighting as the Guide or individual interest may indicate at such points as seem to merit a closer inspection. Among these may be suggested the great Charity Hospital, lying along the route of the Tulane Avenue Belt.

COURTHOUSE AND PRISON.

This car may be taken in Canal Street. It turns thence into South Rampart and thence into Tulane Avenue at the intersection of Rampart and Common Streets. At the corner of Basin and Tulane Avenue stands the new courthouse and jail, erected between 1893 and 1895, at a cost of about $350,000. The criminal courts are on the second floor, overlooking Tulane Avenue. On the lower floor will be found the office of the Chief of Police, the First Recorder's Court and various other administrative offices. The rest of the square is occupied by the Parish Jail. A high brick wall surrounds this portion. A criminal accused of a capital crime enters the institution at the time of arrest, and, if convicted, never leaves it until after sentence or execution. The entrance to the jail is on Gravier Street. Permission must be obtained from the Criminal Sheriff (whose office is in the building) to enter the jail. The executions take place in the large paved courtyard in the angle formed by Basin and Gravier Streets.

The white building on the corner of Tulane and Liberty is the New Orleans Polyclinic.

At Howard Street begins the long façade of the

Charity Hospital.

It is one of the oldest charitable institutions in America. The first hospital was founded by Bienville. In 1727 the Ursuline Nuns assumed charge of the nursing and household management of the establishment, which was located

VIEW OF CHARITY HOSPITAL.

in Hospital Street. In 1737 Jean Louis, a sailor, in gratitude to the Ursulines for their tender nursing, left 10,000 livres for the founding of a charity hospital. This foundation was the precursor of the immense establishment in Tulane Avenue. The present hospital was founded in 1786 by Don Almonaster y Roxas and the main building, as it stands to-day, in the center of the square, was erected in 1832. Other buildings have been added from time to time. Prominent among these are the Richard Milliken Memorial Hospital for Children, founded by Mrs. D. A. Milliken, at a cost approximating $130,000, in memory of her husband, and the Home of the Training School for Nurses, costing $50,000, which was the gift of the late A. C. Hutchinson. On the large tract of ground recently acquired near the hospital the management proposes to erect a hospital for consumptives, and an important bequest of $80,000 from the late William Richards will be utilized, possibly, in the erection of a building for the exclusive treatment of infectious diseases. The Charity Hospital is admirably managed by a Board of Administrators appointed by the Governor; the household management and nursing have for over sixty-eight years been in charge of the Sisters of Charity. The hospital has a capacity of 850 beds, and handles about 7,000 cases annually. It has a fine system of free

RICHARD MILLIKEN MEMORIAL HOSPITAL FOR CHILDREN.

clinics; its ambulance service for emergency cases is unsurpassed, and its amphitheatre is said to be the most perfectly equipped of any in the United States. Competent judges from all parts of the country and Europe have pronounced the New Orleans Charity Hospital one of the most complete of its kind in the world, and one of which any State may be proud. It well repays a visit.

Across the street, on the corner of Freret, is the building occupied by the Ambulance Corps, or the resident students of the Medical Corps.

The Claiborne Market stands at the corner of Tulane Avenue and Claiborne Street.

St. Joseph's Church

is the immense structure of brick on the corner of the avenue and South Derbigny Street. It is noted as being the second largest church in the United States. During the construction of the walls in 1871 the foundations settled, and the building was greatly injured, but the defects being overcome, the structure was completed in 1892, with the exception of the spires, which were to have been 200 feet high. The church is Gothic-Romanesque in style.

The rose window in the organ loft was made in Munich, is 21 feet in diameter, and cost $1,800. It represents Christ and the twelve apostles. The church has seating capacity of 1,900. The iron cross that surmounts it is 25 feet high.

The Lazarist Fathers purchased recently almost the entire square on the Roman Street side of the Church, and will erect thereon, during the present year, a magnificent parochial school and convent. The cost will be $70,000. The school will be called the "S. Pizatti," after the generous donor.

The Hôtel Dieu, an admirable private hospital under the direction of the Sisters of Charity, occupies the square between Bertrand and Johnson Streets. The institution is the outgrowth of the old "Hôtel Dieu," established by the Ursulines in Barracks Street in 1727. The only Medical Gymnasium in the South for correction of deformities in children was recently established in connection with this Hospital.

The large brick structure in Tulane Avenue, between Broad and White Streets, still in course of erection, is the House of Detention, and is intended to replace the City Workhouse.

The visitor can return by Tulane Avenue to Rampart Street. Leaving the car here, he may walk over the continuation of the avenue known as Common Street, into the heart of town. By doing so he will be enabled to see the Chinese Quarter, located in the vicinity of Rampart and Common. The Chinese Mission, a unique religious establishment, is at No. 215 Liberty.

In the square bounded by Canal, Baronne, Common and Dryades Streets there stood, until recently, the buildings occupied by the old University of Lousiana; they were stately edifices, supported by Greek columns and porticoes. One of these, fronting on Common Street, was the home of the Medical College from 1847 to 1893. When the University of Louisiana was reorganized under the name of Tulane University, in 1882, "University Place" was the name bestowed upon the first square in Dryades Street, from Canal to Common. Upon the removal of Tulane University to its present quarters, in St. Charles Avenue, all of these old historic buildings were demolished, with the exception of one, and theaters and stores erected upon their sites. The building that still remains was known for some years after the Tulane purchase as Tulane Hall, and was the official place of business of the Tulane University. Upon the erection of the Tulane-Newcomb Building in Camp Street, the offices of the University were removed to this site, and the old hall was sold to the Grunewald Hotel proprietor for the sum of $90,000, and by him leased to a theatrical stock company. The building stands in University Place, between Canal and Common Streets; it is a handsome structure and is exceedingly interesting from an historic point of view. It was formerly Mechanics' Institute and was built early in the fifties for technical and literary purposes. During the Civil War, when a State Government was formed under the protection of the Federal troops, this building was made the capitol. It was used for this purpose until 1866, when the July riots, as they were called, dissolved the soi-disant government. These riots were caused by the unauthorized assembling of the old Radical State Convention of 1864. The members, supported by some colored adherents, barricaded themselves inside the building. They refused to open the doors when the Sheriff demanded admission. The building was taken by assault and several were killed and wounded on both sides. The Legislature met in this building in 1872, in special session, to count the election returns. The aspiring Republican Governor, W. P. Kellogg, tried to enjoin the State Officers and Legislature from carrying out this purpose, knowing that fraud had been perpetrated. E. H. Durell, Judge of the United States District Court, claiming that his injunction would most probably be disregarded, signed at midnight an order directing the United States Marshal to seize the capitol. The marshal took a company of United States soldiers, seized the hall and refused to admit any but Kellogg's partisans. From this action resulted complications through which Kellogg became de facto Governor of the State, and was maintained in that position for several years, mainly through the help of the Federal troops.

The State Library is in the left wing of the building. The Library contains about 40,000 volumes, of which 5,000 are in foreign languages. A magnificent edition of Audubon's works, illustrated by himself, may be seen in this Library. Audubon studied the form, color, plumage and habits of every bird in the Louisiana forests, and all are faithfully given in this wonderful work. The Library is open daily from 9 a. m. to 5 p. m., except on Sunday. Tulane Avenue is finely paved and is rapidly growing into favor as a residence section.

One of the most delightful rides that can be taken through any Southern city, is had over the St. Charles Belt, which traverses Canal Street, and turns from the direction of the river into Baronne Street. This line carries the visitor 'through the most beautiful and picturesque section of the American Quarter.

But before boarding the car visit the famous

Jesuits' Church,

in Baronne Street, near Canal. Baronne Street at this point marks the limits of the old Jesuits' Plantation of 1727, and just where the beautiful church now rises, with its magnificent dome, was the spot where the fathers of this order first attempted the cultivation of sugar cane in 1751. As the car turns the corner of Baronne the stately dome of the church rises to view. The hand-

JESUITS' CHURCH AND COLLEGE.

some structure occupies the site of an unpretentious little chapel built in 1848. The church is known officially as that of the Immaculate Conception. It is in the Moresque style of architecture, and was designed by a Jesuit priest. The building is 133 feet long and 60 feet wide. The twin steeples have never been built. The interior is graceful, with galleries resting on a series of horseshoe-shaped arches, supported by slender iron columns of Moorish design. The subjects represented in the small, round, stained-glass windows are the stations of the cross. The stained-glass in the lower windows represents scenes from the history of the Jesuits. The main altar is of gold, and was executed in Paris at a cost of $14,000. A dome 180 feet high rises above the altar; and in the wall is a niche in which stands a white marble statue of the Virgin Mary. This statue was ordered by Marie Amelie, Queen of France, for the royal chapel in the Tuilleries; but the Revolution of 1848 drove the Queen from France, and caused the statue to be offered for sale. It was purchased by a Creole gentleman and brought to New Orleans. At his death it was purchased for this church at a cost of $5,000. Its original value was estimated at $30,000. In the chapel on the right is the altar of St. Joseph, and on the left is the altar dedicated to the Sacred Heart of Jesus. The bronze statue of St. Peter, near the main entrance, is modeled from the famous figure in the Church of St. Peter, in Rome. In the galleries are many beautiful memorial windows, among others one erected by the soldier-Jesuit, Father Hubert, to the Confederate dead. The church is celebrated for the excellence of its music.

Adjoining the church is the College of the Immaculate Conception, conducted by the Jesuit Fathers since its establishment by them in 1848. The school contains a library, in which is one of the largest and best collections of books on canon law in the United States, also the largest and best collection of French authors in the United States. The T. J. Semmes Memorial Chapel, a handsome specimen of Moorish architecture, is in this building. To the right of the Church stands McCloskey Hall, a fine brick structure erec-

CRESCENT AND TULANE THEATRES.

ted and donated by the Messrs. McCloskey to the Jesuit Fathers for College purposes.

Just across from the Jesuits' Church is the Hotel Grunewald. Adjoining the hotel, toward the rear of the square, near the corner of Baronne and Common, stand the

Crescent and Tulane Theatres.

These handsome new edifices were erected in 1898, at a cost of over $200,-000, on the site of the old University buildings. The Crescent Theater has a large seating capacity. About twenty-two feet from the Crescent stands the Tulane. It is of almost equal size and a match in beauty for its twin sister. Over 1,000 electric lights illuminate these theatres, and the effect on gala nights is surpassingly brilliant. The splendid new playhouses offer every advantage for the finest scenic display. The stages have a depth of 65 feet, and enable the managers to put up the most elaborate productions. The interiors are finished with the finest staff plaster, the same that made the White City of Chicago famous.

Taking the car at this corner, the Newsboys' Home is seen at No. 840 Baronne Street.

The Poydras Market is on the right hand side of the car as it goes uptown. It occupies the central part of Poydras Street. Its name is derived from Julien Poydras, a famous planter of early days in New Orleans, after whom, also, the street is named. The market is very picturesque. On week days there may be seen standing in the middle of the market rows of colored women waiting to be employed to wash or scrub. The market was a famous slave mart of antebellum days.

In Baronne, corner of St. Joseph, is a large four-story brick plumbing manufactory, erected recently at a cost of $74,000.

LEE MONUMENT.

The next point of interest is

Lee Circle,

in which stands the imposing monument to the great Confederate General Robert E. Lee. This monument cost $40,000. The shaft is over 106 feet high, and

RESIDENCE—ST. CHARLES AVENUE.

is composed of white marble blocks, resting on cypress piles driven deep into the earth and bolted together. The column contains a staircase, and just under the statue, which is of bronze, is an observatory. The Circle was formerly called Tivoli Circle, and Howard Avenue was once called Triton Walk, but was renamed in honor of a public-spirited citizen.

At the Lee Monument the cars turn into St. Charles Avenue, which is a continuation of St. Charles Street. Here the street broadens out; there are double drives and a neutral ground, and the avenue is said to be one of the finest in America. The cars traverse the thoroughfare from the Circle to Carrollton Avenue, continuing out Carrollton Avenue to its intersection with Tulane Avenue, through which they return to Canal Street, thus forming "the St. Charles Belt." The "Tulane Belt" cars traverse the same route in the opposite direction. This line, which was recently absorbed by the New Orleans Street Railways Company, was built in 1833, and was the first line of horse railroads in the United States. The cars were then two-storied, the upper deck being covered with a canvas in the summer time. The upper story was reached by a staircase. There was a great deal of life and excitement about this second story, and many old residents declare that the two-storied cars were much pleasanter than the cars of the present day, as the breezes were cooler and fresher aloft.

At the corner of Calliope Street and St. Charles Avenue is the Northern Methodist Church, founded just after the Civil War by Bishop J. P. Newman. It was here that Gen. Grant worshipped while in New Orleans.

The Young Men's Hebrew Association occupies the stately structure at the corner of the Avenue and Clio Street. The building was erected in 1896. It contains a public hall called the Athenaeum where concerts theatricals and balls are often given.

At the corner of Jackson and St. Charles Avenues is the Harmony Club. The clubhouse is of white marble, and was erected in 1896. The club virtually dates from 1862, having been formed by merging together the "Deutscher Company" and "The Young Bachelors' Club," organized about 1856. Its membership is mainly among the wealthy and refined Hebrews of the city.

Along the line of this demarcation are many of the handsomest private residences in New Orleans, the beautiful open gardens and palms giving this section the title of "Garden District."

PALMS ON ST. CHARLES AVENUE.

The First German Church is on St. Charles, corner of St. Andrew.

The beautiful Whitney residence is at No. 2233 St. Charles.

The mansion at No. 2508 St. Charles is not only a handsome specimen of a Southern home, but was the residence of E. Richardson, the most celebrated cotton merchant of his time. He was known as "the Cotton King." It is now the home of Frank P. Hayne.

At No. 2618 is the residence of the late A. C. Hutchinson, who left a fortune of upwards of a million dollars. He made several large bequests to charitable institutions, and left about $700,000 for the extension of the work of the Tulane Medical College. He bequeathed his beautiful home, with its many art treasures, to his friend, Mr. J. P. Blair.

There has recently been a revival, along the Avenue, of the old colonial style of architecture whose stately columns and general classic effects have added much to the beauty of the thoroughfare. Notable types are the T. J. McCarthy and the remodeled Blair residences.

At the corner of Third and St. Charles Avenue is the house where resided John A. Morris, famous as the head of the Louisiana State Lottery Company.

Christ Church Cathedral

is the fine brick and stucco edifice at the corner of St. Charles Avenue and Sixth Street. This church represents the pioneer Protestant organization of the Southwest. It was organized in January, 1805. At this date the Protestant

CHRIST CHURCH CATHEDRAL.

population of New Orleans was so small and belonged to so many denominations that it was found impossible to build churches to accommodate each unto itself. A meeting was, therefore, called of all the Protestants, and it was decided that a church be erected. The decision as to what denomination the church should belong was settled by lot. The Episcopalians won, the church was built, and all Protestants united in their house of worship. The church was originally attached to the Diocese of New York. It stood at the corner of Canal and Bourbon Streets. In 1847, as the old church was found to be too small, a new one was erected, at the corner of Dauphine and Canal Streets, at a cost of $50,000. In 1886 this church was sold and the congregation moved to the present beautiful edifice. The interior is very handsomely frescoed. The stained-glass windows include memorials to the Slocomb family and the late Bishop Galleher. The entrance to the lower floor of the tower contains old tablets of the former wardens. Christ Church is the pro-cathedral of the Diocese, and the dean acts as rector. The residence of the bishop, Rt. Rev. D. Sessums, adjoins the Cathedral, with which it communicates through vine-grown cloisters. The dean's residence is in the rear of the church in Sixth Street.

Adjoining the church is the J. L. Harris Memorial Chapel, erected by Mrs. J. L. Harris in memory of her husband.

At 3607 is the gray stone Newman residence.

At the corner of General Taylor and St. Charles is the Rayne Memorial Methodist Church, erected by Mr. Rayne, a wealthy citizen, at a cost of $50,-000, in memory of his son, who was killed at the battle of Shiloh.

The beautiful Southern colonial-looking structure on St. Charles, between Jena and Cadiz, is the Academy of the Ladies of the Sacred Heart, a boarding school for young ladies.

PALMER AVENUE.

At the corner of St. Charles Avenue and Valence Street is the palatial home erected recently at a cost of $150,000 by W. P. Brown, who became famous in the great Bull Cotton Campaign of 1903.

St. George's Episcopal Church is at the corner of St. Charles and Cadiz Street.

The Asylum for Destitute Boys is the large brick building between Dufossat and Valmont streets.

VIEW ALONG THE LAKE—AUDUBON PARK.

Between Leontine and Peters is the New Orleans University, a well equipped institution for the education of colored youth.

At the corner of Peters Avenue and St. Charles is the commodious

Jewish Orphans' Home,

which was erected and is maintained through the generosity of the Jews of the city. The home was founded in 1855. The present building was erected in 1886, and is one of the best regulated orphanages in the city. The nursery and kindergarten departments are particularly interesting. In the yard is a magnificent fountain built by the wealthy Jewish children of the city as an offering to their less fortunate sisters and brothers. The children of this asylum are admirably equipped, educationally and otherwise for their future duties in life.

At 5705 St. Charles Avenue is the home of Mr. Lawrence Fabacher, on the grounds of which stands his private Casino, also one of the finest hot houses in the South.

AVENUE OF OAKS—AUDUBON PARK.

A block or two from St. Charles, and visible from the car in the perspective of Nashville Avenue, is seen the Shakspeare Almshouse, where the penniless and decrepit poor may find a refuge. It was built by Mayor Shakspeare ten or twelve years ago. The large brick building in the almshouse inclosure was erected for the use of the Boys' House of Refuge, but has recently by an act of the City Council been diverted to public school purposes.

Two squares this side of Audubon Park, is Palmer avenue, so named in honor of Dr. Palmer, the noted Presbyterian divine who resided in this street.

HORTICULTURAL HALL—AUDUBON PARK.

His family still reside in the old home. The avenue which was formerly a section of Henry Clay avenue, is one of the most beautiful and picturesque residence streets in New Orleans.

Audubon Park,

which is to the residents of the American section of New Orleans, what the City Park is to the French quarter, is the most important point along this route. The entrance to the park in St. Charles avenue leads the visitor over an immense tract upon which magnificent live oaks were sacrificed in 1884, to admit of the erection of the buildings of the World's Cotton Centennial Exposition. The park is a beautiful spot and covers 280 acres. It was originally the plantation of the French patriot, Masson, who in 1768 was condemned to ten years' imprisonment in Moro Castle for resisting the cession of the colony to Spain. The plantation was subsequently owned by Etienne de Boré, the

WASHINGTON OAK—AUDUBON PARK.

first great sugar planter of Louisiana, and grandfather of the historian, Charles Gayarre. It was on this land that Mr. De Boré succeeded in introducing the permanent manufacture of sugar into New Orleans, and raised the first commercially profitable crop of sugar ever grown in the South. Just above this historic plantation was that of Pierre Foucher, a son-in-law of M. De Boré. The entire property finally fell into the hands of the Marquis de Circé Foucher, by whose heirs the present site of Audubon Park was sold to the city. The land was allowed to lie unimproved till the Cotton Centennial Exposition, when the managers of that enterprise greatly beautified the spot. All the Exposition buildings were removed except the Horticultural Hall, which still stands. In 1886 the park was placed under the control of a Commission, which is devoting itself to beautifying the grounds, planting trees to replace those that were cut down, etc. The Horticultural Hall is over 300 feet long and contains a remarkable collection of rare plants, tropical palms and exotics. It is perhaps the

TOWARD THE BRIDGEWAY—AUDUBON PARK.

largest greenhouse in existence. The section of the park lying between Magazine Street and the river is kept in perfect order. The task of improving the rest of the park is progressing slowly. The live oaks are very fine, especially the long avenue in front of and behind the Hall. The single magnificent specimen standing in solitary majesty beside the lake is called the "George Washington" oak. The park is reached by several lines of cars, the most convenient of which are the Coliseum and the Magazine. In summer time a band plays on alternate evenings in a stand under the oaks near the Horticultural Hall. The park is a favorite resort at all times of the year, especially for children. The visitor gets a view of the most barren portion of the park from the St. Charles car.

THE TULANE UNIVERSITY.

In the vicinity on St. Charles Avenue are Audubon Place and Rosa Park, which are beautiful private residence sections.

The handsome colonial-looking residence with the stately white portico at 5809 St. Charles Avenue is the home of Mr. Nicholas Burke. It is a beautiful type of pure Southern architecture. Nearly opposite the entrance to Audubon Park is the beautiful little Church of the Holy Name of Jesus, which is under the direction of the Jesuit Fathers. Around the corner at No. 1930 Calhoun Street, is the convent and school of the Sisters of Notre Dame, who also conduct the parochial school of St. John Berchmans, attached to the church.

Adjoining the church grounds are the extensive buildings of

The Tulane University

of Louisiana. The University was founded through the generosity of Paul Tulane, a wealthy merchant, who, at his death, left a bequest of over $1,000,-000 for this purpose. The University has since received other bequests; among recent donations are those of Mrs. F. W. Tilton, who gave $50,000 to erect the Library Building, and the munificent bequests of the late A. C. Hutchinson. The buildings contain University and Collegiate Departments, both for men and women, and Law, Medical and Technical Schools. The Medical Building is in Canal Street, and is called the Richardson Memorial. In the Arts and Science Building is a copy of "Tripitka," presented to the University by the King of Siam.

Leland University, for colored males, occupies the square on the avenue between Audubon and Walnut.

St. Mary's Dominican Convent is on the avenue, between Broadway and Pine.

Beyond the University, where St. Charles Avenue has, properly speaking, its head, there formerly ran a beautiful road called Naiads Street. The grounds were handsomely laid out and were called the Carrollton Gardens; there was a restaurant where General Boulanger and Thackeray were both entertained on their visits to New Orleans. Some years ago it was found advisable to build a Levee through the gardens, and the old restaurant was dismantled and sold.

The car here turns out Carrollton Avenue to Jeannette Street, the way being through a very choice residence portion.

All this section of New Orleans was formerly the municipality of

Carrollton,

and still bears the ancient name. It was separated by long uninhabited spaces from the nearest city of Jefferson. Carrollton was in early days a plantation and was the property of the brave patriot, Lafréniere, who with his six associate leaders of the Revolution of 1768, was shot in Jackson Square by order of the Spanish Governor O'Reilly. The plantation subsequently became the property of Mlle. De Macarty, who was the famous "bas bleu" of colonial days in New Orleans. She belonged to the school of "Les Dames Précieuses," so amusingly caricatured by Moliére in his "Précieuses Ridicules." She was very brilliant, and declared a thousand times that she had never yet met a man who could please her and was determined to die in single blessedness. She managed her vast estates with masculine ability and her name has come down as the historical "Vielle Fille," or old maid of the Faubourg. All traces of the old plantation have long since passed away.

At 602 Carrollton Avenue is St. Andrew's Episcopal Church.

The Jackson Avenue car, which may be taken in Canal Street, runs from Canal Street up St. Charles to Jackson Avenue, and thence to the terminus in Jackson Avenue near the river. It passes through a handsome residence district.

On the corner of Coliseum and Jackson is

Trinity Church.

Trinity is an Episcopal Church, and so many of its rectors have passed from this parish to the bishopric that it is often called "The Church of the Bishops." It is of Gothic architecture. The congregation was organized in 1847. The present structure dates from 1851, and was built at a cost of $22,-

500. Bishop Polk was called to take charge of the parish in 1855. He left it during the Civil War to become a Major General in the Confederate service, and after serving gallantly was shot and killed while out with a reconnoitering party on Pine Mountain, near Marietta, Georgia, June 14, 1864. A beautiful stained-glass window has been erected to his memory and contains scenes from the life of the Savior—the Last Supper, the Crucifixion and the Ascension. In 1865 Dr. J. W. Beckwith, afterwards Bishop of Georgia, became rector. During his incumbency the church was extended and improved at a cost of $25,000. In 1868 Rev. J. N. Galleher, afterward Bishop of Louisiana, became rector. He was succeeded by the Rev. S. S. Harris, afterwards Bishop of Michigan. In 1873 the front of the church was remodelled at a cost of $16,000 . Dr. Hugh Miller Thompson, the late Bishop of Mississippi, was the next rector. The present rector is Dr. Beverly Warner. Trinity is reputed to have the best choir among the Protestant Churches in the city.

The late Ambassador Eustis, when in town, resided in the handsome red brick house, with the wide verandas, on the corner opposite Trinity Church.

The little French Church of Notre Dame de Bons Secours is on Jackson Street. near Constance.

Near the corner of Jackson and Chippewa stands the

Children's Home (Protestant Episcopal),

an admirable asylum conducted under the auspices of the Episcopal diocese of Louisiana. It is a home for orphan girls, but also receives small boys. The institution is in charge of the Sisters of Bethany, a local diocesan organization of the Episcopal faith. It is well worth a visit. The chapel is very pretty, and the children's festivals, especially at Easter and Christmastide, are very beautiful.

Directly across the street is McDonogh High School No. 2, a brick building originally erected for the Jewish Orphans' Home, but purchased by the city seven or eight years ago for use as a public high school for the girls of the upper districts.

On St. Thomas, near Jackson Avenue, is the Seamen's Bethel.

St. Vincent's Haven for Seamen is on Tchoupitoulas, near Josephine.

At the junction of Napoleon Avenue and St. Charles Street the Napoleon Avenue car, a branch from the St. Charles, may be taken. The car runs thence to the river for the accommodation of residents along the avenue.

This line of cars has developed a large area which is rapidly building up with beautiful residences.

St. Elizabeth's Industrial Home for Girls in charge of the Sisters of Charity is at the corner of Prytania and Napoleon Avenue. The home is the climax in a trinity of institutions, under the charge of this sisterhood in New Orleans.

From the Infant Asylum, at Race and Magazine Streets, the children pass to St. Theresa's Asylum in Camp Street, where they are given a good common school education. Thence they graduate into this industrial home, where they are trained for active work by which they may become self-supporting in the world without. St. Elizabeth's is noted for its schools of needlework, the products of which are in great demand throughout the country. Among its graduates have been many wonderfully expert needlewomen.

At the corner of Camp and Napoleon Avenue, is St. Stephen's Church, a handsome edifice in brick. It has been in course of construction for some years and still lacks the steeple. The interior is not yet completed, but for the past ten years services have been held in the edifice. The pictures over the altar represent the martyrdom of St. Stephen.

The power-house of the street car company at the end of the line is interesting, and may be visited upon application to the foreman.

<hr>

CHAPTER XIII.

Camp, Prytania and Magazine Streets.

Camp Street is an important business thoroughfare of New Orleans, many stores, banks and insurance companies having their offices in the section be-

VIEW DOWN CAMP STREET FROM POYDRAS.

tween Poydras and Canal. The newspaper offices are also in Camp Street, hence this distinct section is often called "Newspaper Row."

The Prytania Street cars run from Canal into Camp Street, and continue up the latter to Calliope, where Prytania Street begins.

The large, brick hardware store on the river side of Camp and Common Streets occupies the site where at one time stood the City Hotel, in its time a famous resort. It played a conspicuous part in the stirring drama of reconstruction days, but was demolished to make way for the present structure. Opposite is the handsome marble front building known as the "Tulane-Newcomb," which has been lately erected by the administrators of the Tulane

University Fund. The business offices of the University are in this building. The remaining portions are let as offices.

On Camp Street, in the middle of block, between Gravier Street and Natchez Alley, stands the four-story granite building occupied by

The Picayune.

The Picayune is, with the exception of the French daily, L'Abeille, the oldest
paper in Louisiana. It shares with L'Abeille and the Deutsche Zeitung the
honor of being the only publications which survived the Civil War. The Picayune was founded in January, 1837, by George Wilkins Kendall and Francis
Lumsden, two practical printers. The paper was at first a four-page folio, with
four columns to the page. It was so successful that it was found necessary

PICAYUNE'S BUILDINGS.

within a few months to enlarge the sheet, and it continued to grow till it has
reached its present dimensions. The present site has been occupied since 1847.
After the death of Mr. Lumsden, who was drowned in Lake Erie, in 1860, Mr.
Kendall continued the publication of the Picayune with Messrs. Holbrook and
Bullitt. Upon the death of Mr. Kendall, in 1867, Mr. Holbrook acquired the
sole control. Mr. Holbrook died in 1876, and his widow, whose maiden name
was Eliza Jane Poitevent, known to the world of letters as the sweet Southern
poet, "Pearl Rivers," took charge of the paper and managed it successfully,
with the assistance of Mr. George Nicholson, a man of exceptionally fine business talent, who had been business manager of the Picayune for many years.
In 1878 Mrs. Holbrook and Mr. Nicholson were married and the firm name
became Nicholson & Co. Mr. Nicholson died in February, 1896, and within
ten days his wife followed him to the grave. Side by side they sleep in Metairie
Cemetery. The Picayune is now managed under the title of "Estate of Mrs.

E. J. Nicholson," in the interest of her two sons, Leonard K. and Yorke P. Nicholson.

The Picayune has had a most eventful history during its long existence of sixty-five years. Mr. Kendall brought the paper into great celebrity during the Mexican War, representing it in the field with the army of invasion, and thus being entitled to the honor of being the first of the now numerous tribe of war correspondents. He succeeded, by means of a pony express, in getting news to the Picayune, and through it to the world, in advance of even the Government dispatches. Mrs. Nicholson's management of the paper was exceptionally brilliant, and she is entitled to the honor of having been the first woman in the world who successfully managed a great daily. The recent enterprise of the Picayune, equipped as it is with the most modern and improved machinery that science has devised for newspaper production, has been worthy of its early fame. During the great and disastrous storm at Chénière Caminada, in 1893, it was not only the first to give the full news of the catastrophe, but chartered a steamboat to send food and clothing supplies to the sufferers. It took the initiative in New Orleans in providing and securing subscriptions for the sufferers of the late great disater at Galveston, helped to organize the ladies of the city into a relief association and sent money, clothes and medicine valued at $50,000 to the relief of the storm-stricken people.

During the recent war with Spain it was represented in the field by two staff correspondents, and by alliance with the New York Herald secured unrivaled special cable service. In the midst of all the changing events of more than sixty years the Picayune has appeared regularly every morning except during the year 1864, when, for a brief period, the offices were in the hands of the military authorities and the publication was suspended. In addition to the daily, the Picayune issues a twice-a-week edition, and annually at Mardi Gras publishes several beautifully illustrated editions, known far and wide as the "Carnival Editions." Within the past ten years the Picayune has devoted itself sedulously to educating the South in the importance of building cotton mills in the regions where the staple is produced. In this crusade it has, at large expense, sent members of its staff to various parts of the Union, and especially to North Carolina and New England, to study the milling enterprises, which have been so successful there. Entirely at its own cost the Picayune sent Mr. Hargrove, one of these correspondents, to deliver addresses in Mississippi and Louisiana, setting forth the result of his investigations. The Picayune reprinted the articles and letters of these correspondents in two pamphlets, of which more than 45,000 copies were distributed, free, throughout the South. Nothing can be more gratifying to the Picayune than the appreciation of its efforts in its home city. It may interest the tourist to know that the Picayune derives its name from an old Spanish coin called "picayon," which was in circulation in New Orleans in the early part of the century. Its valuation was about 6 1-4 cents. The price of the paper when originally published was a picayune. The five cent coin that superceded the Spanish under American coinage was designated by the Creoles as a picayune. The term, so picturesque and quaint, is still heard frequently in New Orleans among buyers and sellers in the old French Quarter.

Parties not exceeding eight or ten in number, who desire to view the Picayune's complete composing room, with its rows of linotype machines, the wonderful press and the stereotyping department, which are among the most instructive sights in the city, are welcome.

Poydras Street is worth a visit. It is particularly interesting near the river. Lively traffic is maintained on the sidewalks in country produce between the retailers and the commission merchants.

The Produce Exchange is at the corner of Poydras and Front.

Odd Fellows' Hall, on Camp Street, between Poydras and Lafayette Streets, houses many of the lodges of that order. The second floor is occupied by a large hall, often used for concerts, theatricals and balls. One of the most remarkable scenes in the history of the State was enacted here in 1877. It was the last act in the tragic drama of the so-called "Reconstruction Era." On Jan. 1, of that year the Legislature assembled and the Democratic members who constituted the lawfully elected majority, marched in a body to the Hotel Royal, which was then the State House. They were refused admission by the Radical Administration, and found the entrance guarded by armed men. They retired to St. Patrick's Hall and organized, and on January 8, swore in the legally elected Governor of Louisiana, Francis T. Nicholls.

At the same time the Radical usurper, Packard, was inaugurated in the same office in the Hotel Royal. The day after inauguration, Governor Nicholls directed the citizen soldiery as they took possession of the public buildings of the city. The Packard Government was besieged for two months, and Federal support being withdrawn, finally yielded to the popular voice. The inauguration of Governor Nicholls was the turning point in the later history of the State.

In the square between Poydras and Lafayette Square there stood, until destroyed by fire some years ago, the famous "Moresque Building," considered one of the most beautiful specimens of Moorish architecture in the South. The exterior was of iron, cast at Holly Springs, Miss., and wrought into beautiful Oriental designs in keeping with the style of architecture.

Immediately in front of Odd Fellows' Hall is

Lafayette Square.

It was named after General Lafayette,. In the centre of the square stands the monument erected in 1856 to the "Mill Boy of the Sloshes," Henry Clay. The statue is 12 feet high and is of bronze. It was sculptured by the famous Kentucky artist, Joel T. Hart. Until recently Clay Statue stood on the neutral ground at the intersection of Canal, St. Charles and Royal Streets. This spot is commonly regarded as the center of the city. Clay Monument figured in the

HENRY CLAY MONUMENT—LAFAYETTE SQUARE.

annals of New Orleans as the great gathering place of the people when bent on business of serious public import. The great revolution of 1874 was precipitated by a speech delivered at Clay Statue, and the lynching of the Mafia members in 1891 resulted from two addresses pronounced on the same spot.

The increasing car traffic of the city, and the network of railroad lines that circled about the monument made the vicinity dangerous to human life, and finally, sentiment yielded to reason and the monument was removed by act of the City Council in 1901 to this abiding place in Lafayette Square. It replaced the statue of Benjamin Franklin, which was moved from the center of the square to the east side. This work is from the chisel of Hiram Powers, and was presented to the city and erected in 1872. In the square stands the geodetic stone erected by the Coast and Geodetic Survey. By it is located exactly latitude 29:50:58 N. and longitude 90:04:09 W.

On the west side of the square, facing the City Hall, is the monument erected by the public school children of the city to the great benefactor of the public school system of New Orleans, John McDonogh.

Once a year, on the anniversary of McDonogh's death, the public school children gather here and strew the mound with flowers.

This thought is symbolized in the design of the monument.

At this point the visitor should cross the street and visit the

City Hall,

which stands at the corner of Lafayette and St. Charles Street, overlooking the square. The hall was erected in 1850 and is an imitation of the Temple of Minerva, on the Acropolis, at Athens. It is built of marble. The noble Ionic portico with its beautiful columns is very imposing. The pediment is ornamented by a bas-relief of Justice, surmounted by figures emblematic of Commerce and Manufacture. A spacious marble hall extends the entire length of the building. To the left of the entrance are the Mayor's offices. Magnificent portraits of George Washington, Andrew Jackson and former Mayors of New

CITY HALL.

Orleans adorn the walls. The handsome apartment on the right was formerly used as a library. Just beyond the stairs on the right is the Council Chamber. Here the body of Jefferson Davis was laid in state previous to temporary interment in Metairie Cemetery. The City Archives are on the fourth floor. In the basement are the offices of the City Treasurer, Comptroller, etc. An interesting room in this section is the headquarters of the fire-alarm telegraph. Many stirring events have transpired in and around the hall. In 1861 the many Confederate regiments departing for the war received their colors in front of this building. From the steps they heard soul-stirring addresses, notably those of Dr. Palmer and Father Hubert, distinguished members of the New Orleans clergy, who followed as chaplains. In 1862 Captain Bailey came hither at the command of Admiral Farragut to demand the surrender of the city to the Federal forces. An angry crowd assembled about the building while Bailey was within and it was only by barricading the doors with furniture that it was kept out and the gallant sailor saved from its fury. He made his escape unobserved by a rear door.

During Mardi Gras time a spacious platform is built over the steps of the hall, on which hundreds sit to witness the parades. The Mayor receives the King of the Carnival in the hall on Mardi Gras Eve, and delivers to him the keys of the city on a velvet cushion, and in return receives from the merry monarch a decoration and the title of Duke of the Realm.

At the corner of Camp and Lafayette stands the

City Library.

The building it occupies was formerly known as St. Patrick's Hall. The new library was opened in January, 1897, and was created by the merging into one of the library established under the Fisk bequest and the old city library, which formerly had its quarters in the City Hall. The library has an annual circulation of about 100,000 books. Seven hundred of its volumes are in foreign languages. It is said to have the most perfectly lighted reading-room in the world. Here may be seen carefully preserved in a glass case two volumes of the "Vie de Caesar," by the Emperor Napoleon III, which were presented by the author to the city.

The location of the new Post Office will be on Camp and Lafayette Streets, upon the site now occupied by the City Library. The latter building was sold by the City to the United States after the Post Office Commission had decided that this would be the most eligible site for the erection of the new building. From the proceeds of the sale a new library, complete and modern in every detail, will be built. The site will probably be in the vicinity of Lafayette Square. The location of the new Post Office will be an ideal one, good and convenient especially for business purposes. The erection of the building will vastly improve the vicinity of Lafayette Square and the whole of lower Camp Street. The erection of a separate Post Office building has become an actual necessity in New Orleans, so great has been the progress within the last few years. The United States, appreciating this fact, appropriated a sum sufficient wherewith to purchase a site. The appropriation of the building proper has yet to be made by Congress.

The Christian Woman's Exchange is diagonally across from the library on the corner of South and Camp Streets. The handsome brown edifice on the upper side of the square is the First Presbyterian Church. It was over this congregation that the noted divine,, the late Dr. B. M. Palmer, presided from 1856 to May, 1902. The First Presbyterian Church, in its eventful history as a congregation, represents the growth of Presbyterianism in New Orleans. The first effort to plant Presbyterianism in New Orleans originated strangely enough with the Congregationalists of New England. In 1817 the Connecticut Missionary Society engaged a missionary to tour the Southwestern States and inquire into religious conditions. As a result of his investigations, the Rev. Sylvester Larned was sent to New Orleans in January, 1818. The City Council gave a plot of ground on St. Charles Street, between Union and Gravier, as a site for a Presbyterian Church, and Dr. Larned succeeded in negotiating a loan of $40,000 for the erection of the edifice. In 1820, Mr. Larned placed the number of communicants in his church at 40. Dr. Larned died in 1820. Eighteen months later Dr. Theodore Clapp, a famous graduate of Yale and of the Theological Seminary at Andover, came to preside over the Church. Dr. Clapp liquidated the debt of the church by means of a lottery which he established, and by a personal donation of $20,000, which he received from Judah P. Touro, a princely merchant of Jewish faith, who became his warm friend through life. Dr. Clapp's ministry was a very troubled one, from the suspicions entertained of his doctrinal unsoundness. In 1824 he declared his faith was shaken in the doctrine of future punishment, and doubts thickening upon him through years, he was at length forced to plant himself in open hostility to the whole Calvanistic theology. Twice he was called before the "Sessions" of the Presbytery. Finally, he was declared deposed from the ministery of the Presbyterian

Church. But Dr. Clapp was a very brilliant man, and he carried the bulk of the congregation and his church property with him, and founded the Unitarian Church in New Orleans. Presbyterianism had received a great blow. It had to make a new start, and from beginnings quite as small as the first, for only nine of the old congregation seceded from Dr. Clapp, and sought to reorganize the First Church. These nine worshiped in a warehouse on Lafayette Street, that was owned by Mr. Cornelius Paulding, and which was located on the site now occupied by Dr. Palmer's Church. In 1835 Dr. Parker came to minister to the congregation, and through his efforts a church costing nearly

VIEW OF DR. PALMER'S CHURCH FACING LAFAYETTE SQUARE.

$70,000 was built. In 1854 the roll of communicants had reached 600. That same year the church was destroyed by fire, and the present handsome structure was begun. In the meantime Rev. B. M. Palmer was called to the pastorate. He arrived in December, 1856, and in 1857 the beautiful edifice, which still stands the pride and monument of Presbyterianism in New Orleans, was completed and dedicated. It cost in all its appointments, the sum of $87,000. No man ever wielded a greater or more beneficent influence among his people than Dr. Palmer, and his name and memory are inseparably associated with the church.

On Camp Street, between Girod and Julia, is

St. Patrick's Church.

The structure, which is Gothic in style, is worthy of the attention of the artist or student, whether considered merely for its size or for the splendor of its architecture. The plan of the church is an imitation of the famed York Minster, and is regarded as being the happiest effort in this field in the United States. The material is brick, rough cast, to simulate uncut stone. The church was erected early in the fifties by the Irish colony in New Orleans. The tower is 250 feet high and for many years "the four points of St. Patrick's steeple" were the guiding compass for New Orleans. The interior of the church is pure Gothic, with comparatively little ornamentation, except the reredos, which is very beautifully wrought. Back of the main altar is a very effective copy of Raphael's "Transfiguration." On the right is a picture of St. Peter walking on the waves, and on the left, St. Patrick baptizing the Kings and Queens of Ireland in Tara's Hall, Among the beautiful pieces of statuary is the "Mater Dolorosa," which created such interest in the religious art exhibit at the World's Fair in Chicago.

On Camp, between Julia and St. Joseph, is the Naval Brigade Armory, a handsome structure recently erected at a cost of $20,000.

The Confederate Memorial Hall

occupies the grassy mound near the corner of Howard Avenue and Camp Street. It was presented to the city by Mr. Frank T. Howard, a philanthropic citizen. The hall is a neat structure of pressed brick, now overgrown in many places by creeping vines. The interior is finished in hard woods, and contains a magnificent collection of relics of the Civil War. Among the more interesting may be mentioned the uniform and sword of General J. B. Hood, the saddle of General Bragg, the cradle and library of Jefferson Davis, portraits of Confederate Generals, etc. Washington's telescope is in one of the cases in the center of the hall.

Shortly after the death of Miss Winnie Davis her mother placed in Memorial Hall the most precious souvenirs that she possessed of her lamented daughter. Among these are all the childhood toys and school books, and paintings of the "Daughter of the Confederacy," her robe and crown and sceptre when she was Queen of Comus in New Orleans in 1892, and the badges presented to her by the various camps. Mrs. Davis also sent many personal souvenirs of Mr. Davis, among others all the important documents of the Confederacy in her possession, and the last suit of clothes and hat worn by Mr. Davis.

The cannon in front of the hall is the "Lady Slocomb," and was used at Mobile in the Civil War. The building is used by the camps of the United Confederate Veterans as a meeting place.

The Howard Memorial Library

is a beautiful structure, erected in 1887 by Mrs. Annie Howard Parrot, as a memorial to her father, the late Charles T. Howard. The interior is finished in polished woods. The reading-room is circular in shape, exquisitely paneled, with carved rafters and ornamented in an extremely beautiful manner. The library contains about 35,000 books, including many extremely rare volumes. There is a collection of works bearing on the history of Louisiana, the like of which can nowhere else be found. Among the treasures of the library are

HOWARD MEMORIAL LIBRARY.

copies of almost all the original works of Audubon, many of which are now very difficult to find. The collection of early maps of America is unique and very valuable. Mr. William Beer, the librarian, is always pleased to exhibit his treasures.

Two squares further on the car turns into Prytania Street. This is one of the most beautiful residence sections in New Orleans. In the triangular-shaped square which marks the entrance to the street stands a monument from which looks down a woman with a little child at her side. This is

Margaret Place,

and the statue is that of Margaret Haughery, the humble baker woman who toiled all the long years of her life for the support and maintenance of the little orphans of this city. She erected the asylum that faces the square, St. Vincent's Infant Asylum, at the corner of Race and Magazine Streets, helped to build St. Elizabeth's Industrial Home for Girls and gave everywhere and to every needy child. Her small bakery grew through her exertions into an immense steam bakery, right in the center of the business life of the city, and she became a great factor in that life. Everyone, from the banker to the

MARGARET MONUMENT.

newsboy, would salute her as she sat at the door of her office of a morning, for everyone honored and respected her. They knew the great golden heart that lay beneath her plain and simple garb. She had never learned to read and write, and yet she died as no woman in New Orleans ever before had died, giving away thousands of dollars to the poor little orphans of the city. A simple "Margaret Haughery (her mark)" was the signature to her will. No orphan asylum was forgotten, Jew and Protestant and Catholic were all remembered, for "they are all orphans alike," said Margaret, "and I was once an orphan myself." She had a funeral such as no woman in New Orleans had ever had, and almost before anyone could ever exactly tell how it began, the idea of a monument seemed to be in every mind. The ladies of New Orleans met and

A VIEW IN PRYTANIA STREET.

undertook to raise the money, and one morning, almost before the people of New Orleans, whom her presence had ennobled, and the little orphans whom she loved so well could realize it, they woke up to see their good friend Margaret sitting just as she used to do in life, in the same old chair apparently, in her old familiar dress, in the grassy plot in the square where she used to watch the orphans playing, in front of the home which she had built for them; and around her shoulders the ladies had thrown, not the old shawl that she used to wear every day, but "the state occasion shawl," as Margaret used to call it, and which had been crocheted for her by the little 6-year-old tots of St. Vincent's Infants' Home. The City Council, by a special act, called the spot "Margaret Place." The monument is the first ever erected to a woman in the United States.

The asylum overlooking the place is called the "New Orleans Female Orphan Asylum." It was first founded in 1850 as a home to which the children from St. Vincent's Infant Asylum may be transferred and educated, and these in turn, as they grow older, are sent for special training in womanly work and art to St. Elizabeth's Asylum.

St. Anna's Asylum,

is a handsome stuccoed structure at the corner of St. Mary and Prytania Streets. It was founded by Dr. Mercer, in memory of his only daughter, Anna, as a retreat for poor gentlewomen, and was well endowed by him.

It is impossible to point out all the handsome houses on Prytania Street, which thence on is principally a residence street, but several may be particularly mentioned. At the corner of First and Prytania stands the mansion formerly occupied by Bradish Johnson, and now owned by Mr. W. D. Denegre. It is a rare specimen of Southern architecture. At the corner of Prytania and Second is the home of Mrs. Ida Richardson, surrounded by grounds exquisitely kept and filled with the rarest order of tropical vegetation, including many palms from far Eastern climes. The hothouses are considered the most beautiful in the South.

At Washington Street the car runs between the Washington Street
Cemetery on the one hand and the

Southern Athletic Club

on the other. This Club was one of the first founded in the South for the promotion of athletics and amateur sports. It has a large membership among
the best classes. It belongs to the National Amateur Athletic Union. The
clubhouse is of wood, the interior being finished in hard native woods. The
gymnasium is 120x77 feet, and is fully equipped with every appliance for athletic training. There are hot and cold baths, a swimming pool, boxing and
fencing rooms, Turkish and Russian baths, etc. In 1889 Kilrain trained at
this Club for his fight with Sullivan at Richburg, Miss., and in 1892 Corbett
trained here for his celebrated battle with Sullivan. It was to this clubhouse
that Corbett returned after the fight, to receive the congratulations of his
admirers. The visitors' book contains the autographs of many celebrities of
the sporting world.

Touro Infirmary,

an admirable institution sustained by the Jews of the city, and managed by
the Touro Infirmary and Hebrew Benevolent Association, occupies a square
on Prytania Street, between Delachaise and Aline. The Association undertook the management and enlargement of Judah Touro's bequest for the
relief of the suffering and needy of New Orleans. The original hospital was
in the cotton press district, at the corner of Gaiennie and South Peters Streets,
but when the city grew away from this section the Association decided to build
a model hospital uptown, about twenty-seven years ago. Subsequently the management made many improvements, and a debt of $20,000
was incurred. To relieve this burden a great fair was given, in February,

TOURO INFIRMARY.

1895. The entire South contributed liberally, and the magnificent sum
of $60,000, net profits, was realized. This enabled the management to carry
out many cherished plans for the further improvement of the infirmary. The
hospital is built on the pavilion plan, amid lawns and gardens beautifully
kept. It has free clinics, and all nationalities and creeds are admitted to
their benefits. The hospital has accommodations for about 400 patients. Recently the Infirmary management decided to still further extend its facilities,
and a new and more modern hospital building is contemplated.
    Within the grounds stands a magnificent fountain, erected at a cost
of $500, by the little Jewish children of New Orleans. On the same

PALMS IN PRIVATE GARDEN—PRY-   PALM TREE IN PRIVATE GARDEN—
TANIA AND SECOND STS.   PRYTANIA AND SECOND STS

grounds as the Infirmary was built, in 1899, at a cost of $35,000, the
handsome three-storied brick structure known as the Julius Weis Home for the
Aged.

It was the generous gift of the philanthropic Hebrew whose name it
bears. The Touro Infirmary Training School for Nurses is located in this
building.

In the block above the Infirmary is the Home for the Aged and
Infirm, conducted by the Little Sisters of the Poor. This is the uptown
branch of the noble institution, corner of North Johnson and Laharpe
Streets, in the French quarter. Between the two institutions nearly 600
old men and women, every one of whom is over 60 years of age, are cared for.
Both houses are well worth a visit.

The car now passes through a section full of small and pretty houses set
in gardens and shaded by trees. The line terminates at Audubon Park.

Upper Camp, for the purpose of this Guide, comprehends that section of the
thoroughfare lying above Calliope Street. The Magazine car will take the
tourist up Camp as far as Calliope, and thence through Upper to Old Camp, to
Louisiana Avenue, to Laurel Street, and thence to Audubon Park.

Beginning at Calliope Street, the visitor's attention is drawn to the handsome stone church occupied by the Episcopalian congregation of St. Paul's.
It stands at the corner of Camp and Gaiennie Streets.

St. Paul's Church

was erected in 1893, on the site of an older structure, which was destroyed by
fire a year or so before. The interior of the church is very beautiful. Its most
remarkable feature is its tower, which is a reproduction of a famous structure
at Oxford, England. The church is expensively finished with pavements and
wainscot of colored marbles, and has a pleasing interior. This building was
erected under the efficient management of the late Rev. H. H. Waters, who
was for twenty-seven years in charge of the congregation. This church has a
fine surpliced choir of boys and makes strangers welcome at its services.

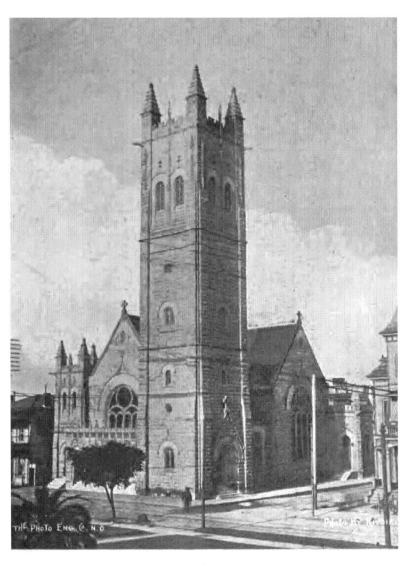

ST. PAUL'S CHURCH.

The asphalted walk in the center of the street, bordered with grass plots and shaded with small trees, is called Margaret Walk, in memory of Margaret Haughery.

At the corner of Camp and Erato is St. Theresa's Church, a quaint specimen of Dutch architecture.

The car then skirts

Coliseum Place,

a large, irregular park, almost a half a mile long, and beautifully laid out and shaded with trees. It is a great playground for children and a fashionable promenade in summer.

At the corner of Camp and Terpsichore is the Coliseum Place Baptist Church, one of the oldest worshiping places of that denomination in the city.

Miss Sophie B. Wright's Free Night School for Boys is at the corner of Camp and Race.

The Felicity Street Methodist Church, plainly visible from the cars, is at the corner of Felicity and Chestnut Streets. It is a handsome brick struct-

COLISEUM PLACE.

ure and stands upon the site formerly occupied by a stately edifice of brick, which was built about 1850, in the Grecian style, and which was burned about eleven years ago.

At Felicity Street Camp divides; one branch retains the name of Camp, running uptown, and the other continues for two blocks, and intersects at St. Andrew Street with Magazine. The latter Branch is called Old Camp. The Magazine car runs through Old Camp and turns into Magazine just beyond the lower Magazine Market. This market is smaller than the French market, and not so interesting.

The visitor will do well to leave the car at St. Andrew Street and visit the

"Ecclesiastical Square."

This comprises the group of schools, convents, churches and provincialate of the Redemptorist Order on or near the corner of Josephine and Constance Streets. There are the churches of St. Alphonsus and St. Mary's Assumption; the residence of the Redemptorist Fathers, who have built these churches, the Convent of Mercy, St. Alphonsus' Free Library, the school for colored children and other parochial schools and clubs.

St. Alphonsus' Church is on Constance Street, between St. Andrew and Josephine. It is of pure Renaissance architecture, with two towers, the steeples of which have never been completed. Over the main door, in a niche, is a statue of St. Alphonsus,, to whom the church is dedicated. The edifice has a seating capacity of 1,200. It was begun in 1855 and dedicated in 1858. The visitor is struck immediately upon entering, by the profusion of ornamentation and the beautiful frescoes on which the painter and the gilder have exhausted the resources of their art. The main altar cost $8,000. Over this altar is a very beautiful painting of St. Alphonsus, the work of a Roman artist. The large building used for the parish school, library, etc., stands in the open area on the downtown side of the church. The building cost $100,000, exclusive of its artistic embellishments.

St. Mary's Assumption Church is on Josephine, between Constance and Laurel Streets. The belfry is 190 feet high, and is considered very beautiful. It stands in the courtyard, near the side door of the

ANOTHER VIEW IN COLISEUM PLACE.

church. The church is Renaissance in style, with an exterior the plainness of which contrasts well with the highly ornamental interior. The ceiling is covered with stucco traceries. The main altar, designed and executed in Munich, cost $10,000 and is considered one of the handsomest in America. The stained glass windows are very expensive and beautiful. The pulpit is hung in a remarkable way.

The Convent of the Sisters of Mercy, on St. Andrew, between Magazine and Constance, was erected in 1858. Attached to the convent is a Boarding Home for Working Women, an orphanage and a Home of Mercy, where any poor woman may find shelter and food till she can obtain employment.

Upper Magazine Street.

On Magazine, between Jackson Avenue and Philip, stands the second oldest Presbyterian Church in the city—the Lafayette Church, built in 1843. For over half a century Rev. Dr. Thos. R. Markham, who was a great Confederate chaplain, was the rector. He was buried from this church. His monument is in Metairie Cemetery.

On Magazine, between Washington Avenue and Sixth Street, is a building known formerly as the Garden District Theatre, now owned and occupied by the First Baptist Church.

At the corner of Seventh and Magazine Streets is the upper Pythian Hall, built about 1893 for the use of the Knights of Pythias.

On Magazine, between Seventh and Eighth Streets, is a handsome brick structure, about which the vines clamber, suggesting peace and content. This is the Seventh Street Protestant Orphans' Home; it is under the management of a board of lady directors, and is ably conducted.

The Ninth Street Market stands at the corner of Ninth and Magazine.

At Louisiana Avenue the car leaves Magazine and runs out to Laurel. It proceeds up Laurel to the Audubon Park, stopping near the entrance to the Horticultural Hall. This is the best line to take to reach the park.

The German Protestant Home for the Aged and Infirm is at No. 5919 Magazine. At No. 6126 will be found the Monastery of the Poor Clares. This is a cloistered community of nuns, similar to the Discalced Carmelite Nuns, whose home is in the old French quarter.

Adjoining the monastery on Henry Clay Avenue is the Home for Incurables.

Three years ago the Louisiana Kings' Daughters undertook, through the offering of a cent a day for blessings received, to build an annex to the Home. The sum of $10,000 has been raised through these "blessing boxes." The new edifice will be erected during the year and will serve as the Administration Building of the Home.

In returning by the Magazine line, St. Vincent's Infant Asylum, "Margaret's Baby House," is passed. This interesting institution is at the corner of Magazine and Race Streets. It is in charge of the Sisters of Charity. It is the foundling asylum of the city, and contains at almost all times at least 200 children, infants in arms or babies just beginning to walk. No little motherless or abandoned babe is ever refused admittance here. The neatness, order and general perfection of the management are often commented upon admiringly. One of the most interesting features of the Asylum is the perfectly equipped kindergarten and the nursery, where several hundred little tots play about the floor or sleep in the pretty white-curtained beds, all unconscious of what life has in store for them. In the pretty parlor on the first floor is a picture of Margaret holding a babe in her arms. The memory of this gentle mother of the orphans is very fragrant in the Asylum.

The lower portion of Magazine Street is occupied largely by factories or wholesale grocery and produce stores.

The Maginnis Cotton Mills, which were incorporated in 1881, are on the corner of Annunciation and Calliope Streets, and their warehouse is at the corner of Magazine and Lafayette Streets. Originally the mills had 15,360 spindles and 360 looms, making sheeting, shirtings, drills and osnaburgs. The ready market for its product resulted in an enlargement of the plant in 1888, when the most modern English machinery was purchased, increasing the capacity of the mills three-fold. Even greater improvements have been made since then, and there are now over 40,000 spindles and nearly 1,500 looms in operation. These are kept going the year round, giving employment to over 1,000 people, many of whom are girls. The mill's output finds a ready market from Boston to San Francisco, from Chicago to Texas, and certain grades are shipped to China.

The Board of Trade has an entrance through the archway of Magazine Street, between Natchez Alley and Gravier Street. The archway passes through a three-story brick building, formerly known as the St. James Hotel. The rotunda of this hotel was, before the War, the principal slave mart in the city. The building is now occupied by offices.

The main office of the Southern Pacific Railroad is in the large gray building, with massive Greek portico, at the corner of Natchez Alley and Magazine Street.

CHAPTER XIV.

Along the Coliseum Line, St. Charles, Carondelet, Upper Magazine and Other Streets.

An interesting portion of New Orleans is that through which the Coliseum car passes. The car starts at the Louisville and Nashville depot, near the foot of Canal Street, and traverses the great boulevard as far as the corner of Carondelet Street, into which it turns, proceeding thence to Clio, to Felicity, to Coliseum, to Chestnut, to Louisiana Avenue, to Magazine and Broadway, to Maple and Carrollton Avenue. It returns by way of Maple Street to Broadway, to Magazine, to Calliope, and thence proceeds down St. Charles to its starting point in Canal Street. From the many turns and zig-zags along the winding route, it has often been called the "Snake Line."

Before beginning this long ride, which leads really through a very beautiful and important section of New Orleans, the tourist will find it interesting to walk from Canal Street to Poydras, stopping en route to inspect leading points in the great commercial thoroughfares of St. Charles and Carondelet Streets.

Carondelet is the Wall Street

of New Orleans. The cotton and stock brokers for the most part are established along this street. Almost all the railroads have their offices in the neighborhood of St. Charles and Common streets, as also the express and telegraph companies.

On St. Charles, one square from Canal, between Common and Gravier, is the

St. Charles Hotel.

The present hotel is the phoenix of three structures bearing the same name that have successively risen upon this historic spot. The first St. Charles Hotel was erected in 1835, at a cost of $700,000. It took three years to build it. It was characterized by a magnificent portico of Corinthian columns, from which a flight of marble steps led to the hotel. Its rotunda was world-famed. A dome forty-six feet in diameter surmounted the edifice, which was considered at that period one of the most beautiful in the world. Its erection marked the beginning of the great hotels of America, and it was only after some years that it was rivalled by the Astor House, of New York City. A. Oakey Hall, afterwards Mayor of New York, wrote of it shortly after its erection: "Set the St. Charles Hotel down in St. Petersburg, and you will think it is a palace; in Boston, and, ten to one, you would christen it a college; in London, and it would marvelously remind you of an exchange. In New Orleans it is all three."

The hotel was the resort of the wealthiest planters of the South. Its weekly balls were famous. In 1851 the building was destroyed by fire. Many other buildings which were historic landmarks also passed away, among others the First Presbyterian Church. The total loss was $1,000,000. Within two days the directors of the hotel met and decided to rebuild. In twelve months the new hotel was finished. This building was the scene of many stirring events of the decade between 1851 and 1861. In its parlors Jefferson Davis and a number of Southern leaders met on their way to the Charleston Convention of 1860, and decided on the course they would pursue. The building had been leased to Messrs. Hildreth and Hall. In 1862 the course of Mr. Hildreth in refusing to give General Butler accommodations in the hotel came near resulting in a serious street disturbance. Hildreth was a Northern man and a relative of General Butler's wife. But he was intensely Southern in his sympathies, and was an active member of the Confederate Guards. When Butler reached the city, on May 2, he sent messengers to the hotel to ask for rooms for himself and his staff. He soon followed, accompanied by a large military guard. Mr. Hildreth declined to admit him, declaring that the hotel was closed. Butler demanded the keys, which were refused him. In the meanwhile the angry crowd had gathered in the neighboring thoroughfares, hooting the General and threatening him with personal violence. The crowd interfered with the officers who were trying to force their way into the hotel, but was finally dispersed. Butler took refuge in the barroom, and there held a conference with Mayor Monroe and the City Council. These gentlemen agreed to do all in their power to maintain the peace. Butler finally succeeded in obtaining possession of the hotel and opened it to his officers. A few days later he moved to the Twiggs House, and the lessees again obtained possession of their property. During the remainder of the war it was kept open. In 1865 many of the impoverished Confederates were entertained here free of charge. The books showd that bills contracted by them to the amount of $30,000 had never been sent out for collection. This historic building was destroyed by fire April 28, 1894. A great deal of sentiment was attached to the old hotel, and its destruction moved many to tears. From the ruins of the famous old hostlery like magic sprang up the new St. Charles Hotel, superb and modern in all its appointments. From the first glimpse of its chaste red exterior, with palms and banana trees waving amid its colonaded walks, to the beautiful palm gardens glowing with tropical verdure, the stately parlors and marble-floored dining-halls, the hotel is a perpetual delight to the artistic observer. It is the palatial fin-de-siècle hostlery of the South. The most important event in its history was the entertaining of President and Mrs. McKinley and the Cabinet suite during their visit to New Orleans prior to the President's assassination at Buffalo. Just back of the hotel are the two annexes which give it a capacity for 1000 guests. The hotel now ranks as the fourth in size in the United States.

Directly opposite the Cotton Exchange, at the corner of Carondelet and Gravier, will be seen in course of construction the handsome new building of the Hibernia Bank and Trust Company. The building is twelve stories high, and has a frontage of 140 feet on Carondelet Street, and a depth of 100 feet on Gravier Street. It is not only the largest building as to the amount of floor space offered in New Orleans, but one of the most handsomely appointed edifices in the city. The first two floors are of granite, and the remainder of the building of light brick or terra cotta The total estimated cost is about $850,000. Work began on October 1, 1902. The Hibernia Bank and Trust Company occupies the first floor, and the remainder is utilized as business offices, On the twelfth floor a Merchants' Noonday Club will be put in, the membership of which is expected to reach seven or eight hundred.

At the corner of Common and Carondelet Streets, on the river side, stands the handsome building owned and occupied by the

Liverpool and London and Globe

Insurance Company. As will be seen by the accompanying illustration, it is one of the most notable of the city's business buildings. It was erected at great expense and is viewed with great interest by strangers on account of the architectural beauty and finish of both exterior and interior. The company's general offices are on the first floor, and here is handled the large business coming to it from the six States under the jurisdiction of the local office. In erecting this building the company has shown its desire to be regarded as a local institution and its great faith in the future of New Orleans. A second building has recently been erected as an annex, similar in point of architecture and finish to the main building. During the fifty-four years of its honored existence in this country this great corporation has paid out $90,000,000 in losses. Such a record, added to a wide-spread reputation for liberal dealing and undoubted solvency have gained for the company the full confidence of the insuring public.

The State Board of Health has its office on the second floor. This Board controls the elaborate quarantine system by which contagious diseases from the Latin-American ports are prevented from entering the United States.

The handsome building with classic exterior at the north-west corner of Carondelet and Common is the headquarters of the Commercial Bank and Trust Company, recently erected.

LIVERPOOL AND LONDON AND GLOBE INSURANCE CO.'S BUILDING.

On the lake side of Carondelet and Common Streets are the Hennen Building and its annex, the Cora Building, which were erected at a cost of $300,000 in 1895 by Alfred Hennen Morris, son of the late John A. Morris. The buildings are used for offices. The City Board of Health has its office in the Cora building, which is just back of the Hennen.

The Stock Exchange is located in the Denegre Building, which is at No. 221 Carondelet Street.

At the corner of Gravier and Carondelet stands the

Cotton Exchange,

which is a fine specimen of the Renaissance style of architecture, and is considered very beautiful. It is built of cream-colored stone. The cost of erection was $380,000. The Cotton Exchange was organized in 1871, with a membership of 100. It has now about 500 names on its roll. The Exchange proper occupies a beautiful apartment superbly frescoed with scenes from the history of Louisiana. Futures are sold around the small fountain at one end of the room. The Exchange enforces obedience to its rules for sampling, buying, selling and delivering cotton, and settles all disputes by arbitration. Reports of the receipts of cotton at all ports, exports and imports, meteorological and crop reports, and other indispensable information are daily posted on the blackboards. The upper floors of the building are occupied by business offices. A small gallery, accessible from the stairway or elevator, is open to visitors. A fine view is obtainable from the roof of the building. There is a time-ball on the roof,

COTTON EXCHANGE.

regulated by telegraphic communication with Washington. It is dropped daily at noon. The Bureau of State Engineers, where the engineering work of the Louis iana Levee system is done, is located in this building.

Immense commercial interests combine to make all this section of Gravier, Common, Carondelet and St. Charles one of the busiest business sections of New Orleans.

The United Fruit Company occupies the large building at the corner of St. Charles and Union Streets. This site is famous as the one occupied for so many years by the Louisiana State Lottery Company.

Adjoining is the building of the People's Homestead Association, the oldest of the homestead associations in New Orleans, the success of which gave inspiration to the many other homestead companies that are now established in this city.

The Masonic Temple, a stately edifice in brick, is at the corner of Perdido and St. Charles Streets. The statue on the upper corner pinnacle is of bronze and represents Jacques de Molay. The upper floors are reserved for lodge rooms. The Grand Lodge of Louisiana has its offices here.

The St. Charles Orpheum,

one of the finest of the new modern theatres of New Orleans, occupies the site of the famous St. Charles. Theatre, so often called the "Old Drury." The history of this old theatre, which was destroyed by fire in 1899, extended back over a period of sixty years. It was erected in 1835 by James Caldwell, the scholar and actor, who built the first American theatre in this city in Camp Street in 1823. The cost of the old building was $350,000. Its history was in a great measure the history of the English drama in New Orleans. Such famous stars as the elder Booth, Keane, Macready, Ellen Tree, Patti, Tom Placide, Joseph Jefferson and Mr. and Mrs. Vance acted here. From the ruins of the old theatre there rose this splendid modern playhouse, superb in all its equipments, and erected at a cost of $150,000 by Dr. Geo. K. Pratt. It fully sustains the reputation enjoyed by its ancient ancestor.

The ruins of the Audubon Theatre, known in other days as the

Academy of Music,

are in the same square. The building was erected in 1853, and that same year the renowned circus man, Dan Rice, opened the theatre. It had a portable stage, and its character as an amphitheatre was retained until 1854, when the Old Varieties, where Mr. and Mrs. Dion Boucicault were to act, burned down. The late David Bidwell, who had assumed their management, and who subsequently became the owner of this, as well as the St. Charles Theatre, immediately leased and renovated the building and named it the Pelican Theatre. Shortly after he gave it the name of "Academy of Music," which it bore until the appellation "Audubon," was given it by a popular vote. In former times its attractions included a museum of natural curiosities. The theatre was destroyed by fire, February 11th, 1903.

The Hotel Denechaud, noted for its excellent Creole cuisine, is at the corner of Carondelet and Perdido Streets.

In Perdido Street, between Carondelet and Baronne, is the Pythian Hall, where most of the Pythian Lodges are located, and where the Grand Officials of the Order have their offices.

Taking the car at this point in Carondelet Street, one passes en route, between Poydras and Lafayette, the "Jewish Right Way" Synagogue. This is the worshiping place of the orthodox Jews.

Between Lafayette and Girod is the Carondelet Street Methodist Church, the oldest Methodist Church in the city. It was built shortly before the Civil War, through the liberality and the exertions of Messrs. McGehee and Hill, two prominent Methodists. The church is of brick, and has an Ionic portico, and is covered by a graceful cupola, modeled after the monument of Lysicrates, in Greece. Bishop J. C. Keener, the Senior Bishop of the Southern Methodists, often preached here.

At 731 Carondelet is the New Orleans Sanitarium and Training School for Nurses. A handsome addition was recently erected at a cost of $39,000.

The Touro Synagogue

is situated on Carondelet Street, between Julia and St. Joseph. It is of Grecian design, and is named after the philanthropist, Judah Touro, who settled in New Orleans in 1801, and died in 1854, leaving an immense fortune, over $400,000 of which was, by the terms of his will, distributed among the religious and charitable institutions of the city. Mr. Touro was a sincerely religious man, and associated himself with a body of Jews who were accustomed to meet for religious services at the home of a gentleman named Andrews, which occupied the site adjoining the Howard Library, on Camp Street, where now stands a neat, one-storied frame residence. In 1845 Mr. Touro

TOURO SYNAGOGUE.

purchased the building on the corner of Canal and Bourbon Streets, which had up to that year been occupied by the Episcopal congregation of Christ Church. This was converted into a synagogue and presented to his coreligionists. They used it for several years, but disposed of it to remove to the present structure, which is interesting as reproducing with considerable exactness the original home of the venerable and wealthy congregation. In 1882 Touro Synagogue and the old congregation of the Gates of Mercy, organized in 1828, and the oldest in the city, consolidated.

The congregation has subsequently been known as the "Gates of Mercy of the Dispersed of Judah." In memory of its great benefactor, the name of Mr. Touro was bestowed upon the place of worship. A special prayer for Mr. Touro has been inserted in the memorial services on the Day of Atonement, and at each annual recurrence of the ceremony the entire congregation rises and remains standing while the rabbi pronounces the solemn sentences.

Rev. I. L. Leucht is the presiding rabbi. The synagogue is noted for its beautiful music and excellent choir.

The Temple Sinai

stands on Carondelet Street, near Howard Avenue. This congregation was founded in 1871. The first rabbi of the congregation was Dr. J. K. Gutheim, one of the most eloquent and learned men of his time. This congregation, like that of Touro Synagogue, is composed of reformed Jews. The building is decorated in the Byzantine style, and is very beautiful. The music and chanting here are always very fine. Rev. Max Heller is the presiding rabbi.

The third Hebrew congregation was founded in 1850, and erected a synagogue, which it still retains, corner of Jackson and Chippewa Streets.

TEMPLE SINAI.

The German Evangelical Lutheran Church is on Clio, near St. Charles Avenue.

Further up along this line are many handsome residences. It is the most beautiful part of the Garden District, and the visitor should notice the luxuriance of the flowering shrubs, which blossom even in the depths of winter.

At Washington Street the car passes

The H. Sophie Newcomb

Memorial College for Young Women. This is the female department of the Tulane University. The college occupies a whole square. The handsome central building facing on Washington Street was formerly known as the Burnside residence, having been the home of an eccentric millionaire of that name. It was built originally by James Robb. a great banker of ante-bellum days, in imitation of the country seat of an English nobleman. The house at one time contained a celebrated collection of pictures, including many paintings from the gallery of Prince Jerome Bonaparte, at Bordentown, N. J. These pictures were sold to local dealers some eight years ago. The upper story of this building was added after the purchase by the' University. The lower floor contains several rooms with the original frescoes.

The H. Sophie Newcomb Memorial Room is worth a visit, if only to see the magnificent reflecting mirrors of old Moorish design, said to be the finest in the United States. This room also contains all the childhood souvenirs of Haryott Sophie Newcomb, who died at the age of 15, in 1866. She was an only child, and her mother, Mrs. Josephine Louise Newcomb, has commemorated her in this magnificent gift. Mrs. Newcomb first donated upward of $450,000 to the college, which she placed under the auspices of Tulane University; at her death, in 1900, she left her vast estate to the college. The grounds contain magnificent live oaks, a tennis court, and grouped around are the Newcomb High School, which is preparatory to the college, the art building, gymnasium, pottery building and chapel. The pottery building, which is directly opposite the Camp Street entrance to the college, has its own kiln, and the manufactures are all of Louisiana clay. In the art building is a rare collection of òld paintings, and some quaint curios, among others illuminated missals from the fourteenth century. A marble statue of St. George, costing $5,000, adorns the art building. The beautiful little chapel,

H. SOPHIE NEWCOMB MEMORIAL COLLEGE.

in which services are yearly held in memory of H. Sophie Newcomb, contains several handsome stained glass windows by Tiffany, among others a representation of the "Resurrection Morn," said to be the finest piece of work ever sent out by Tiffany, and which adorned the chapel exhibited by this company at the World's Exposition in Chicago, in 1893. The Newcomb library is constantly growing, and now numbers about 10,000 volumes. Opposite the college is the Newcomb dormitory, recently built and donated to the college by Mrs. Newcomb as a home for the students, and just around the corner stands the private residence of the generous donor, which, since her death, has been made an annex to the college dormitory.

At the corner of Chestnut and Louisiana Avenue is the Catholic Church of Our Lady of Good Counsel, built in 1892.

The Cumberland Telephone Company has recently erected a handsome new building in the square bounded by Coliseum, Foucher, Camp and Chestnut.

At the corner of Louisiana Avenue and Magazine is the Louisiana Avenue Methodist Church, erected in 1895.

The Valence Street Baptist Church is on the corner of Valence and Magazine.

At No. 5116 Magazine, between Soniat and Dufossat Streets, is the Southern University, for the education of colored persons. Coeducation is in force here. The school is excellent and the instruction of an advanced character.

The handsome brown brick building embowered in foliage, on Magazine Street, between Leontine and Peters, is the

Poydras Asylum,

founded in 1817, through the liberality of Julian Poydras. The Asylum was the outgrowth of a peculiar and pathetic incident dating back to the year 1817, when an immigrant vessel came to New Orleans with cholera on board and twenty little children who had been rendered fatherless and motherless by the ravages of the terrible scourge while the vessel was at sea. A kind-hearted gentleman stated the circumstance to Mrs. M. A. Hunter, mother of the celebrated Commodore Hunter, and she at once sought to enlist the sympathies of other women in their behalf. She gathered the little waifs into a rented house, when Julian Poydras heard of their condition and donated a home for them on the corner of Julia and St. Charles Streets, where the house known as the Spofford property stands. The property was subsequently leased out for a period of fifty years, and in 1905 it will revert to the Asylum.

POYDRAS ASYLUM.

Julian Poydras was a young Frenchman who came to New Orleans from San Domingo in the days of Governor Galvez. He was a poet and a scholar, but he was very poor. He was not ashamed, as the old traditions run, to carry a pack on his back, and furnished himself with a peddler's stock and traveled up the coast on foot all the way to St. Louis, thus beginning the commercial connections of the great Mississippi Valley. Out of his industry came wealth, honors, slaves, plantations and a colonial home. He is recalled in Creole traditions as a courtly gentleman, who always dressed in the Louis XV style. At his ancient villa, near where the Poydras market now stands, he entertained the most distinguished persons, among others the sons of Philip Egalité, when they came to New Orleans. But it is also related of him that his villa was ever open to peddlers, and an old Creole chanson says that "no man with a pack on his back was ever turned from the door of Julian Poydras." In 1817 he founded the Poydras Asylum, erecting it out of his own means. He munificently endowed the Asylum at his death. In 1836 the present building was erected, at a cost of $90,000. It was first placed in the charge of the Sisters of Charity, but at his death the institution passed entirely under the control of the Presbyterian Directory, and the government was transferred to a Board of Lady Managers. The institution is beautifully kept. In the rear are extensive vegetable gardens, which supply the Asylum. Upon the walls of the reception room hang the pictures of Julian Poydras and Mrs. Hunter.

Parker Chapel is the small wooden church at the corner of Magazine and Peters Avenue.

The German Protestant Home is at the corner of Magazine and Eleonôre. The German Orphan Asylum is on State and Magazine.

Audubon Park is the site of the Cotton Centennial Exposition of 1884, and the Horticultural Hall, where many beautiful tropical palms and exotics bloom, is passed. The terminus of the line is at Carrollton Avenue.

Returning, at No. 3043 Camp Street, the

Fink Home,

or Asylum for Widows is passed. This asylum was founded through the bequest of Mr. John Fink, a wealthy but eccentric gentleman, who died some years ago. Mr. Fink was an old bachelor, and the story runs that in his youth he fell in love with a beautiful New Orleans girl, who rejected his suit, declaring that she did not believe in girls marrying. She told him that she thought that they should become old maids, and thus remain free to work out their own individual destinies. It is related that Mr. Fink pleaded and pleaded, but in vain. The lady remained firm. He therefore shut himself off entirely from the society of ladies, and at his death left a large sum of money to found the "Fink Home for Widows." Down at the end of his testament he added a special restrictive clause, forbidding the entrance into this Home of "any old maid, no matter how aged or dependent she was or necessitous her circumstances." He closed this singular testament with the words, "Let every old maid work out her own individual destiny." It was thus, the Faubourg Ste. Marie declared, Mr. Fink revenged himself upon the fair but cruel sweetheart of his youth.

At the corner of Camp and Foucher Streets is the Frank T. Howard School No. 2, recently erected by Mr. Howard at a cost of nearly $60,000 as a memorial to his mother.

At the corner of Camp and First Streets is a large old-fashioned brown mansion, surrounded by magnificent trees. This is the home of Judge Charles E. Fenner. It was in this house that Jefferson Davis, President of the Confederate States, died in November, 1889.

At No. 815 St. Charles, near Julia, is the

Young Men's Christian Association

Building. This commodious structure was erected in 1895, partly through the liberality of Mr. J. H. Keller, a wealthy manufacturer. The reading-room on the first floor, is free to the public. The members of the Association have access to an excellent gymnasium, swimming tank and baths, the use of the parlors, dining-hall, etc. On the second floor is a large hall called the Helme Memorial Hall. An observatory on the roof affords a splendid view of the city.

Near the corner of St. Charles and Julia Streets, in the beautiful cultivated garden spot on the river side of the street, there stood until 1902 the famous Church of the Messiah, which was erected by the Hebrew philanthropist, Judah P. Touro, in 1854, for the use of his friend, the celebrated Unitarian minister, Dr. Theodore Clapp, when the latter's church was destroyed by fire after his secession from Presbyterianism. The church cost $60,000, and was a very curious piece of architecture. It was octagonal in form, and the aisles and clerestory gave it a pleasing effect. This church was sold in 1902, and from the proceeds of the sale the new edifice, corner of Dryades and Peters Avenue, was erected. The old church was demolished.

Between Julia and Girod Streets stands the

Washington Artillery Hall,

where the famous Washington Artillery has its headquarters. It was away back in 1838 that the "Native American Artillery" was organised in New Orleans. In 1841 it attached itself to the Washington Battalion, and in 1844 this battalion was augmented by the transfer from the Louisiana Legion of three companies, the Orleans Cadets, the Louisiana Grays and the Orleans

Grenadiers. Francis A. Lumsden, one of the founders and proprietors of the Picayune, was the Captain of the latter company. The battalion became known as the Washington Regiment, with General Persifer F. Smith as the commanding officer. In 1845, when the "Army of Occupation," under General Zachary Taylor, was dispatched to Texas, General Gaines, of the United States Army, Department of the South, issued a call for troops. The Washington Battalion responded and went to Mexico, near the Rio Grande. Shortly after the Mexican War the battalion adopted the name of the Washington Artillery. When the Civil War broke out the battalion was among the first to respond. It was mustered into the service in Lafayette Square, and, marching to the old Christ Church, in Canal Street, received a flag, presented by the ladies of New Orleans, costing $1,000. Mr. Judah P. Benjamin made the presentation. The command fired the first gun at Bull Run and brought up the rear at Appomattox. After the collapse of the Southern cause, the survivors returned to their homes, but the tie of comradeship and the pride of the old corps were too strong to be kept down. As it was the reconstruction era and the Confederate soldiers were not allowed to continue their military organization, the company took the name of a benevolent association, whose object was to care for the needy and to erect a monument to its dead. The handsome monument in Metairie Cemetery tells its own story. Before the war the company's arsenal was located on Girod Street, but this building was confiscated while the battalion was in the Confederate service. In 1875 the Battalion of the Washington Artillery was reorganized, and in 1880 Colonel John B. Richardson, who had been promoted to the command, succeeded in purchasing the present spacious arsenal. This hall was erected in 1872 as an exposition building, to afford a permanent place for the exhibition of all the manufactured articles used in the South. The building has a frontage of 85 feet and a depth of 341. The ballroom, on the second floor, in which the Rex balls are given, is 200 feet long. The arsenal contains some valuable relics of the Mexican and Civil Wars. Among the latter are the magnificent flag, on which are the names of the sixty battles in which the command participated, and a famous painting by Julio, valued at $5,000. It represents the last meeting of Robert Lee and Stonewall Jackson at Chancellorsville. The catafalque upon which the remains of Jefferson Davis were borne to the grave occupies a conspicuous place in the arsenal.

Soulé's Commercial College is at the corner of St. Charles and Lafayette Streets. The college was founded in 1856, and occupies a leading place among the educational institutions of the city. The handsome new building, erected in 1902, occupies the site of an ancient structure which was one of the landmarks of the American quarter.

Thence to Canal Street the car passes directly in front of the City Hall, the magnificent mansion of the well-known public benefactor, Mr. Frank T. Howard, which adjoins it, business houses and theatres, the St. Charles Hotel, and railroad offices, and, turning from St. Charles into Canal Street, passes the Crescent Billiard Hall, a resort celebrated for the past forty years.

Tchoupitoulas Street.

Tchoupitoulas is mainly a business street, and the best way to see it is to take the car which runs up the street from Canal to Audubon Park. The lower part of the street nearest Canal is lined with immense groceries and warehouses. Further up are a number of foundries and metal working establishments. Throughout the route glimpses may be caught from time to time of shipping lying alongside the wharves.

The shot tower is at the corner of St. Joseph Street. It is the highest tower in the city.

The heart of the cotton press district is next passed.

Near Louisiana Avenue are several grain elevators.

The Stuyvesant Docks are on the river front, between Delachaise and Foucher Streets, and are of great interest. The elevator is of gigantic size. A very elaborate system of grain carriers and railway terminals exist. The elevator has a capacity of 1,000,000 bushels, or about 1,200 cars. If coupled together these cars would make a chain eight miles long. The elevator can unload 250 cars a day; and at the same time deliver, through an unequaled system of conveyors, to four steamships

STORING COTTON IN THE PRESSES.

at once. It is the largest, the best-equipped and busiest elevator in the United States. In addition to the other facilities, there are wharves 1,500 feet in length.

Annunciation Street.

The Annunciation Street car follows the line of the Coliseum car, from Canal as far as Erato Street. It diverges there to Annunciation. It will take the visitor through a picturesque part of town. In the vicinity of Annunciation Square it passes through the cotton press district, where, in the season, thousands of bales of the fleecy staple are pressed and stored. Long rows of bales may be seen banked along the sidewalk. The dull rumble of the presses is constantly heard. If the visitor has never seen the presses in operation, it will be well for him to visit one of the yards, where he will willingly be admitted to see its wonders.

St. Simeon's School is the fine old colonial building occupying the entire square on Annunciation, near Erato Street. It is in charge of the Sisters of Charity.

A detour is made around Annunciation Square. This square was presented to the city by a private citizen. On the woods side is the beautiful residence of the late E. J. Hart.

Just opposite the square, on the river side, are St. Michael's Church, presbytery and parochial schools.

At the corner of Orange and Annunciation the visitor will notice an old-fashioned wooden residence, with pillared veranda and dormer windows. This was formerly the Stanley residence.

Mr. Stanley was a cotton merchant of a charitable disposition. He adopted Henry M. Stanley, the famous explorer, who at that time was a destitute

INTERIOR OF A COTTON PRESS.

orphan. Stanley's name was assumed by the boy in lieu of his own, which was originally John Rowlands.

Clay Square is on Annunciation, between Second and Third Streets.

Peters Avenue and Dryades.

These cars, which start on Canal, near the river, traverse the least attractive part of the city. Going up town, the route is through South Rampart and South Liberty Streets. Above Louisiana Avenue, where the car enters Dryades Street, and in Peters Avenue, there will be noticed indications of the rapid growth of the city. A few years ago these two streets boasted very few residences of any sort; now they are being rapidly built up, and within a brief period will be numbered among the most attractive in the city.

At the corner of Peters Avenue and Dryades Street is the new

Unitarian Church.

This building was erected in 1902, and represents the congregation founded oy Dr. Theodore Clapp when he seceded from the Presbyterian Church in 1833, and carried the bulk of his congregation and the church property with him. The history of this congregation has already been referred to, as also the old church edifice which stood for so many years near the corner of St. Charles and Julia Streets; from the proceeds of the sale was erected the present building. Though much smaller than the old church, it is better adapted to the needs of the Unitarian congregation.

At the corner of Peters Avenue and South Rampart stands the Isidore Newman Manual Training School, the gift of a philanthropic citizen of that name to the Jewish Widows and Orphans Home Association for the manual training of the orphans in the Jewish Home.

The cars stop at the upper station, corner of Arabella and Magazine, within sight of the huge rectangular brick building, the Louisiana Retreat, an insane asylum conducted by the Sisters of Charity. This building stands at the corner of Henry Clay Avenue and Coliseum, and is visible from all the street car lines which run to the Audubon Park.

Returning, St. Mary's Dominican Convent, at No. 1107 Dryades Street, and the Turnverein Hall, at No. 116 Clio, are passed.

At the corner of Calliope is the handsome Church of St. John the Baptist. This is a Catholic Church; it stands between the Dominican Convent and St. John Parochial School and Presbytery.

At Howard Avenue the car passes within sight of the Illinois Central Passenger Station and the head of the New Basin Canal. This canal, by the way, is exceedingly picturesque, filled almost all the time with schooners, and lined with sawmills and wood yards.

At the corner of Lafayette and Dryades is a building of large proportions and obviously once of aristocratic appearance. It was formerly the Turners' Hall, but long ago was abandoned by that organization, being subsequently used as a manual training school by Tulane University, and more recently by a manufacturer of tinware.

Other points of interest are the Poydras Market and the office of the State Medical Society, and the New Orleans Medical and Surgical Journal, over the way.

CHAPTER XV.

The Port of New Orleans—Scenes along the Levee.

The visitor to New Orleans will have missed the most interesting as well as important feature of this city should he fail to make a personal inspection of the magnificent harbor known as the Port of New Orleans. For a distance of fifteen miles along the city front there extends an almost unbroken line of wharves and docks, sufficient to accommodate a vast fleet. Owing to the great depth of the Mississippi River, ships are able to lie close alongside the bank and load cargoes through all hatches at once. There is an equal stretch of fifteen miles along the west bank of the river within the port limits, although as yet only a moderate portion of this space available for shipping is used.

Along the harbor front there are five great grain elevators, extensive railroad terminals, including the famed Stuyvesant Docks, belonging to the Illinois Central Railroad. There are several fruit docks, with covered sheds, for the handling of tropical fruit. Another conspicuous feature is the fine new coffee dock, with its immense iron shed to protect freight from the weather. Along the city's wharves will be seen some of the largest freight ships afloat.

The best way to see the river front is to walk along the levee. It is called the levee because it consists of a great bank of earth thrown up to protect the city from the invasion of the Mississippi, which at flood rises far above the level of the streets. For many years, however, the river along most of the front has withdrawn itself a good way from the original channel, so that many solid blocks of buildings now stand where the Mississippi flowed when Bienville first looked upon it. The constant additions made to the levee in consequence cause a gradual slope up to the river front. The slope begins at a considerable distance back, and the ascent up hill is so gradual as to be imperceptible.

Many interesting sights attract along the river front.

Near the foot of Canal Street is the

Steamboat Landing,

where boats of all sorts and sizes, from the stately river packets which trade up the river to Vicksburg, Memphis, Cairo and St. Louis, to the little stern-wheelers which run up Red River and into Bayou Atchafalaya and along the lower Mississippi coast, are to be seen the year round.

Here the packets lie, busily receiving and discharging freight. The immense loads of cotton and sugar which they take on, make them especially interesting to the stranger. It is very picturesque to see the throngs of darkies handling these cargoes, and singing old plantation melodies or camp-meeting hymns as they work away. When the vessels are loaded to the guards and are ready

ON THE MISSISSIPPI IN THE BUSY COTTON SEASON.

to leave a great shout goes up from the throng of laborers and roustabouts. Then they turn their attention to the next big cargo.

The Sugar Exchange,

where the members conduct many of those operations which regulate the price of sugar throughout the country is on the corner of Front and Bienville Streets. The Exchange is a building of magnificent proportions. Facing the levee are the salesrooms, vestibule and telegraph offices; on the second floor are the library, reading-room and museum and committee rooms. The building throughout exhibits exquisite taste in ornamentation. Upon the walls hang the portraits of Etienne de Boré, the first great sugar planter of Louisiana, Don Antonio Mendes, who first granulated sugar from cane in the old Parish of St. Bernard, and Jean Joseph Coiron, who in 1818 put up on his plantation in Terre-aux-Boeufs the first steam engine ever used to grind sugar, and in 1820 introduced from Georgia the red-ribbon cane in place of the tender Creole variety. The New Orleans Sugar Exchange has

LEVEE SCENE—HANDLING SUGAR.

about 211 members, and wields a powerful influence in the commerce of the State. In the vicinity of the Exchange are several great refineries, where the crude products of the sugarhouses on the plantations are changed into the beautiful white sugar that is seen on the table. They are worth a visit. Trees and shrubbery adorn the triangular islet near the Bienville side of the Exchange.

The Fruit Landing

is just above Canal, near the head of Thalia Street, where almost any day may be found vessels discharging great cargoes of tropical fruits, bananas, oranges, lemons, mangos, pineapples, cocoanuts, etc. These are brought from ports on the Gulf of Mexico and the Caribbean Sea. A large quantity of this fruit, especially the ripest of it, stops in New Orleans, where it finds a ready sale in the markets at ridiculously low prices; but the great bulk of it is loaded into cars right at the fruit wharves, and in a few hours after the arrival of the ship is flying northward towards Louisville, Cincinnati, Chicago, St. Louis and other cities, to be sold there.

At the corner of Levee and Toulouse stood until 1826, when it was destroyed by fire, the old French Colonial "Government House."

LEVEE SCENE—HANDLING COTTON.

At the head of St. Louis Street are the wharves of the Southern Pacific Railroad Company, which runs a regular line of steamships from this point to New York. The steamships come here loaded with miscellaneous cargoes, and carry off immense cargoes of cotton, sugar, molasses, rice, cotton seed oil and other characteristic Southern products. Immense sheds will be erected during 1904.

At a short distance below are the wharves of the Harrison Line, which trades between New Orleans and Liverpool, running two and three steamers a week, and sometimes one a day, when the trade is very brisk.

Just in front of the French Market, along the Levee line, is the

Lugger Landing, or "Picayune Tier."

Here the Dago fishermen from the lower coast land their cargoes of oranges and oysters, and here gathers a swarm of luggers, with motley crews of traders, hustling about unloading cargoes of oysters, fish, oranges, vegetables and all the various offerings of the land and water along the bayous and lakes of the lower Louisiana coast. When waiting for a cargo of some sort to set sail again they loiter idly about, smoking cigarettes or cooking their meals over queer little charcoal furnaces. The "Tier" is a picturesque sight.

At the foot of Hospital Street is the landing of the New Orleans and Porto Rico Steamship Company, a line that has been established since the American occupation of Porto Rico, and which is already bringing large consignments of coffee from this tropical island, carrying back principally cargoes of Louisiana rice, which is fast finding a market in the island.

The Morgan Ferry Landing, where the Southern Pacific Company's freight cars are transferred by ferries to the Algiers side of the river, is at the foot of Elysian Fields Street. Transfers of passengers are made now at Avondale, about nine miles up the river.

The ferries which ply between New Orleans proper and Algiers all have their houses along the river front, at such convenient points as the foot of Canal Street, the French Market, the foot of Esplanade, Jackson, Louisiana Avenues and the foot of Richard Street.

Towards the lower limits of the port, on the Algiers side, is situated the

New Naval Station,

with its mammoth floating dry dock, the next largest dock of the kind in the world. This immense structure is capable of raising high and dry a vessel of 18,000 tons displacement. It is over 500 feet long, and its inside measurement between the side walls is 100 feet.

While the great dock was designed primarily to care for the ships of the Navy, it is available for docking merchant ships of a greater size than the local private docks can accommodate. By permission of the Navy Department, a number of merchant vessels have already been docked, and other vessels can

NAVAL DOCK—NEW ORLEANS.

have the use of the dock whenever they desire, provided no naval vessels are at the time waiting to go in the structure.

The British Government has recently built a dock for the Naval Station at Bermuda, which is slightly larger than the dock here, but it has not as great lifting capacity. A visit to the dock and Naval Station will prove instructive and interesting. New buildings, making vast improvements, were erected at the Station during 1903.

Quaintest of all in this ever-changing panorama along the levee are the

Batture Folks,

a queer people who live outside the revetment on the river side. The batture is an alluvial elevation of the bed of the river caused by the constant washing of the great stream towards the Algiers side. The batture is continually being enlarged by the sandy deposits from the river, especially along the front from Louisiana Avenue up the stream. As far back as 1807 this batture land was the subject of controversies between the owners of the soil along the river front

LEVEE SCENE—UNLOADING RICE LADEN STEAMBOAT.

of the Faubourg Ste. Marie and the folks who came and made their homes there. In September, 1807 there occurred the "Batture Riots," and the eminent jurist, Edward Livingston, represented private claimants, but was opposed by the public in two distinct outbreaks.

ALONG THE LEVEE.

The batture is peopled by quaint shifting people who come down the river in skiffs looking for homes. They build their houses along this deposit, under the shadow of the levee, the most interesting settlements being from Louisiana Avenue towards Carrollton. The houses are built like flatboats, on stilts, in such a way that they are enabled to rise and float; for the batture is dry or submerged, according to the season. Numerous floating galleries connect the houses with the shore. When the batture is dry the people lay out little vegetable gardens and pretty flower plots, that make their homes very picturesque and attractive. They keep chickens and goats, and gain their living by going out in skiffs, picking up driftwood and selling it in town. The batture is considered outside the city's limits, and is no man's land. The people living there take advantage of this, paying no taxes or rentals. No sight in New Orleans is more picturesque than these floating houses under the big wharves, rising and falling with the stream. The batture people are very good-natured and kind, and have a hospitality that is all their own.

CHAPTER XVI.

The Cemeteries.

Unique among the cemeteries of the United States are those of New Orleans. Owing to the dampness of the soil, which long ago caused the authorities

ENTRANCE TO THE OLD ST. LOUIS CEMETERY.

to agree that burial beneath the earth was unsanitary and impracticable, the custom here of burying above the ground has brought to the assistance of nature all the graces which money and art can combine in producing to make fair and beautiful the resting-places of the dead. In many of the cemeteries small fortunes have been expended upon a single tomb, and throughout the homes of the dead, wherever the purse permits, no expense is considered too great, in this city where sentiment so largely sways that Love, mounting on the wings of Faith, may follow in beautiful outward expressions of human thought the course of the dead in their trackless flight. And so everywhere our cemeteries breathe the lesson that the dead still live, and their spiritual influence, hidden, but felt, still abides.

A day should be devoted to visiting the cemeteries, which are, curiously enough, scattered over the city, marking historically the progress of its growth. One comes unexpectedly across a city of the dead in the heart of the metropolis, and learns that this once marked a line of demarcation outside the city's limits, but which, as New Orleans in time spread far beyond this prescribed line, was eventually swallowed up in the city's growth. The most historical cemeteries are those of the old French quarter, the most beautiful those which are on both sides of the New Basin Canal, near and around the terminus of Canal Street.

THE DEAD LIE CLOSE TOGETHER—OLD ST. LOUIS CEMETERY.

The tombs are built of brick or marble or granite, and consist generally of two vaults, with a crypt below for the reception of bones. The vaults or crypts are carefully cemented to prevent the exhalation of decaying animal matter, and there is a law forbidding any one to open a tomb before a certain time shall have elapsed after burial. Sometimes, as in the old St. Louis Cemeteries, the tombs are built in tiers, along walls of extraordinary thickness. These walls surround the cemeteries, and the vaults are called "ovens," the name being derived from the primitive form of tombs in the St. Louis Cemetery, which were made of brick and shaped like an oven. Over many of these ancient oven-shaped tombs a second story has been erected. As years pass on and deaths multiply in a family, the vaults are needed for the reception of other bodies. The slabs are then removed from the tombs, the old coffins broken up and burned and the remains of the dead are deposited in the crypt. If the coffin is of metal, it is simply transferred to the crypt. In this manner a long series of burials may take place in a single tomb. In the St. Louis Cemeteries generation after generation mingle their dust in the same crypt.

Very beautiful are the new cemeteries, with their spacious grounds, lovely walks and magnificent monuments. Yet, with all their beauty, the new homes of the dead lack the mysterious charm of tradition and romance, association and age, which are the heritage of the old cemeteries.

The four oldest of these are the St. Louis, which lie in close proximity to one another, along the line of the Claiborne cars and the Dauphine as they traverse the old Creole line of fortifications, Rampart Street. It is like turning a page of Louisiana history to walk through these cemeteries. The most ancient is

St Louis No. 1,

which lies in the square bounded by Conti, St. Louis, Basin and North Liberty Streets. The cemetery is just one square's walk from Rampart Street. This is the old burying-ground of the French quarter, the cemetery laid out by Bienville in 1718, when he came to found his city of New Orleans. He placed the cemetery outside of the city's ramparts, and loyally named it "St. Louis," after the patron saint of his royal master, Louis XIV, of France. The place is so old and crumbling in decay that it never opens its vaults now except to an heir of the soil. Further building of tombs has long been prohibited here. But the old, old families still cling to their dead—the dead who gave New Orleans a history and a name—and the Government respects these time-honored ancestors. The dead lie so close to one another along the narrow aisles that there is not an inch of available earth that has not offered a home in death to some one of the old New Orleans families. Even to the "Vieux Carré" of to-day, the very names on some of these old and crumbling tombs seem strange and foreign, for years ago many of the families became extinct, and their very names passed from the records of the city. But the old St. Louis must ever hold the title of mother of all the Louisiana cemeteries, and by reason of its very antiquity must ever be a place of peculiar interest to strangers. The tombs are scattered irregularly over the inclosure, and form tortuous alleys, through which it is very difficult for the uninitiated to find their way. Strange histories lie buried here. A Russian prince finds a last resting-place in a corner of one of the old ovens against the walls, and, as the French legend runs on the marble slab, "This tablet was placed here by a broken-hearted mother, who supplicates in tears, all ye who pass this way to kneel and say a prayer for the repose of her son's soul." Almost in juxtaposition will be found the tomb of Benedict Van Preebles, "an officer of the Revolution under Lafayette, who died in 1803," and of Paul Morphy, the great chess player. In the rear of the cemetery will be found a curious old-fashioned oven tomb, hardly two feet above the ground. It is the last resting-place of Etienne de Boré, the first great sugar planter of Louisiana, and of his grandson, Charles Gayerre, the illustrious Louisiana historian. In an alley to the right is the tomb of Stephen Zacharie, founder of the first bank established in the Mississippi Valley, and a little further on that of Daniel Clark, the American Consul in Spanish times in New Orleans, who was claimed by Myra Clark Gaines as her father: out of this claim grew the famous litigation which extended over nearly half a century, and which involved immense tracts of property claimed by the City of New Orleans. The magnificent tomb of "La Societé Italienne," with the commanding white marble statue of "Faith," attracts attention, as also that of "La Societé Française," erected in 1848. Just beyond the Canal Street side of the Cemetery is a plot containing a quaint chapel where the Jesuit priests are buried. Passing from aisle to aisle in the old cemetery, on many tombs will be found the legend, "Mort sur le Champ d'Honneur" (Died on the Field of Honor), or "Victime de l'honneur," indicating that here sleeps some one who has fallen in a duel. At the back of the cemetery, beyond a board fence, which separates the consecrated from the unconsecrated ground, will be found the original monument erected to the memory of General Claiborne, the first American Governor of Louisiana. It possesses merely an historic interest, as the remains of the Governor were long since removed to a costly tomb in the Metairie Cemetery.

As the French quarter grew, another cemetery was added to the city's repository for its dead, and this was placed beyond the limits allotted to the mother cemetery. It is very ancient, and is called the

St. Louis No. 2.

It is within sight of the old cemetery, on St. Louis, between North Robertson and North Claiborne Streets, and is best reached on the Claiborne Avenue
car. It is built very much on the same style as the first cemetery. Interesting monuments are those to General J. B. Plauché,
a friend of Andrew Jackson's, who commanded the Orleans Battalion in the
War of 1812, at the Battle of New Orleans; Alexander Milne, a philanthropic
Scottish resident of New Orleans, who died in 1838, leaving a large fortune to

A STUDY IN OVENS—OLD ST. LOUIS CEMETERY.

endow the Milne Asylum for Boys; François Xavier Martin, Chief Justice o
Louisiana in 1815, and one of the earliest historians of the State; Pierre Soulé,
statesman and orator, and once Ambassador to Spain; the fine Association tomb
of the "Spanish Cazadores," erected in 1830, and that of the Iberian Society,
erected in 1848. At the end of the aisle, towards Claiborne Street, is the tomb
of a young man named Barelli, who was killed in the burning of the steamer
Louisiana many years ago. The accident forms the subject of a bas-relief on the
tomb, which always attracts much attention. The large mortuary chapel at the
end of the cemetery is that of the Carriere family. It is very beautiful. But
most unique of all the tombs is that of Dominique You, one of Lafitte's pirates,.

who commanded a company of cannoneers on the Chalmette battle-field. The tablet bears no date, but beneath the name inscribed thereon is a stanza from Voltaire's famous "L'Heriade," which speaks of "the intrepid warrior," "the new Bayard," "sans peur et sans reproche."

An interesting relic of the days of reconstruction is the tomb of Oscar J. Dunn, colored, who was Lieutenant Governor under Warmoth in 1871.

Just across the street lies the annex of St. Louis No. 2, and immediately beyond lies

St Louis No. 3.

This cemetery is devoted to the uses of the colored people. From the advent of slavery into the colony, which was, indeed, in the first days of the

A CEMETERY AISLE.

Biloxi establishment, the lines between the two races were very closely drawn. When Bienville laid out the old St. Louis Cemetery for the use of the white population, the open space which stretched beyond as far as Bienville Street was reserved for the colored population. As time passed on, many of the early Creole slave owners purchased burying plots for their slaves in the ancient reservations, and erected special tombs for them. When the San Domingo Revolution drove even the free men of color to seek refuge from the fury of their own slaves on Louisiana shores, the necessity arose of providing a special cemetery for these colored folks, for the proud, blue-blooded Creoles refused, even in death, to be placed on equality with the inferior race, though represented by freemen. Still they recognized a line of distinction between the "gens de couleur," as the free blacks were called, and the slave proper, and so the authorities walled up this ancient reservation of the slave dead and marked off the allotted spaces for the burial of slaves and of free men of color by the erection of a great iron cross in the center of the grounds. The cemeteries were systematically numbered, and this colored burying ground was dignified by the title of St. Louis No. 3. When the war emancipated the negroes, the question arose as to what rights the erstwhile slaves, whose relatives were buried in these grounds, possessed to the tombs; but the matter was settled by the masters and mistresses themselves still holding the titles to the ground and tombs, and giving the right of burial as the occasion arose to the members of their households and their descendants. More than this, one hears every now and then, even in these latter days, of some old serving-men or women who had scornfully rejected freedom when it was proffered, and who had clung through long years of trial and rehabilitation to the fortunes of their ancient masters, being honored in death with interment in the "family tomb" in St. Louis Nos. 1 or 2, while the gentlemen of the family act as pallbearers and the ladies follow with tears the faithful old servant to the last resting-place.

Out in Esplanade Avenue, near the Bayou St. John, lies the

New St. Louis Cemetery,

a young sister of the older ones, and laid out some forty years ago to accommodate the growing French Quarter. As the population of New Orleans continued to increase and the tide of immigration to flow in, it will be noticed from the location of the cemeteries that the "outskirts" of the city in one decade became a densely populated section in the next, both above and below Canal Street; here as early as 1813 the Americans had built their own cemetery. Soon it became apparent that the city would have to locate its cemeteries at a great distance from the populated centers, and so the Americans began to lay out beautiful burying grounds at the furthest end of Canal Street; but the "Vieux Carré," still jealous of its ancient rights and loath to lay its dead so far from the olden cemeteries where their ancestors lay sleeping these hundred years and more, resolved to keep them within its own bosom. A square of ground at the furthest end of Esplanade Avenue was reserved as a cemetery, and, still clinging to the old name, sacred in the early annals of New Orleans, they called the place the new St. Louis Cemetery. It is reached by means of the Esplanade Avenue cars, which may be taken in Canal Street or in Rampart just after leaving the old cemeteries. Beautiful in its ancient aspect, though comparatively new, the cemetery holds its own as a repository for the remains of ancient families. The central avenue is shaded by handsome trees, and many of the tombs are very fine. Father Turgis, the soldier-priest and veteran Confederate chaplain, is buried here under a beautiful monument erected to his memory by the Army of Northern Virginia. A notable tomb is that of James Gallier, a famous architect of Creole days, who, with his wife, Marie, was drowned in the wreck of the Evening Star in 1866. It was Gallier who built the French Opera House and the City Hall.

Leaving the old French and Spanish cemeteries, one turns instinctively to

St. Roch's Cemetery and Shrine.

The old Gothic chapel of St. Roch is one of the most quaint and picturesque edifices in New Orleans, or in the world, for that matter, as the opinions of such distinguished travelers as Marion Crawford, Charles Dudley Warner, Joaquin Miller and other noted writers attest. The shrine is best reached by taking the Villeré or Claiborne Avenue car in Canal Street, or after leaving the old St. Louis Cemeteries. Alight at St. Roch's Avenue and walk a short distance out the avenue, and the beautiful chapel, overgrown with ivy, bursts upon the view. The chapel was erected by a pious priest, with his own hands, in fulfillment of a vow, that, if none of his parishioners would die during a prevailing epidemic in early days, he would, stone by stone, build a chapel in thanksgiving to God. He and his parish united in a novena or nine days' prayer to St. Roch, the patron of health. His prayer was heard. The city to a great extent was decimated, but not one of this congregation died. Then the old priest built this chapel and called the spot "Campo Santo," or "Place of Health." Soon from all parts of New Orleans pilgrims sought out the chapel, and it became a favorite shrine for the suffering and afflicted. In time it acquired the prestige of the miracle-working shrines of Europe. No one comes to New Orleans without visiting it, not once, but many times. Hundreds of tapers, the offerings of devout pilgrims, are always burning before the altar, and on all sides of the dim chapel are seen "ex votoes" or thank-offerings, placed there in gratitude for favors granted. The shrine is surmounted by a military statue of St. Roch, and at his side is

ST. ROCH'S CHAPEL.

the representation of the good dog, which fed him miraculously when he lay afflicted and abandoned with the plague in the forests of Munich.

The chapel is designed after the old mortuary chapels still extant in German and Hungarian countries, and which, in ages gone by, were used for the burial of the elect. Each morning the bell hanging in the quaint belfry is tolled in accordance with a curious Hungarian custom, and every Monday morning mass is offered in the chapel for the repose of the souls of all those interred within and about the consecrated grounds.

The history of the spot as a cemetery dates back to 1871, when, owing to the passage of the May Laws, many of the religious orders were expelled from Germany. Some sought refuge in New Orleans, and were followed by many earnest German Catholics, who settled for the most part in the rear of the old Faubourg Marigny. The section was called the "German Quarter." The pastor was Father Thevis, the builder of St. Roch, who, like the newcomers, had been a refugee in the days gone by. Seeing that they had no cemetery of their own, Father Thevis determined to convert the Campo Santo into a burial spot where the exiled children of the Fatherland might rest side by side. And

OLD VIEW IN ST. ROCH'S CEMETERY.

so a few lowly graves, marked by wooden crosses, rose here and there among the grasses. By degrees more pretentious monuments were erected, and it is now one of the most picturesque burying grounds of the city. Beneath the sanctuary of the chapel, in a crypt built with his own hands, lies the saintly founder of St. Roch's, who had indeed builded better than he knew. For the place, with its open-air stations of the cross, its crowd of kneeling worshipers, its well-authenticated legends of miracles and answered prayers, seems rather the remnant of a mediaeval abbey, which philosophy and reason have never invaded, and where Faith, clad in the pure and simple garb of her early years, still lives in all her freshness and beauty, and offers to all the sorrows and afflictions of humanity a positive and effectual remedy in prayer.

Just back of the old lies the new Cemetery of St. Roch. It is carefully and beautifully laid out, and therefore lacks the romantic picturesqueness of the older shrine. A mortuary chapel, frescoed by two Carmelite monks from Munich, adorns the center.

Leaving the cemetery, walk down St. Roch's Avenue to St. Claude Street, and, taking the Claiborne car, ride as far as Louisa Street, where the

St. Vincent de Paul Cemeteries

may be seen. These cemeteries were laid out by Pepe Llula, the famous fencing master of old Creole days, who has already been mentioned in connection with the story of the "Dueling Oaks" in the City Park. After having taught the "jeunesse doré" of New Orleans how to meet in mortal combat as "swordsmen and gentlemen," and led the most famous fencing masters to do the same thing, and kill one another "just for the sake of showing the art," Pepe Llula settled down in this old truck farm section of ancient New Orleans, and, after the erection of the parish church of St. Vincent de Paul, over forty years ago, he cut up his ground into cemeteries, and named them after the patron saint of the parish. The tombs are built on the same order as those of the ancient French cemeteries. The old fencing master, with his wife and only daughter, is buried here. Just over the way, overlooking the cemeteries, in a handsome house, bounded by Clouet, Louisa and Urquhart Streets, is the ancient home of the famous swordsman, where his grandchildren still reside. One room is kept sacred.. It is filled with the trophies of Pepe Llula's great battles.

Across Canal Street lie the American cemeteries, and the oldest of these is the

Girod Street Cemetery,

which is the first Protestant burying ground ever laid out in New Orleans. It lies on Girod Street, between Cypress and Perriliat, and was named for Nicholas Girod, who formerly had his plantation along this line. Away back in 1844 the cemetery was one of the handsomest and swellest in the city, but after the great epidemics of '53 and '66 it was mainly abandoned, and is now given over principally to the very poor, to negroes and emigrants. The only families of note who still have their tombs there are those who acquired the ground in the early days of the cemetery's history. Historic monuments are those erected to Colonel S. W. Bliss, who was a son-in-law of President Taylor, and of Dr. Thomas Leacock, who for thirty years was rector of the old Christ Church. Glendy Burke and his wife are buried in the central aisle, in a tomb which was erected in 1832. Some of the old graves date as far back as 1821, and are in utter decay. One ancient tomb bears the legend, "Mammy, aged 84, a faithful servant, who lived and died a good Christian, 1829."

Lafayette No. 1,

also called the Washington Street Cemetery, is on Washington Avenue, between Prytania and Coliseum Streets. This cemetery succeeded the Girod as the aristocratic burial-place of the American Quarter. Henry W. Allen, War Governor of Louisiana, was buried here; the body was subsequently removed, but the monument remains. General John B. Hood and General Harry T. Hays, distinguished Confederate commanders, rest within these ancient aisles. A magnificent monument is that erected to Captain Charles W. McLellan, a Louisiana boy, who in 1861, at the early age of 19, enlisted in the Crescent Rifles. Captain McLellan took part in twenty-three engagements, the most noted of the war, but it was at the Battle of Sharpsburg that he signally distinguished himself. General Jackson found it necessary to protect his left flank, and ordered a detail from the Second Louisiana Brigade to go forward. McLellan was put in command. He was only twenty years of age. To reach the point indicated it was necessary to pass through a narrow valley called by the soldiers "The Valley of Death," and over which the Federals were pouring shrapnel and shell to such an extent that it seemed impossible for any one to go through alive. Yet McLellan with his men gained the point amid the cheers of their comrades and to the delight of General Jackson, who then and there recommended him for promotion.

It was the first instance where an officer of the line in the volunteer service received a commission direct from the President. Captain McClellan was killed in the vicinity of Meadow Bridge, before Richmond, June 1, 1864. His remains were removed from Hollywood Cemetery, Richmond, to this beautiful plot in Lafayette Cemetery in 1867. The monument, which is very costly, was erected by his parents. Near by is one of the most picturesque cemetery corners in New Orleans. Dr. Palmer, the celebrated Presbyterian divine, sleeps in one of the narrow old-fashioned aisles towards Prytania Street. The remains of Dr. Palmer will be removed during 1904 to a magnificent monument erected to his memory, in Metairie Cemetery, by the congregation of the First Presbyterian Church.

From the cemeteries of the French and American Quarters that seem like bits of old world painting set down in the heart of New Orleans, take the car in Canal Street labeled "Canal Belt," and ride out to the new and beautiful cities of the dead, lying at the extremity of the ancient street. Six or seven of these cemeteries will be found grouped together on Metairie Ridge, near the Half-Way House. The first one, on approaching the Ridge, is a Jewish cemetery, called "Tememe Direch," or "Hebrew Rest." Near by is another Jewish cemetery that belongs to the congregation "Dispersed of Judah." The Hebrews

VIEW IN WASHINGTON CEMETERY.

still adhere in New Orleans to the ancient custom of burying their dead in the ground. The Charity Hospital burying ground and "Potter's Field" are on the left, and to the right is Cypress Grove Cemetery, the beautiful trees indicating the name.

St. Patrick Cemeteries,

so fresh and clean in their snow-white garb and pebbly walks, always attract attention. Here lie the sturdy Irish pioneers who came to New Orleans in the early part of the last century and helped to make her history the proud tale it is. Many of the best old families in the city have their tombs in these cemeteries. They breathe throughout the spirit of Catholic faith. Special attention is directed to the beautiful Calvary shrine at the further end of St. Patrick's No. 1 and the Mater Dolorosa that marks the entrance to St. Patrick's No. 2.

The Firemen's Cemetery

will be recognized from the gateway, modeled upon the Egyptian pilon or temple gates. This cemetery stands a monument to the efforts of the old Volunteer Fire Department of New Orleans, which did such effectual service from the foundation of the city till a few years ago, when the old volunteer system was replaced by a paid Fire Department. All through the cemetery will be seen the tombs belonging to these old Volunteer Fire Companies, and some chronicle the deaths of heroes who gave up their lives for the protection of the city. Notable among these is the lofty shattered column that commemorates the sacrifice of Irad Ferry, the first martyr of the Department, who was killed at a fire on Camp Street in 1837; of Maunsell White, a leading citizen and planter, now remembered as the inventor of the pepper sauce that bears his name; in the central aisle is a column commemorating John T. Monroe, the War Mayor of the city. It might be mentioned here that the Volunteer Fire Department included the best men in New Orleans, socially and commercially. Indeed, all through the old cemetery the inscriptions on the tombs show the character of the firemen as citizens.

The Masonic Cemeteries are in this section. They are shaded by beautiful avenues of trees, and the effect is very picturesque.

Greenwood Cemetery,

whose very name suggests fresh pictures of woodlands and verdure, lies just over the way from the firemen's burying-ground. Almost at the very entrance, towards the New Basin Canal, stands the monument erected by the women of New Orleans to the memory of the Confederate dead. The monument is surmounted by the figure of a private soldier, and around the four corners of the shaft are grouped the busts of Robert E. Lee, Albert Sidney Johnston, Stonewall Jackson and Leonidas Polk. Beneath the mound repose the bones of over 600 Confederate soldiers, gathered several years after the War from many a battlefield, where they lay moldering and neglected. This was the first monument ever erected to the Confederate dead. At the unveiling Father Ryan's beautiful poem, "The March of the Deathless Dead," was read. The monument is in the custody of the Ladies' Confederate Memorial Association of Louisiana, which erected it. A. D. Crossman, Mayor of the city 1846 to 1854, is buried in Greenwood. A gallant soldier and journalist, Dan C. Byerly, who fell during one of the heated political conflicts which grew out of the Reconstruction period, sleeps peacefully in Greenwood's aisles. At the lower end of the cemetery is an artistic monument to the firemen in the form of a lofty pavilion, in which stands the marble figure of a volunteer carrying a line of hose. Two martyr volunteers, D. S. Woodruff, Ex-Foreman, and William McLeod, Foreman of Mississippi Fire Company No. 2, who were both killed at the same fire in 1854.

are nobly commemorated here. A notable tomb is that of the Typographical Union, inaugurated in 1855. The tomb of W. T. Richards, who left a bequest of $80,000 to the Charity Hospital, is in Greenwood.

MONUMENT TO CONFEDERATE DEAD—GREENWOOD CEMETERY.

For a number of years Greenwood stood unrivalled as a fair and verdant resting-place for the dead, but just across the bayou there arose in time, on the site once occupied by the famous Metairie Race Course, the beautiful

Metairie Cemetery,

a fair and lovely spot, that seems to rob death of half its terrors to leave the loved one sleeping there. The old Metairie Jockey Club went out of existence in 1870, and the race track, which for thirty years was the most noted in the United States, was purchased by a wealthy citizen and turned into a cemetery. The Metairie Cemetery Association, organized in 1872, now owns the place. It has greatly beautified the cemetery. The system of lakes and lawns was executed in 1895 at a cost of $30,000. The first lake, near the main entrance, is called the "Horseshoe." A carriage drive thirty-two feet wide extends around the lake, and there is a shady promenade for pedestrians. The second lake is 1,200 feet wide, or one-half as long as the Horseshoe, and the third lake is 2,700 feet long. The grounds are beautifully laid out, and many handsome and costly mausoleums and monuments mark the resting-places of the dead. Near the entrance stands the magnificent monument-tomb of the Army of Tennessee, surmounted by Doyle's famous equestrian statue of Albert Sidney Johnston.

The trophy of arms over the entrance was modeled from the badge of the Association. At the entrance to the vault stands a marble statue of an orderly "Calling the Roll." It is also from the chisel of Doyle. The burial vault, in the heart of the mound, contains a tablet to the memory of General Johnston, on which is inscribed Dimitry's famous epitaph, said to be one of the finest mortuary inscriptions in the English language. Within the mound, along with many of the soldiers he led, sleeps General P. G. T. Beauregard, the great Confederate chieftain.

Over the way from the entrance is a massive monument, surmounted by a granite shaft, along which are grouped several life-sized figures. This monument was erected recently by Mr. Moriarity in memory of his wife. The cost was $50,000. A special railroad leading to the cemetery had to be built to transport the heavy granite blocks of which the monument is constructed.

Near the main aisle of Metairie, as one passes down the shady avenue, is the granite monument beneath which repose Mr. and Mrs. George Nicholson,

TOMB OF THE ARMY OF TENNESSEE—MONUMENT TO ALBERT SIDNEY
JOHNSTON—METAIRIE CEMETERY.

the late proprietors of the Picayune. Dying within ten days of each other, side by side under the grassy mound they sleep the last eternal sleep. Mrs. Nicholson's maiden name was Eliza J. Poitevent. She was known to the world of letters as "Pearl Rivers." She was one of the sweetest poets who ever touched a lyre and woke it into song.

Among other interesting tombs are those of Thomas Jenkins Semmes, who was the last of the Confederate Senators to answer the great roll call; Dr. Thomas R. Markham, a noted Confederate chaplain; A. C. Hutchinson, who left a bequest of nearly a million dollars to the Tulane University; Patrick O'Brien, who so magnificently endowed the Catholic University at Washington; General Fred N. Ogden, a conspicuous figure of Reconstruction days, and commander of the famous White League. The latter sleeps beneath the most expressive monument in the cemetery, a great granite bowlder, lying under a gigantic live oak, towards the western end. Mr. John T. Gibbons, brother of Cardinal Gibbons, has his family tomb in Greenwood, as also the Stauffer, Slocomb,

Aldigé, McCan, Morris, Hernandez and other prominent families. These monuments cost thousands of dollars. Especially beautiful are those located on the Ridge, just around the curve of the old race course, and overlooking the lake. The tomb of the Army of Northern Virginia is surmounted by a shaft crowned by a statue of General Stonewall Jackson. Aside from its own historic interest, the tomb has acquired a sacred character in the minds of the people of the South, for within its mound reposed for two years the remains of Jefferson Davis, prior to final interment in Richmond, Virginia. During this period special detachments of Confederate veterans acted as a guard of honor about the tomb by night and day, and when the remains of Mr. Davis were at length carried to the capital of the Confederacy, there to await the last réveille; the vault in which they had lain was hermetically sealed and a bronze tablet placed without, telling to future generations that it marked one of the last chapters

TOMB OF ARMY OF NORTHERN VIRGINIA—METAIRIE CEMETERY.

in the great tragedy of the South. Near by is the monument of the Washington Artillery, surmounted by the figure of a Confederate artilleryman in uniform, guarding the rest of his comrades, who sleep below. Upon the four sides of the tomb is the roll of the dead of this ancient command who "fell on the field of honor."

And last, but not least, in this cemetery of beautiful monuments, is the first tomb ever erected within its limits, that of the owner of the soil, Mr. Charles T. Howard. It is a large structure of granite, with iron gates, through which the visitor may see the interior and the statue of "Time," seated, with a finger pressed to the lips. The face of this statue is said to have been modeled from that of Mr. Howard himself,

Metairie Cemetery is a great promenade of a Sunday evening. Flowers are always blooming upon the graves, and the freshness and verdure lead the mind from the contemplation of death to the thought of God.

Other cemeteries in New Orleans are St. Joseph's, on Sixth Street, near Liberty, in which may be seen the old wooden structure that first served as a

WASHINGTON ARTILLERY MONUMENT—METAIRIE CEMETERY.

church to the Redemptorist Fathers, in Constance Street, and which was transferred to this plot and turned into a mortuary chapel when the splendid new churches were erected; the three St. Vincent de Paul Cemeteries, in Soniat and Dufossat Streets, and the ancient Carrollton Cemetery, which marks the resting-place of the first settlers of this now beautiful suburb of New Orleans.

All Saints' Day.

All Saints' Day, which always falls on November 1, is observed in New Orleans as the general day for the decoration of the graves of the dead. It has been said that New Orleans has two great festivals—the Carnival, when she invites strangers from all parts of the world to come and make merry with her, and "All Saints," the great home festival, when, heart to heart, the entire city meets on common ground to pay its tribute to the loved and lost. Together the rich and poor, the high and low, recognize that barriers of caste and class have no place in the all-embracing dominion of death; for each home has its heart history written somewhere out in the white cities of the dead. It may be on the marble tablet of some stately mausoleum, or only on the rude wooden headboard of some grass-grown mound. But the dead are there, and the heart is there, and so the city unites in its work of love and remembrance.

A CEMETERY VIEW—ALL SAINTS' DAY.

All Saints' is a legal holiday, and all the banks, stores and places of business are closed. For weeks before its advent the florists are busily engaged preparing for the immense sale of flowers which the day always brings, and the patient workers in beads and wax, down in Royal Street, place on exhibition their wonderful creations of months of labor to remind the passersby that All Saints' is approaching, and that these designs are not so perishable as those made of natural flowers. The cemeteries, too, are filled with faithful workers, cleaning the tombs and planting fresh flowers. The day dawns and enfolds the city in its hallowed influence. From every home the people go forth, bearing

DECORATING GRAVES ALL SAINTS' DAY—METAIRIE CEMETERY.

their fragrant offerings. From morning till night the cemeteries are thronged, and it does one good just to look at the vast, soulful, heart-throbbing multitude, so different from the gay, rollicking crowds of Carnival time, and all linked together by one thought, "the dead, the dead," who are everywhere. The florists, the cake vendors, the praline women, the perambulating refreshment stands, all do a thriving business, for the people spend the day in the cemeteries, going quietly and decorously from one to another, after having paid their tributes at their own individual shrines, for death sanctifies the day.

The observance of All Saints' dates away back to the year 998, when the Abbott of Cluney instituted it for the monasteries of his congregation, holding services for the dead, and going from grave to grave and lighting blessed candles before them, decking them with flowers, and blessing them with holy water. All these customs are still observed in the old French cemeteries of New Orleans. Some of the tombs resemble miniature altars on All Saints', with their numbers of lighted candles and sacred images. In all the Catholic Cemeteries services are held, and at a certain hour the priests with a train of acolytes pass up and down the aisles, sprinkling the graves with holy water and singing litanies, just as the old French Jesuits and Capuchins used to do in the first days of the old St. Louis Cemetery.

Though distinctly Catholic in its origin, the thought underlying the celebration of All Saints' is so beautiful that the custom of setting aside this one day for communing with the dead has been instinctively adopted by all the nationalities of New Orleans, and poor indeed must be the home that fails to respond to the call of this consecrated day, when Love and Memory walk hand in hand along the borderland of time and eternity, strewing the way with flowers.

CHAPTER XVII.

New Orleans Suburban Resorts.

In addition to Audubon, the City, the Athletic Park and the numerous pretty squares that stud the residence section of the city, and which are favorite haunts of the people at all seasons of the year, New Orleans is especially well supplied with open air resorts. In front is the river, the levee running along which is always a great promenade of an evening, particularly during the summer season, while the ferries that ply between the city proper and Algiers are thronged till far into the evening with fathers and mothers taking the children for an airing, or young folks enjoying the freshening breezes, the music that floats over the water and the glorious sunsets on the Mississippi. Back of the city are the lakeside resorts, West End, Spanish Fort and Milneburg, where the salt breezes blow, giving strength and vigor with every passing breath. And so it will be seen that this is another most charming feature of this delightful old city, the fresh water in front, the salt water in the rear; all combine, together with proximity to the gulf, to make New Orleans an ideal place during the summer season. While the thermometer is registering over 100 in the shade in Northern cities, here in New Orleans a pleasant temperature is maintained. We have always a delightful breeze on the warmest day, and we do not have to go very far to get to the lakeside, to enjoy a salt water bath or a pleasant boat sail.

The most popular of the lake resorts is

West End,

so called from its position on Lake Pontchartrain. The lake itself is a body of brackish water, about twenty miles in diameter, being nearly round in shape, and at no place very deep. It affords yachtsmen a splendid opportunity for small yachts. The series of regattas which are held in the summer are among the pleasant features of life in New Orleans. Lake Pontchartrain communicates with Lakes Maurepas and Borgne, and, through the latter, with the Mississippi Sound.

West End is beautifully laid out. The large music plaza on the other side of the bridge is built on pilings over the water, and forms what is perhaps the largest work of the kind in existence. There is a splendid music stand, and during the summer months thousands congregate here to enjoy the music that is always furnished by the finest orchestra that can be obtained. The gardens are beautiful. The pretty winding paths and intricate puzzles are the delight of the younger folks. The most beautiful tropical flowers are always keen blooming luxuriantly in the open air. The crest of the levee beyond the plaza has been utilized for this garden, which terminates at the Parish line. The beautiful sward beyond extends into the Parish of Jefferson. The various restaurants at West End are famous for their excellent cuisine.

West End is reached by means of the electric cars, which start from Canal and Carondelet Streets. The train runs out Canal Street to the Half-Way House, makes an abrupt turn and follows the course of the New Basin

GARDEN AT WEST END.

Canal to the resort. Another way is by carriage drive out Canal Street to the Half-Way House, and thence out along the beautiful Shell Road.

The New Basin Canal was built to enable schooners and other small craft to reach the heart of the city. The canal, which is State property, terminates at the New Basin, alongside the Illinois Central Railroad Depot, on South Rampart and Howard Avenue. On the railroad side of the canal are the clubhouses of the St. John's Rowing Club and the West End Rowing Club, while, leading out from the plaza is a long wharf, at the end of which is the home of the Southern Yacht Club, under whose auspices many celebrated races have taken place.

Spanish Fort

is a small village with pleasure gardens, situated at the mouth of the Bayou St. John. The fort was erected by the Spaniards during the days of the Spanish domination in Louisiana, and was called by them "Fort St. John." It was armed and garrisoned as long as the Spaniards ruled in Louisiana, but after the cession of the colony to the United States the Americans found that the fort was too far inland to be of any great service, and it was abandoned. The ancient fortifications, built of small bricks, are fairly well preserved. The embrasures were filled up and the ramparts leveled to give space for seats when the place became a pleasure resort. Behind the fort are four cypress trees, standing near the gate leading into the gardens. Tradition says that these trees mark the grave of a young Spanish officer who was killed in a duel on this spot. It was at this fort that General Jackson first landed, when he hastened from the Indian War in Tennessee, in 1814, to take command in New Orleans. General Jackson came across Lake Pontchartrain in a schooner, and, riding from the Fort to Bayou Bridge, rested there before making his entry into the city the following day. During the Civil War the fort was again garrisoned; and the old guns still to be seen there, some of which date from colonial times, were mounted and used in two or three encounters which took place under these walls. The foundations of some of the old houses which formerly stood within the walls may still be seen. The old torpedo boat, which may be seen near the bayou, was fished up out of that stream a few years ago. The torpedo boat was an abortive experiment made during the Civil War in the line of submarine navigation. A fine restaurant which was built on one side of the fort was burned some years ago and has not been replaced. The resort is closed at 9 o'clock at night. It is reached by a train from a depot at the corner of Canal and North Basin Streets. On the right are the St. Louis Cemetery and the Basin, into which the Bayou St. John discharges. The bayou is navigable for schooners, and connects with Carondelet Canal, one of the waterways leading into the heart of the city. At Hagan Avenue the train passes one of the city's draining machines, by means of which rain waters are moved through canals and expedited in their course to Lake Pontchartrain. At Metairie Ridge the upper end of City Park is passed, affording an excellent view of the old duelling ground. Thence the road follows the course of the Orleans Drainage Canal to the Fort.

The last of the lakeside resorts is the

Old Lake, or Milneburg.

It is reached by the Pontchartrain Railroad, which starts at the depot, corner of Elysian Fields and Chartres Streets. The Old Lake was once the most fashionable of the lake resorts, and stood alone in its glory for over half a century. The resort was exceedingly primitive at first, but was gradually built up. At the time that the Pontchartrain Railroad, which, as has already been noted, was the second railroad ever built in the United States, began its operations, all the freight cars on the railroads were unloaded just as wagons are; but the Superintendent of the Pontchartrain invented the simple platform, which may now be seen everywhere. The road runs in a straight line for four miles along what is the shortest distance between the river and the lake. Milneburg is a very old town. It is named in honor of Alexander Milne, a philanthropic Scotch citizen of New Orleans in the old days. It became a famous resort, and was noted for its splendid caterers, the most famous of whom, named Boudro, managed the celebrated restaurant in which a banquet was given to Thackeray while he was in New Orleans. The dining made a great impression upon Thackeray; he made allusion to it in one of his books, paying at the same time a famous tribute to New Orleans cookery. The restaurant remains, but the old caterer is dead, and the glory of Milneburg has departed, it having been superseded in popularity by West End, or the New Lake, as it is often called, in distinction from the old resort.

CHAPTER XVIII.

Education in New Orleans—The Story of John McDonogh—Social Literary and Philanthropic Effort—The Military.

The educational system of New Orleans is unsurpassed.

It is estimated that there are upwards of 75,000 educable children in the City of New Orleans. Of these, some 32,000 attend the public schools; about 16,000 attend the Catholic parochial schools, convents, academies and colleges.

A large proportion of the remainder attend the many excellent private schools scattered over the city, which are, for the most part, under the direction of talented Southern women.

Tulane University has an attendance in all its departments aggregating about 700. Its sister institute, the H. Sophie Newcomb Memorial College, has about 350. The Jesuits' College has an attendance of about 600 students. These institutions have already been noticed in this Guide, but throughout the city the visitor will come unexpectedly upon some beautiful building surmounted by a cross or statue, and surrounded by extensive grounds. Through the grating in the gate one may catch sight of demure maidens moving about with book in hand, or engaged in recreation beneath the trees, and at their side is ever a black-veiled nun, for the most part a woman thoroughly educated in the best schools of Europe, and who has taken the vow to devote herself forever to the education and guidance of youth. These are the convent schools and academies of New Orleans, for many years the only higher institutions of learning in the far South, until the public high schools were established in the forties. The convents still hold their own in the progressive march of the age, and young ladies come from all parts of the South to enjoy the benefits of higher education and acquire the accomplishments in music, art and the languages for which the New Orleans convents have ever been famous.

The Public School System

of New Orleans is also unexcelled. There are about seventy public schoolhouses, which have cost on an average of $40,000 each. The public school enrollment averages 32,000. 1903 witnessed the addition of public night schools to the general system.

McDONOGH SCHOOL No. 14.

Ten of the public school buildings are reserved for the education of colored youth. Thirty of the public school buildings were either bought or built and are kept in repair through the noble endowment of John McDonogh. For this reason the visitor will see inscribed on many of the finest public school buildings the name "McDonogh," followed by the number of the school.

Romance of John McDonogh.

The history of John McDonogh reads like a romance in these later days. He was of Scotch-Irish parentage, and was born in Baltimore in 1779. He was liberally educated, and early in life embarked in commercial pursuits. In 1800 he came to New Orleans, where he opened business on his own account, and was soon regarded as one of the most successful and wealthy men.

In 1806, young, gay and dashing, and a general favorite, not only in business circles, but in the most exclusive homes of the old Creole noblesse, he retired from commercial life and devoted himself to the management of his large estates. He opened a magnificent house at the corner of Chartres and Toulouse Streets, kept a numerous retinue of slaves, fine horses and equipages, and was considered one of the most desirable matches in the French Quarter. But young McDonogh aspired high, and none pleased him so well as the beautiful daughter

ROBERT E. LEE SCHOOL—LATEST TYPE OF PUBLIC SCHOOLS.

of Don Almonaster, the Spanish Colonial philanthropist and magnate of old New Orleans. The proud old nobleman indignantly rejected the suit, declaring that a daughter of his noble race should never ally herself to a poor plebeian. Stung to the heart, McDonogh withdrew. The lady subsequently became the wife of the Baron de Pontalba, and McDonogh's grief and mortification weighed so heavily upon him that he swore he would have more money than all the Almonasters and Pontalbas put together, and that his name would live when their proud titles would have sunk into oblivion. From that hour his habits and nature changed. In his bitter anger he sold the contents of his magnificent house in Chartres Street, and moved to a small house on his plantation in McDonoghville, on the other side of the river, where, for nearly half a century, he led a lonely, penurious life, with seemingly one ambition—the amassing of money. He seemed, to all appearances, cold, hard, selfish, and the prejudice of New Orleans against the close, miserly life he led was great.

Wherever he passed he was pointed out as a miser. At his death, in 1850, he left his immense fortune to be divided, share and share alike, between the Cities of New Orleans and Baltimore, for public educational purposes.

No condition was attached to the gift to the City of New Orleans, except the simple request at the bottom of the will that the little children of the public schools should come once a year and strew his grave with flowers

McDonogh was at first buried in a marble sarcophagus on his estate on the other side of the Mississippi, above Algiers. His body was subsequently removed to Baltimore, in accordance with his last request, and laid beside his father and mother. But the old tomb over the river is still to be seen. The inscriptions, which were the rules of Mr. McDonogh's life, were composed by him-

McDONOGH MONUMENT—LAFAYETTE SQUARE.

self, and are exceedingly characteristic of the man. The public school children of New Orleans built the monument to his memory in Lafayette Square. May 1, "McDonogh Day," is annually kept in the schools, the children devoting the afternoon to memorial exercises in his honor, and sending delegations from each school to strew the monument with flowers.

The Social Life of New Orleans

is very beautiful, but, as remarked in the beginning of this Guide, the stranger must come with letters of introduction, else he will gain his impressions of the city from the streets alone, seeing nothing of the inner life of the people, which is the most charming and distinctive feature of this old Southern metropolis.

New Orleans is rich in social clubs, educational, literary, benevolent and charitable organizations.

The social clubs are, of course, exclusive organizations, and admission is by invitation or by presentation of a card from one of the members. The most prominent of these are the Boston Club, which has its home at No. 824 Canal Street, the Pickwick Club, 1028 Canal Street, the Varieties Club, with rooms at the Grand Opera House, in Canal Street, the Chess, Checkers and Whist Club, with quarters at 108 Baronne Street, Louisiana Club, 122 Carondelet Street, French Opera Club, which meets in the French Opera House, the Harmony Club, an exclusively Hebrew organization, occupying the beautiful home, corner of Jackson Avenue and St. Charles, the Cotillion Club and the Carnival German Club, which give very swell and exclusive social evenings during the Carnival season.

Among

Organizations of Women

are the Woman's Club, which meets the first Monday of each month at 1446 Camp Street, the Arena Club, which meets at the residence of the President, 610 Julia Street; the Era Club, devoted to the extension of suffrage among women, which meets at Gibson Hall, Tulane University, every second and fourth Saturday of the month. At the meetings of these several clubs visiting club women are cordially welcomed upon presentation of credentials, as also at the meetings of the Daughters of the Confederacy, in Memorial Hall, on the first Monday of the month, and the quarterly meetings of the Ladies' Confederate Memorial Association, held in the same place. The Daughters of 1776-1812, meets every first Tuesday at Washington Artillery Hall Armory, St. Charles Street, the Daughters of the American Revolution hold reunions every first Wednesday morning in the reading room of the Howard Memorial Library, the Colonial Dames meet at the residences of members. Among distinctively literary organizations are the Round Table, the Book Club, Quarante, Geographics, Tea and Topics Clubs, which are very exclusive and which hold their meetings at the residences of the Presidents or members. Along

Educational Lines

is the Catholic Institute, which has succeeded the Catholic Winter School, the Church Club (Episcopal), the New Orleans Educational Association and the Kindergarten Club; the latter meets the first Monday and second Saturday of the month, respectively, at the Boys' High School, in Calliope Street, near St. Charles. The New Orleans Free Kindergarten has five kindergartens under its direction, located respectively at 1203 Annunciation, 1534 Poydras, 610 Camp, 2218 St. Thomas, and 3327 Laurel Street.

The Athletic Clubs

are located as follows: Young Men's Gymnastic Club, 224 North Rampart Street; the Southern Athletic Club, corner of Washington Avenue and Prytania Streets; the Audubon Golf Club has its links and clubhouse at the upper end of Audubon Park; the New Orleans Golf Club at the lower end of the City Park; the New Orleans Tennis Club has its clubhouse and court on Saratoga Street, between General Taylor and Constantinople; the Walnut Street Tennis Club has its court at the upper end of Audubon Park. The golf and tennis clubs are composed of ladies and gentlemen.

Very prominent socially and otherwise are the

Yachting and Boat Clubs.

The Southern Yacht Club, which was organized in 1849, and is the second oldest in the United States, the St. John's Boat Club and the West End Rowing Club have their clubhouses at West End. Regattas take place annually under the auspices of these clubs, the admission to the clubhouse on such occasions being by card from the members.

The Young Men's Gymnastic Rowing Club has its house on the Bayou St. John, at the terminus of Esplanade Avenue.

The Victoria Cricket Club plays in Audubon Park, and the New Orleans Polo Club has its field in the City Park.

New Orleans has numerous rifle clubs. Thirty-five organized private hunting and fishing clubs, with handsome camps and many game preserves, are located within thirty miles of the city, along the lines of the railroads and waterways. Public institutions of this character are also plentiful. Philanthropic and benevolent associations and mutual aid societies, missionary and church societies, abound in New Orleans. Every asylum and orphanage has its organized body of auxiliary women workers, who devote themselves to sewing and assisting in providing for the wants of the inmates. It is said that for its size and population New Orleans does more charity work in comparison than any other city of the United States.

New Orleans is the

First Military District,

and most of the military organizations are comprehended in the First District. It comprises the Division Staff, the Battalion of Washington Artillery, the Louisiana Field Artillery, the Naval Brigade, the Jefferson Guards, the First Troop of Cavalry and the Signal Corps. The district is commanded by Major General John Glynn, Jr., with Colonel E. C. Fenner as Chief of Staff.

The oldest of these military organizations is the Washington Artillery, whose armory is located in the Washington Artillery Hall, on St. Charles Street, near Julia. It comprises five batteries, all under excellent management. The battalion is under the command of Lieutenant Colonel John B. Richardson. The Louisiana Field Artillery, commanded by Lieutenant Colonel John P. Sullivan, consists of five batteries. Its armory, on St. Charles, near Felicity Street, was destroyed by fire in 1902. The erection of a new armory, which will probably be located on the old site, is contemplated. The First Troop of Cavalry is commanded by Lieutenant Churchill. Its armory is on Eighth and Carondelet Streets. The Jefferson Guards, com-

U. S. NAVAL TRAINING SHIP, "THE STRANGER."

manded by Captain Kantz, has its armory in Gretna. The Signal Corps is commanded by Captain Warner, and is located at St. Charles, near Gravier Street. The Naval Brigade, which is attached to the First Military District, was organized in 1895. This organization, familiarly called the "Naval Reserves," did splendid service in the war with Spain. It furnished 240 officers and men to the United States Navy. The brigade has eight divisions, two of which are engineer divisions. The organization recently erected a handsome new Armory in Camp Street, between Julia and St. Joseph, abutting the sidewalk, with a large drill and recreation ground in the rear. The cost was $20,000. The Commanding Officer and other officials have their offices in the building. Strict military regulations prevail within the barracks. The Naval Brigade is now one of the largest organizations in the Naval Militia service in the country. The membership is now above 400. The United States Steamship Stranger is the training ship of the organization, and is ordinarily anchored in the river at the foot of Henry Clay Avenue. Captain J. W. Bostick is the commander of the brigade.

The only other military organization in the city is the Continental Guards, organized in 1854, and which did excellent service during the Civil War. The organization is an independent command, permitted to bear arms. The armory is in Odd Fellows' Hall, on Camp Street.

Not ranking among the military organizations, but dear to the people of New Orleans because of the heroic part they bore in the memorable struggle of '61 and '65, are the New Orleans Camps of

The United Confederate Veterans,

whose headquarters are at Memorial Hall, in Camp Street. New Orleans is justly proud, of the fact that the organization of the United Confederate Veterans had its birth here, the survivors of Confederate Cavalrymen holding the first reunion in this city Feb. 13, 1888. As a result, a joint call of the New Orleans Camps was issued for a general Convention to be held in New Orleans June 10, 1889, the purpose of which was to form a confederation for the assistance of the widows and orphans of fallen comrades, and to hand down to future generations the true history of the Southern cause, etc. Ten camps of veterans were represented at that first convention, the Army of Northern Virginia of New Orleans being designated as Camp 1, the Army of Tennessee as Camp 2, and the New Orleans Confederate Veteran Cavalry as Camp 9, and permanent organization was effected, the title "United Confederate Veteran Association" adopted with General John B. Gordon as the unanimous choice for Commander-in-Chief. Eighteen camps were represented at the first reunion. The second reunion was held at Jackson, Miss., June 2, 1891. Twenty-six veteran camp delegates responded. The third reunion was held in New Orleans April 8, 1892, and there were delegations from 172 camps. There are now 1492 camps. The reunion held in New Orleans in April, 1903, brought together delegate survivors of the cause, numbering some 65,000. Over $65,000 was raised by the people of New Orleans for the entertainment of the veterans, and the reunion was voted the grandest and most successful ever held.

Working in sympathy with the veterans are the United Daughters of the Confederacy and the Confederate Southern Memorial Association. Here again New Orleans patriotically points to the fact that her women were the first to organize in 1861, and the first to build a monument to the Confederate dead. The United Sons of Veterans is an organization pledged to the noble principles laid down in the constitution of the parent organization.

The Department of Louisiana and Mississippi of the Grand Army of the Republic has its headquarters in New Orleans, at 164 South Rampart Street. Colonel C. W. Keeting is Department Commander and Rudolph E. Baquie is Adjutant General. The members are mostly soldiers who came to Louisiana and Mississippi after the close of hostilities between the States, or came with the Federal Army during the latter years of the war.

CHAPTER XIX.

The Carnival and Mardi Gras.

The Carnival is New Orleans' most distinctive social feature, and no guidebook to the city would be complete without reference to this world-famed fête, so magnificent in its conception, so gorgeous in its pageantry, so thorough in the perfection of even the most minute detail of its marvelous scope, that competent historians and critics have declared that the famous spectacular triumphs of ancient Rome, with all their barbaric wealth and splendor, never surpassed in beauty the wonderful parades of New Orleans.

Year after year thousands of spectators travel hundreds of miles to participate in the festivities, and the magnificent success of this unique fête has often inspired other cities to attempt to rival it. But New Orleans remains supreme as the "Carnival City." She established the festival on American soil, and made and won the laurels which she wears so proudly. No rival can ever wrest them from her brow. For it is not only money and pageantry that make a carnival. The people themselves must be a part of it. In New Orleans all combines towards the end; the lavish expenditure on the part of a few public-spirited citizens to make all the people happy for just a few days, the hearty response from the depths of the great popular heart, the gracious hospitality with which the stranger is welcomed and bidden to be one of New Orleans' great family of merrymakers, all unite in giving to our Mardi Gras a distinctive character, whose impression remains and yearly adds to the immense throngs that crowd our Carnival streets.

REX PARADE—THE KING OF THE CARNIVAL.

In the average mind the words

"Carnival" and "Mardi Gras"

are supposed to be synonyms. But there is a fine distinction. The "Carnival" properly speaking, begins with the grand ball of the "Twelfth Night Revellers," on January 6, and culminates with the magnificent festivities of "Mardi Gras," or "Fat Tuesday," which is the eve of Ash Wednesday, and marks the close of festivities and the beginning of the Lenten Season. The word "Carnival" is derived from the Latin words "carne," "flesh," and "vale," "farewell," or "farewell, flesh." The great popular features of the New Orleans Carnival are the gorgeous street pageants that take place in the week ending on Ash Wednesday.

Our Carnival parades date back to the year 1827, when a number of young Creole gentlemen, who had just returned from Paris, whither they had been sent to complete their education, conceived the idea of organizing a street procession of maskers. It was a success. The celebration continued year after year on a grander scale, the whole populace taking up the idea. Mardi Gras was, however, in those days essentially different from what it is now. There was more promiscuous masking. The streets were thronged with quaint, picturesque, grotesque bands of maskers of every age, rank, sex and condition, and their costumes ran the whole gamut from the polichinelle or clown, with his jingling bells, monkeys and polar bears, devils, with red horns, and dominoes of all colors, to kings and queens and knights and ladies of the olden time. An exclusive ball in the old St. Louis Hotel or the Salle d'Orleans followed, while the city generally had its festive gatherings, and fun and merriment reigned. Mardi Gras was also a great day with the boys, who, clothed in dominoes, old calico dresses or bagging, masked themselves, and, armed with a stout hickory stick and a bag of flour, promenaded the streets, seeking for victims upon whom to exercise their mischievous spirit. Their depredations, however, were limited to such as wore the Carnival uniform, and consisted principally in throwing flour and confetti. The flour, confetti and hickory sticks have disappeared, and the number of promiscuous street maskers is growing gradually less each year, but many of the ancient distinctive features of the day still remain, the ball at the old St. Louis Hotel having been the inauguration of the grand Carnival balls which are special features of the celebrations to-day.

The various customs that still maintain indicate the

Roman Origin of the Festivities.

Paris derived her Carnival from the Eternal City, and New Orleans derived hers from Paris, so that the historian may trace the genealogy of the celebration far back into pagan times, when the sacrifice of the Lupercalia formed the great festival of ancient Rome. It seems fitting, also, that, since New Orleans derived its old-time Carnival from Paris, the system of street pageants of moving tableaux should also have been introduced into New Orleans from an old French city of the new world.

The idea of reproducing scenes from history, poetry, folk-lore or fairyland on floats drawn about the streets was first inaugurated in Mobile by an organization known as the Cowbellions, in 1831. New Orleans continued her street processions, begun in 1827, on Mardi Gras, having quite an extensive one in 1837, and another still more brilliant in 1839. Attention was now being paid also to the purely spectacular part of the pageant, a feature of the procession of 1839 being an immense cock over six feet high, riding in a carriage and delighting the crowds with stentorian crows. In 1857 a society called the "Mystick Krewe," now known as the

Mystic Krewe of Comus,

was organized. The Picayune especially exploited the extraordinary secrecy which shrouded its movements, and stimulated the curiosity of the public to the highest degree in regard to its appearance. Mardi Gras, Feb. 24, at 9 o'clock, the Krewe appeared for the first time on the streets, coming whence no one could say, and presenting a gorgeous series of moving tableaux representing scenes of the infernal regions, taken from Milton's "Paradise Lost." After the parade the Krewe repaired to the Varieties Theatre, where a series of appropriate tableaux were presented, the subjects, "The Diabolic Powers," "The Expulsion from Paradise," the "Conference of Satan and Beelzebub" and "Pandemonium," being in keeping with the character of the pageant. A grand ball followed the tableaux, far surpassing the first effort in this direction in 1889 in the old St. Louis ballroom, or the exclusive displays which from 1840 to 1845 so delighted pleasure-loving New Orleans. It took rank with the memorable ball of 1852, given in the old Orleans Theatre, and which for gorgeousness of decorations, richness of toilettes and brilliancy of effect has never been surpassed in New Orleans.

The Mystick Krewe of Comus continued to give annual displays till 1861, when the tragedy of the Civil War for a time put an end to the pretty gayeties of the Carnival. In 1866, after the restoration of peace, Comus resumed his entertainments, giving a grand street parade and an exclusive ball annually until 1884, with the exceptions of the years 1875, 1879 and 1883. From 1884 to 1890 Comus did not appear. In the latter year, however, the merry God of Revelry delighted the popular heart by reappearing upon the streets in a magnificent series of tableaux, representing the "Paligenesis of the Mystick Krewe's Life and Work," or a review of its own history. Since that period Comus has never failed to delight the Carnival City with an annual display. It is the oldest of the Carnival organizations,

The Twelfth Night Revelers,

the second of the mystic organizations, came into existence in 1870. It derives its name from the night it celebrates, January 6, or the twelfth night after Christmas. For several years the organization gave annual street pageants, very much on the same style as Comus, but varying in the treatment. The first parade was in 1871, and the subject presented was "Mother Goose's Tea Party." The revellers went out of existence in 1876, but reorganized in 1894, when they gave a grand masquerade ball. Since then the society has annually entertained its friends at the French Opera House on Twelfth Night. The ball is very interesting, reproducing all the old Creole customs and observances of Twelfth Night, such as the cutting of the Twelfth Night or King's Cake, in which are hidden the gold and silver mystic beans. The one who gets the slice containing the gold bean becomes "King" or "Queen," as the case may be, and the finders of the silver beans become the royal attendants.

Rex

made his first appearance in 1872. This organization was started for the purpose of bringing all the maskers of the city together for the entertainment of the Grand Duke Alexis, who was in that year the guest of the City. The Grand Duke reviewed the procession from the portico of the City Hall. Rex has appeared ever since, and is called the "King of the Carnival." His court is composed of Dukes and Peers of the Realm, appointed from the best circles of the City. Like all the other organizations, Rex chooses a Queen, and this lady, invested with royal symbols, is known as the "Queen of the Carnival." The entry of the King into his Carnival City takes place the Monday preceding Mardi Gras, and is a magnificent display, in which are seen all the Dukes and Peers of the Realm, forming the royal escort, the household of His Majesty, the royal baggage, etc. He is supposed to come from a distant country, and a gayly bedecked fleet of vessels of all sorts proceeds down the river to meet him and escort his yacht to the landing-place at the foot of Canal Street. Having arrived, amid the booming of cannon and the clash of martial music, a parade is formed, and the King and his court are escorted through the principal streets by all the local and visiting military to the Carnival Palace. At the City Hall the Mayor of New Orleans presents the King with the keys of the city on a silken cushion, on which are embroidered the royal arms. Rex accepts them, and no ruler enjoys greater privileges or has more loyal subjects than this merry monarch of a day. The annual parades, which have continued since 1872, take place about noon on Mardi Gras, and are gorgeous spectacles. At night Rex gives a magnificent ball at the Royal Palace,

CANAL STREET DURING MARDI GRAS PARADE.

Washington Artillery Hall. The ballroom and throneroom are splendidly decorated, and for three days after the Carnival are open to visitors. Mardi Gras is a legal holiday in New Orleans.

The first appearance of the

Knights of Momus

also made memorable the Carnival of 1872. Momus first gave his parades on the last day of the year, but in 1876 the organization changed the time of the processions to Carnival week. The first parade represented scenes from Scott's romance, "The Talisman." "The Coming Race," a humorous and satirical forecast of the progress of evolution, was the subject in 1873. Momus did not appear in 1874, 1875 or 1879, but the intervening years down to 1886 were marked by displays of great richness and beauty. In 1886, after a magnificent parade and ball, the Knights of Momus ceased to participate in the Carnival. In 1889 the organization entertained its friends at the French Opera House with beautiful tableaux from "The Culprit Fay," by Drake. In 1892 the gorgeous panorama of "Aladdin and the Wonderful Lamp" was given. Annually since then the Knights of Momus have given at the French Opera House a grand ball and tableaux, which attract the élite of the social world. In the Carnivals of 1900, 1901, 1902 and 1903, the society was again represented by a street pageant of great beauty on the Thursday night preceding Mardi-Gras.

The Krewe of Proteus

was organized in 1882, appearing first on Mardi Gras Eve of that year in a series of brilliant tableaux, "The Dream of Egypt." Since that time Proteus has not allowed a single year to pass without adding a brilliant contribution to the Carnival festivities in its magnificent parade and ball. The fancy of the artist, the thought of the historian, the dream of the poet, are allowed free scope in the magnificent portrayal of subjects for pageant and tableaux, whether in "A Trip to Fairyland," as in 1893, or in "E Pluribus Unum," Proteus' idea of the States of the American Union, as expressed in twenty moving tableaux in 1899. Year by year the beauty and grace of the pageantry elicit the admiration of all observers.

The Krewe of Nereus,

organized in 1895. is the most youthful but one of the Carnival societies. For several years the Krewe limited its efforts to giving a ball at the French Opera House. But in 1900 it supplemented this entertainment with a beautiful street pageant, mounting its tableaux on trolley cars, which afforded opportunity for a beautiful display of electric illuminations.

Several other Carnival organizations, the Krewe of Consus, the Atlanteans, the Elves of Oberon, the High Priests of Mithras, confine themselves to giving one ball annually during the Carnival period. The Carnival of 1898 witnessed the revival of the Phunny Phorty Phellows, a society nearly a quarter of a century old, which formerly delighted the populace with a daylight procession on Mardi Gras, the themes selected being always of a humorous character.

The balls given by the various organizations having street parades begin immediately after the parade has concluded, and generally occur at the French Opera House, the maskers being put down from the floats as these draw up before the venerable lyric temple. It is a wonderful sight to see the maskers descending; the flaring torches, the ever-changing colors, the glittering tableaux, the marvelous richness and beauty of the costumes, the managers shouting orders, the staring crowds, all combine to make the scene a memorable one.

Admission to these balls is by invitation only, and the cards are not transferable. Admission cards are distributed only through nomination by members of the secret organizations. Strangers who have no friends through whom their names may be presented and communicated to the societies, may write a note asking for invitations. If ratified by the committee, invitations will be sent to the writer's address. Rex's ball is the popular one, and the attendance often numbers 30,000. Invitations to this ball may also be procured by applying to the Mayor. Nevertheless, the admission is hedged about with many restrictions, and to be honored with an invitation is supposed to confer a certain social rank not otherwise obtainable.

It is the custom of each organization to appoint a lady to preside as its

"Queen,"

and to select one of their number to exercise the brief sovereignty of King, representing "Rex," "Comus," "Proteus," "Momus," "Nereus," etc., as the case may be. The King often exercises the privilege of choosing his consort, and always presents her with magnificent jewels. For a week preceding the ball these handsome ornaments, crown and scepter, necklace and girdle, may be seen in the show window of some Canal Street jeweler, or store on some other principal thoroughfare. The jewels are usually made in Paris, and are very costly. The "Queen" chooses her maids of honor, who occupy with her one of the proscenium boxes at the Opera House during the presentation of tableaux. The box directly opposite is always reserved for the Queen and maids of the preceding year. After the tableaux, the pretty ceremony of the coronation of the Queen takes place, then the dancing of the Royal Quadrille. This is followed by several beautiful dances, in which the maskers lead out the young ladies who have been specially honored with a previous invitation. These ladies occupy special seats in a body in the parquette, and to be "called out" by a masker is considered a great mark of distinction, while to be "Queen" of one of the balls is an honor that clings to the recipient through smiles and tears in this quaint old city. Each young lady who is called out receives from the masker who has so honored her some beautiful gift, generally of jewelry, and the air of mystery surrounding the giver makes it all the more appreciated. Before the ball is over each masker has divested himself of dainty accessories in the way of badges, scepters, rings and other ornamentation, and presented them to the lady of his choice. Of course, she is not supposed to know who the donor is, and many a time she does not. These are only some of the very pleasant courtesies that make these Carnival festivities unique and happy memories. Many a love match is made on Mardi Gras night, and "once Queen, forever Queen," has grown to be a pretty Carnival motto, just as the King's royal anthem always remains "If Ever I Cease to Love."

At the Comus ball the principal event is the visit of the King and Queen of the Carnival to the King and Queen of Comus. All the forms of royalty are studiously observed.

How the Parades are Managed.

The Carnival parades are managed by bodies of private citizens of the highest social standing, who form the famous Carnival organizations. These gentlemen spare no expense out of their own private means to make these street pageants as beautiful, as magnificent and as instructive as possible. The expense of a single display ranges from $20,000 to $30,000, and sometimes higher. The people are not taxed anything. They have only to come from their homes and enjoy; and so with the thousands of strangers who find such a warm welcome in New Orleans.

The work of the Carnival organizations in the preparation of these magnificent street pageants is shrouded in impenetrable mystery. Besides exciting the curiosity of the public to the highest degree, the strict secrecy maintained enables the organizations to begin their preparations for the next parade almost as soon as one is off the street.

In each organization the system of work is as complete, in a way, as an established government, and the discipline maintained is like that of a small army.

Each association has its own floats, ladders, housing for the draft-horses and disguises for the torch-bearers. None of the organizations have any known permanent meeting-place.

The association consists generally of about 250 members, mostly leading clubmen, and it may be remarked that many of them have grown old in the service, and are grandfathers. In getting up the parades about 100 gentlemen are selected to appear in the display; the remainder are utilized for duties, much more onerous than is generally supposed.

MARDI GRAS FLOATS PASSING THE GRAND BOULEVARD,

Mardi Gras is scarcely over before a meeting of the organization is summoned, and plans are taken into consideration for the next parade. A design committee is selected, the head of which is called the "Captain," and he is invested with absolute power. The artist is then summoned for consultation. Each committeeman proposes a subject for treatment, drawn from history, poetry, mythology, fairy lore or modern topics. Often the subject requires extraordinary research to portray it properly and accurately. A half dozen of the best of these suggestions are given to the artist, who makes a series of rough crayon sketches, which are presented about a month after the first meeting. The final selection of a subject is always a difficut problem. Once the decision is made, the work begins in earnest. The artist is directed to make a drawing of each float as it will appear in full parade, and also to prepare sketches of each of the hundred or more costumes to be worn by the maskers. Each study is elaborately finished and inscribed with the name of every material which is to enter into the composition. These undergo the criticism of the design committee. Such modifications or additions as are suggested are made, and the characters are so distributed among the members of the association as to harmonize with individutl peculiarities. Each card is then labeled on the back with a memorandum giving the height, size, girth, etc., of the gentleman who is to wear the costume. The

Designing of the Floats

is the hardest part of the artist's task. Each float is done in water colors on a scale about twenty times as large as the costume card. Several sets are made, one with each figure duly numbered and posted as it is to appear in the street parade, is hung upon the wall of the clubroom in which the meetings are held, there to be scrutinized and criticized diligently by the members. Another set with the individual costume cards as marked, is sent to the manufacturer.

These preliminaries are usually over by July 1. In the meantime, the papier maché workers are busy molding the different accessories required to decorate each float. The costumes are usually received by December 1. As soon as they arrive they are carried with utmost secrecy to the "Den," as the mysterious clubroom of the organization is generally called. Each suit is found packed in a separate case and carefully labeled; they are taken out and arranged on a long table, each surmounted by its own corresponding picture. The members come and try on their individual suits, and for weeks thereafter the Court tailors, armorers and milliners are kept busy making such alterations as are necessary in the fit, makeup, etc. When this immense task is satisfactorily accomplished, each costume is replaced in its proper case, and is duly numbered. It is then locked up and laid aside for the eventful night.

In the meantime, the Float Committee, which has been furnished with a third set of designs, has been busy at the

Float "Den," located in some out-of-the-way place,

usually the yard of an abandoned cotton-press, where the building up of the floats has been going on quietly, noiselessly, and with the most profound secrecy; though numbers of carpenters, painters, gilders, papier maché workers, etc., are employed for months and months, strange to say, the secret of the place is so well guarded that the public has no clue to its location or ever learns aught of the preparations in progress. The "Ball Committee," which arranges for the grand function at the Opera House which invariably follows the parade, is also busy; the balls are opened with a series of tableaux, embracing all the characters that have appeared in the procession. The work of drilling the participants in these tableaux is not the least part of the general preparations.

On the date fixed for the parade

All is Bustle and Excitement at the "Den."

If the parade is to take place at night the preparations begin about 2 o'clock in the afternoon; if during the day, they begin almost at sunrise. All the drivers, torch-bearers, attendants, etc., are on the scene being drilled anew in the various duties that each is to perform with military precision. The boxes containing the costumes were removed during the dead of night to some building in the vicinity of the yard where the floats are waiting. Every precaution has been taken to prevent the public from even guessing to what purpose this building is being applied. Exits from other houses are cut into it, the windows are kept darkened, and the main doorways are never opened.

At the appointed hour the members begin to arrive. They bring their formal evening dress with them. This they place in the boxes in lieu of the costumes, in which they proceed to deck themselves. If it is to be a night parade, by 7 o'clock all are dressed. The roll is called, and the characters, securely masked, take their places in line and undergo a last formal inspection. In the

TITLE BEARER PRECEDING MARDI GRAS FLOAT.

meantime, a committee has traversed the route over which the pageant is to pass, to see that the street is free from all obstructions. The committee reports all in readiness, and shortly after a squad of police makes its appearance. It clears the streets and establishes a cordon around the yard for about four or five squares. The torch-bearers are marshaled on the left side of the open space, under the command of officers, who are stationed at regular intervals. The floats are driven out of the press yard. The "Captain" calls the numbers, and each gentleman, hearing his special numeral, takes his place upon the float to which he has been assigned. This is driven off expeditiously, to make way for its successor. The bands of music are then marched in position, the torchmen surround the cars, and the

Procession is Ready to Move,

in remarkably short order. The "Captain" once more rides along the line to ascertain that everything is as it should be, the signal is given, and the procession moves quietly and in darkness to the nearest large thoroughfare. A rocket, piercing the evening sky with a lurid line of light, announces to the waiting multitudes that throng all the line of march that the mysterious Krewe is once again on the streets to delight their pleasure-loving hearts. Suddenly there is a blaze of light, for the torches are lit and encircle each float in a brilliant parallelogram of fire, and the streets are transformed into pictures of Fairyland. The Krewe has come, whence no one knows; it will return, where, no one can tell; but it is here; it tells its own story of the time, the labor, the thought, the money that have been expended so lavishly, so unselfishly for this pleasure of a few fleeting hours. And it is because of this sweet sentiment underlying all, the utter unselfishness and thought of others, that the Carnival is so dear to our people.

No matter what route has been selected, the parade winds up at the French Opera House at about 10 o'clock. Here the maskers dismount and the floats disappear in the darkness from which they emerged. The boxes containing the dress suits of the members have, in the meantime, been conveyed from the "Den" to the dressing-rooms of the Opera House.

Within the great temple

All is Light and Beauty.

Tiers upon tiers are occupied by the most beautiful and brilliant women of the city and lady guests from other States. The Queen of the evening is there with her court, and the Queen and court of the previous year. Dozens of the

REX PARADE IN ST. CHARLES AVENUE.

most beautiful girls, who expect to be "called out," occupy honored seats within the ribbon enclosure of the parquette. The curtain rises upon a brilliant series of tableaux, after which the royal quadrille is danced, and after three or four dances reserved for the maskers and the young ladies who have received special invitations in advance, the floor is free to all, and the maskers mingle with the brilliant throng. As 12 o'clock strikes the maskers disappear quietly, one by one. A few moments afterwards they return dressed in the conventional evening society garb. They are obliged to present their invitations at the doors like everyone else, so that it is absolutely impossible to obtain a clue to their identity with the character personated during the parade. A great deal of mirth and laughter follow, the rippling echo of some pretty girl who is sure that she has found a clue, the gay badinage, the merry dance, and then the deepening skies without and the shrill crow of some neighboring cock, announce that it is "Ash Wednesday morn."

The ball is over, the masquers have fled; the Carnival of that year is a thing of the past, and New Orleans, with a sigh for the bright hour of sunshine that was hers, puts on onee more a serious garb and says: "Come, children, let us shut up the box and the puppets; turn we to better things."

The Carnival of 1904

will be in many respects the most brilliant ever known in New Orleans. Since 1899 there has been a disposition to prolong and elaborate the ceremonies, in order to still better compensate the enormous crowds that throng our city in Carnival Week. The festivities will begin on February 11, when the Knights of Momus will parade. On Monday, February 15, the arrival of Rex will be made the occasion of a daylight parade, and at night the Krewe of Proteus will parade. The following morning, February 16, is Mardi Gras, and Rex will marshal his court and people in a street pageant. At night Comus will close the Carnival in a blaze of glory. And so with the Carnivals to come; each will outrival the preceding effort.

Special Carnival Editions of the Picayune,

beautifully illustrating the parades of Proteus and Comus can be obtained on application at the Picayune office.

During the next three years Mardi Gras will fall on the following dates: March 7, 1905, February 27, 1906, February 12, 1907.

CHAPTER XX.

Out-of-Town Journeys.

The country about New Orleans is beautiful and characteristically Southern. The land of Evangeline, immortalized by Longfellow, lies just beyond our doorways, and Arcady, sweet Arcady, the old hiding-place of Lafitte, the first campgrounds of Iberville, are near enough to be familiar haunts.

The rude huts of the famous Choctaw Indians are but over the waterway, restling under the pines and bay trees of St. Tammany Parish. The mouth of the Mississippi, the Gulf and the great jetties are a few hours' ride distant, and all about and around the great sprawling city lie orange groves, white with blossoms, or golden with fruit, cane fields and plantations.

Among the out-of-town journeys which the visitor should not fail to enjoy is the trip down the river by steamer to Port Chalmette, over Lake Pontchartrain to Mandeville, Chinchuba, Covington and Abita Springs, the trip along the Mississippi coast to Bay St. Louis, Pass Christian and Biloxi, the trip to Lake Borgne over the Shell Beach Railroad, to the pine hills of Magnolia and Chatawa, Mississippi, on the Illinois Central, over the Mississippi Valley Railroad, a run to the State Capitol at Baton Rouge, a boat trip to Bayou Sara, to Vicksburg or to Natchez. The picturesque Tèche country, in which dwell the peaceful and quaint Acadians, is less than half a day's journey by rail.

Mandeville,

the nearest of the lake coast resorts, is one of the most picturesque of Southern watering places. It was one of the most fashionable resorts of old New Orleans. It lies in the heart of the piney woods district, and nearby is the beautiful village of Chinchuba, noted for its crystal springs. The Mandeville coast may be almost distinctly traced against the horizon from the shores of Milneburg, and is reached by excursion steamers from this point during the greater part of the year. It may be reached daily by the East Louisiana Railroad.

Within a few miles of Mandeville, easily accessible by stage or carriage drive from this resort, are the old towns of

Covington and Abita Springs.

Both lie in the great piney woods belt, on the banks of the Bogue Falla River, one of the most picturesque and beautiful streams in the United States. Abita Springs derives its name from an old Indian legend, and signifies the "Startled Fawn." The waters are medicinal. Cóvington is a noted health resort. It may be reached by the East Louisiana Road or by the steamer Camella, which runs from Milneburg to Mandeville, thence turns into the Tchefuncta River as far as Old Landing. A more beautiful or picturesque trip could not be imagined than along this winding river, with the pine trees singing their everlasting threnody along the banks, and the cypresses almost lapping their branches overhead. A pleasant trip can be made on the Shell Beach Road, which makes a run of an hour and a half to the Gulf, or up the Illinois Central Road to

Magnolia and Chatawa,

the latter one of the prettiest hill towns of Mississippi, lying on the banks of the dark, fern-fringed Tangipahoa.

There are small boats going tri-weekly to the jetties, but the luxury of a river trip is only tested by a journey up the Mississippi River.

The up-river excursion to

Bayou Sara

affords an opportunity of seeing the very best part of the Mississippi River scenery, its orange groves and cane fields, and plantations with negro cabins sprawling in the sunshine, and all occupied the year round. The old town of Plaquemines, the beautiful college and convent in St. James Parish, the imposing State Capitol at Baton Rouge, set on terraced hills, and altogether charming, are worthy of the two days, or perhaps less, time that it takes to make the trip. All along the way the big boats stop continuously, and the tourist has ample time to see plantation life and Southern villages, and know what it means to go boating along the Mississippi.

Another delightful river trip is up the Bayou Tèche to

New Iberia and the Old Town of St. Martinville.

Some of the finest sugar plantations in the State are to be seen along this route. The towns are also directly reached by the Southern Pacific Railroad. New Iberia lies on the dreamy and beautiful bayou, in the heart of the Land of Evangeline. This section of Louisiana is called the Valley of the Tèche, and is famous for the exquisite beauty of its scenery and the great fertility of its land. It is called the "Garden of Louisiana."

From New Iberia to the

Great Salt Mine, on Avery Island,

is only a short distance. A little railroad carries the tourist to the mines. It is situated on Petit Anse Island, and the salt is found between eleven and thirty feet below the surface of the earth. The miners have worked over sixty-five feet into the solid salt, which shows itself on a level with tidewater. The salt is supposed to extend hundreds of miles below the surface of the gulf, and has been found to be superior to any other salt sold in the Southern markets. New Iberia is in the heart of a great duck, snipe and fishing country. The great comedian, Joseph Jefferson, has a summer home not far from New Iberia.

If the visitor is interested in sugar-making, a visit to one of the plantations within easy reach of the city will be found satisfactory. Some of the largest of these estates are on the western side of the river, but if he wants to see the sugar country in its perfection, he should make the trip by steamboat

Down the Bayou Lafourche.

The trip can be made at a small cost in about twenty-four hours by taking a boat to Thibodaux, and thence back to New Orleans by rail. Bayou Lafourche is scarcely less lovely than Bayou Têche. The magnificent stretch of sugar lands, the beautiful plantation homes, the dreamy bayou, the generous hospitality of the people, all combine to make the trip a pictured memory. During the grinding season, which lasts from November to February, a visit to a sugar plantation is delightful.

By going to Morgan City, over the Southern Pacific Road, excursions can be made on boat and steam tugs through the waterways by which the Atchafalaya reaches the gulf. Another very pleasant expedition is by steamer through the swamps and bayous to

Grand Island.

This is a famous Creole summer resort, and is noted for its fine surf bathing. The Caminada Cheniére, the scene of a terrible disaster caused by a storm and tidal wave of 1893, through which over 2,000 lives were lost, is not far from Grand Islans. Further on, outlined like a silhouette against the sky, is a dark strip of land, the last the eye rests upon ere the waters of the Mexican Gulf reach the sea. This is Isle Derniére, or Last Island, which was at that time the most fashionable of all the gulf resorts. Thousands of lives were lost, and half of the island itself buried in the sea. Since that time it has been abandoned. It is a marked spot, and the great tragedy of Last Island has furnished many a theme for poet and romancer.

CHAPTER XXI.

From New Orleans to Mobile—"Across the Lake"—
Short Sketches of the Gulf Coast
Summer Resorts.

Studding the beautiful stretch of Gulf coast that spans the distance from New Orleans to Mobile lie pretty villages, whose many attractions in the way of fishing, boating and bathing have made them favorite resorts among New Orleans people for over a century. Not only do the élite of the city have their summer residences along this pleasant line, but even the poorest seek to spend a day or two, at least, during the summer season, at some one of the gulf resorts. From May to September, especially, these towns are overflowing with the best people of New Orleans: they are the scene of constant gayety. There are yacht races and regattas, and fishing and hunting and boating parties, the yacht races held at Bay St. Louis, Pass Christian and Biloxi enlisting general interest. The salt bathing is delightful, the drives along the beach of surpassing beauty. In front one sees the ever-changing glory of the white-crested sea; in the rear, magnificent belts of pine lands, that give life and health with every resinous breath.

The salubrious climate and balmy winters of these resorts have of late years attracted many Northern visitors and invalids, who spend the winter there. They are finding out that New Orleans itself not only offers peculiar advantages and inducements, both as a winter and summer resort, but at our very doors are the health-giving land of the pine, and white beaches of the Mexican Gulf, famous hunting-grounds and bits of virgin forests, whose beauty and picturesqueness are unlike those of any other section of the Continent.

And so the old city has become the point of departure for many wonderlands, not the least pleasant of which are the pretty resorts

"Across the Lake,"

as the coast line that intervenes between New Orleans and its old French sister, Mobile, was charmingly designated by the old Creole settlers. The Louisville and Nashville Railroad is the only one which reaches these resorts. The passenger station is located at the foot of Canal Street, less than 500 feet from the river. There are usually two morning and two evening trains. During the summer months cheap excursions are a feature, and are patronized by enormous crowds.

The run to Mobile is made in about four hours. By taking a morning train the visitor will have ample opportunity to study the scenery around New Orleans. Following the line of the Pontchartrain for a little distance, the train carries the tourist through the

"Prairie Tremblante," or Trembling Prairie.

This is a swampy expanse lying within the municipal boundaries of the city. It is inhabited by squatters, who eke out an existence by hunting, trapping and fishing. They are mostly of the Austrian, Chinese and Malay races, and live a life peculiar to their class.

Near this prairie, in a spot remote from the railroad, is a large colony of Manilamen, probably the only one in the United States. Quaint negro cabins dot the entire line of the railroad, and every now and then is seen a pretty bit of garden greenery, showing the home of some white resident. At Micheaud and Lee Station small settlements have grown up, but they are still unimportant.

Chef Menteur

is the first noteworthy stopping-place after leaving New Orleans. Chef Menteur signifies "Lying Chief." The French were deceived by the Chief of a tribe of Indians living here. They perpetuated his infamy by bestowing the name "Chef Menteur" upon the place and bayou. The bayou connects Lake Borgne and Lake Pontchartrain, and is a famous place for fishing. Most of the buildings at Chef Menteur are fishing clubs, the members of which reside in New Orleans, but make constant excursions thither to pursue the gentle sport of Sir Izaak Walton. Chef Menteur is 19.4 miles from New Orleans.

Lake Catherine, six miles further, is another settlement of fishing clubs and fishermen. The train pauses here a moment, and then speeds on to the

Rigolets,

a thriving little town, with miniature dockyards and several residences of proportion. The Rigolets is a deep channel which connects Lake Borgne and Lake Pontchartrain. Through the car window is seen an apparently illimitable stretch of marshy meadow, and in the distance white sails flash in the sunshine, as though some boat were sailing over dry land. But in reality the boat is pursuing its course silently through one of the many tortuous, narrow, yet deep, waterways which intersect the marshy ground in all directions, and the very existence of which can scarcely be noticed except when almost directly upon the banks. This series of natural canals crossing and recrossing in all directions afford many excellent channels for schooners, luggers and other small craft. The Rigolets mark the boundary line along the coast between Louisiana and Mississippi. The distance from New Orleans to the Rigolets is 30.3 miles. Between the Rigolets and the next point of interest,

English Lookout,

is a spreading live oak, which is famous as the last tree in Louisiana. English Lookout is so called because in 1814 a post was established here by the Americans to watch the movements of the English fleet moving up the Mississippi Sound on the way to attack New Orleans. Here the train crosses the Mississippi line. Lookout is thirty-six miles from New Orleans. It is also famous as the place where Pearl River, which forms the eastern boundary of Louisiana,

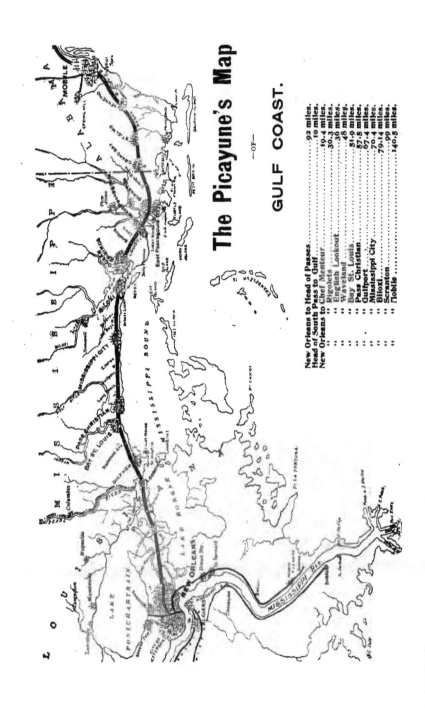

The Picayune's Map

—OF—

GULF COAST.

New Orleans to Head of Passes........92 miles.
Head of South Pass to Gulf...............10 miles.
New Orleans to Chef Menteur...........19.4 miles.
     "   Rigolets.....................30.3 miles.
     "   English Lookout...........36 miles.
     "   Waveland.....................48 miles.
     "   Bay St. Louis...............51.9 miles.
     "   Pass Christian..............57.5 miles.
     "   Gulfport.......................67.4 miles.
     "   Mississippi City...........70.4 miles.
     "   Biloxi............................79.14 miles.
     "   Scranton.........................99 miles.
     "   Mobile.........................140.5 miles.

empties into the lake. The trip up Pearl River is very picturesque. A small steamer plies between Lookout, Gainesville, Columbia, Logtown and Pearling-tcu, the latter being the site of extensive saw mills. Pearl River runs through a section famous for its splendid timber lands. A trip along Pearl River will repay the fisherman.

Gulf View,

which is the first important stop along the Mississippi Sound, has only recently sprung into existence. Some very handsome hunting and fishing clubs and lodges, owned by private citizens in New Orleans, dot the route. The name "Gulf View" was given to the settlement because it is near this point that the tourist catches the first glimpse of the blue waters of the Mississippi Sound stretching away to the right, as the train speeds on through the dense growth of pine forests.

From Gulf View to the beautiful town of

"Waveland"

is comparatively a short distance. Waveland is forty-eight miles from New Orleans. It lies on the banks of the lovely bay that Bienville named for the patron saint of his loyal master, St. Louis. It is just two miles from Bay St. Louis proper, and, indeed, may be said to be the new Bay St. Louis, or a continuation of the old Creole watering place. But Waveland is a distinct town. It is incorporated under the laws of Mississippi, and has its own Mayor. It is populated almost entirely by wealthy people, many of whom have their homes

HOME OF THE POET "PEARL RIVERS"—WAVELAND, MISS.

in New Orleans and maintain beautiful summer residences here. Among the handsome residences, which are distinctly Southern in architecture, and, therefore, quite different from summer residences in Northern resorts, is the summer home of the late proprietors of the Picayune, Mr. and Mrs. George Nicholson, and now the residence of their sons. The train makes a short stop one mile further, at Nicholson Avenue, and in a few moments

Bay St. Louis

is reached. A settlement was founded by the French at Bay St. Louis shortly after the establishment of the French colony at Biloxi. A similar settlement was also made at Pascagoula. In 1727 Governor Perier made a tour of these settlements, reporting upon their condition to the French Government. The real history of the "Bay," as it is commonly called, began in 1820, when General Shields, the United States Lighthouse Inspector, built two houses at the lower end.. One if these original houses still stands, near the Crescent Hotel. The Government considered the site so healthful that for several years it quartered troops there in a barracks, which stood on the beach, between the sites now occupied by the Crescent Hotel and St. Stanislaus College. For a while the place was called Shieldsboro, but the designation was altered years ago. Bay St. Louis is 51.9 miles from New Orleans. It is situated on a high peninsula, comprising some 20,000 acres. The population is about 3,000. Towards the lower end are the homes of many of the ancient Creole families of ante-bellum days. Along the drive towards Waveland, skirting the beautiful beach, are many new and charming homes of a more modern character. In the old town, which was the most aristocratic of the gulf coast watering places before the war, and which still holds its own, stands the Church of Our Lady of the Gulf, erected in 1872 at a cost of $30,000. St. Joseph's Convent, established in 1854, and St. Stanislaus College are interesting educational institutions. The quaint old graveyard is well worth a visit. All along the beach are magnificent live oaks that have defied the ravages of time and tide.

Bay St. Louis has several very good hotels and a number of charming private boarding-houses.

Leaving the town, the train crosses immediately the broad and beautiful expanse of Bay St. Louis. The track is carried on a trestle-work, much of which is encased or sheathed in huge earthenware pipes to protect it from' the teredo worm. The scene in crossing the waters is very picturesque. The beautiful homes nestling amid the trees along the pebbly beach, the fishing smacks and sailing boats, with their white sails flying in the breeze, often as not the glimpse of some Italian fisherman singing a gay bacarole or dreamy opera as he throws his net, are pictures that come floating over the waters with every dancing ray of sunlight reflected in the white-crested waves. Just over the way is the beautiful Pass, and nestling on its banks, like a white-robed Queen, is the fair town of

Pass Christian.

It is also situated on a peninsula, and extends along the coast for nearly six miles.. On the north are Bayou Portage and Bayou D'Or. The latter has been so named on account of the golden brilliancy of the foliage along the banks in autumn. Bayou Portage follows a devious course, at one point approaching within a mile of the sea. The Indians knew this fact, and in the old days used to save a journey of nearly twenty miles by hauling their canoes across the narrow neck of land. The town is named in honor of a Swedish sailor named Christian, who discovered the pass, which leads from the Gulf of Mexico into the Mississippi Sound, near Cat Island. Pass Christian is fifty-seven miles from New Orleans. It has a population of about 2,000. The magnificent trees are the admiration of tourists. The Pass has several fine hotels, and is a very popular resort with Northern visitors.

From the train window a good view is had of

Cat Island,

which, with Ship Island and Chandeleur Island, was the first land that Iberville and Bienville discovered before entering the Mississippi River. The name "Cat Island," then bestowed, has been retained to this day. Its origin is peculiar. When the French first landed there they found large numbers of a strange looking animal that somewhat resembled a fox, but was more like a cat. Not knowing what it was, one of the exploring party exclaimed: "Why, this must be the kingdom of cats." At once the name "Cat Island" was given to the place. The animal is now known as the raccoon. Cat Island is about eight miles long, and practically arid. It lies about ten miles out from Pass Christian.

About ten miles beyond Pass Christian lies the progressive city of

Gulfport,

The latest of the beautiful Gulf coast resorts, but one which has substantiated the proud boast of having grown more rapidly than any other Southern city.

The marvelous growth of Gulfport has been practically within the last three or four years. Twelve years ago there was only one house on its shores. To-day the town boasts of a population of 4,500 inhabitants; it is regularly and beautifully laid out, with wide well-paved streets; it has its own water-work system, its own electric light plant, many large and handsome residences, and the most magnificent hotel on the seacoast. Its wonderful growth is due to the public spirit and enterprise of Capt. T. J. Jones, who believed in the possibilities of establishing a splendid sea-port, right on the Mississippi Sound, connecting the ocean traffic directly with the great west, with sturdy determination set about making his dream a reality, a few years ago. He built the Gulf and Ship Island Railroad, connecting Gulfport with the Illinois Central Railroad at Jackson, Miss. He caused a harbor to be dredged on the west side of his new town, having a depth of 30 feet of water at the wharf. He dug a channel from the harbor to Ship Island, a distance of twelve miles out in the Gulf, thus practically connecting the coast with the ocean. Steamships and sailing vessels, drawing 22 feet of water, now come directly to the wharves at Gulfport. An immense lumber traffic has been established, and timber is being shipped to all parts of the world. Capt. Jones built the Great Southern Hotel, containing about 400 rooms and magnificently equipped in every way. It is one of the largest hotels in the South, the largest on the Gulf coast, and the equal of the famous Florida East Coast Hotel in system. The electric cars run a mile along the wharf leading to an immense pavilion, and to the beautiful Yacht Club House which is modern and complete in every detail. The city of Biloxi intends building an electric car line to Gulfport, and Gulfport has secured the franchise to build a similar line to Pass Christian, thus connecting those celebrated seacoast resorts by easy and rapid transit. Capt. Jones has a magnificent five-story office building. Business activities are continually on the alert, and tourists come from all sections, not only to enjoy the delightful sea breezes and the advantages offered by sojourn in this popular resort, but also to study the growth of the place and its great possibilities for the future.

Just beyond Cat Island, and visible from the Biloxi beach, is

Ship Island,

one of the most imposing landmarks in the history of Louisiana, whether as Colony, Territory or State. It is one of the four low islands (Cat. Chandeleur and Round) that, stretching ten or twelve miles along the gulf coast, form the Mississippi Sound. Ship Island is only seven miles long and three-quarters of a mile wide. It belongs to the State of Mississippi, but is, in fact, ten miles distant from the nearest point of that State. Ship Island was discovered in 1699 by Bienville. In 1814 it served as a rendezvous for the British fleet that was advancing against New Orleans. It was to its white sands and quiet harbor that they retreated for refuge after the disastrous results of the battle on the plains of Chalmette. In the Civil War it was for a while a safe and convenient place of organization. The history of the island as a place of banishment for those who had incurred the displeasure of General Butler during his occupancy of New Orleans has made its name inseparably connected with the later history of the city. The white beach of the island glistening in the sun forms a convenient landmark for mariners.

The train makes a short stop at Long Beach, about six miles from the Pass. It is a recent thriving settlement and rapidly becoming known as a resort. Long Beach boasts of a good hotel. A few minutes' run brings the tourist to

Mississippi City,

which is a very prosperous town and the County seat of Harrison County. As far back as 1830 a great city was projected here, and elaborate plans were made for its establishment. A great harbor was planned, and the older of the two present good hotels was erected soon after. But the extensive scheme required the aid of the United States Government to materialize. This aid was not forthcoming, and the project languished. Mississippi City has a population of about 1,200. Its hotels are considered very excellent. It is 70.4 miles from New Orleans.

BEAUVOIR—THE HOME OF JEFFERSON DAVIS.

Beauvoir,

the old home of Jefferson Davis, President of the Confederacy, is a little over four miles' drive from Mississippi City. Carriages may be taken to this historic place of interest at Mississippi City. Mr. Davis and family lived at Beauvoir during the last years of his life. He died in New Orleans. The old mansion has recently been purchased by the Sons of Confederate Veterans of Mississippi as a home for impoverished Confederate veterans.

The Seashore Campgrounds,

which is quite a large settlement, lies between Mississippi City and Biloxi. The grounds are the property of the New Orleans, the Mobile and the Seashore

District Conferences of the Methodist Episcopal Church, South. Every summer two weeks of religious revivals are held here. The revivals attract visitors from all parts of the far South. The grounds are occupied by wooden buildings called "tents," where many people go to spend the summer. Many prominent Methodists have their special 'tents," or summer houses, here. The bathing at this point is unsurpassed.

Very near the Campgrounds lies the town of

Biloxi,

The town was founded by Bienville in 1718. Though the first settlement by the French was made over the bay in the old town of Biloxi, now known as Ocean Springs, this point stands for the first permanent settlement in Louisiana, all Mississippi and the surrounding country having formed a part of the Louisiana Province. In the year mentioned the capital of the entire Province was transferred to this point. Prior to this date a warehouse and a few other buildings had been erected on the site, which was known to the French as Deer Island. Bienville took up his quarters in the old warehouse. In 1723 the capital was transferred to New Orleans. Nothing of interest marked the history of the Biloxi settlement until 1760, when for a brief sp ce of time it was included in the British possessions, the transfer having been effected by treaty between the European Powers. It became a Spanish town by conquest in 1780. After the cession of Louisiana to the United States, Spain contended that the Districts of Feliciana, East Baton Rouge, St. Helena, St. Tammany, Biloxi and Pascagoula were a part of West Florida, and had not been sold with Louisiana. President Madison held that the District of West Florida belonged, by the treaty of 1803, to the United States, and was a part of the Territory of Orleans.

In 1810 the inhabitants of Bayou Sara, which was a part of the West Florida contention, revolted and declared themselves independent of Spain. The Bayou Sarans attacked the Spanish fort at Baton Rouge and captured it, and asked to be annexed to the United States. President Madison told them quietly that the District of Florida already belonged to the United States, and directed Governor Claiborne to take possession of the district. Claiborne marched at the head of his militiamen to St. Francisville and took possession of the entire district in the name of the United States. The people cheerfully submitted to his authority. Subsequently Biloxi and Pascagoula became part of the State of Mississippi. Biloxi is a great resort for New Orleans people. It is seventy-nine miles from New Orleans. It has a population of 4,500. The town is lighted by electricity, possesses large canning and lumber interests and is supplied with abundant artesian well water. The bathing is delightful, the boating and fishing unexcelled. Its hotels, clubs, residences and churches are numerous and handsome.

A long trestle reaches from Biloxi to

Ocean Springs,

the oldest town in all the area of what was known to the French of old Louisiana. This is the settlement founded by Iberville in 1699. He found on this spot an old Indian village called Biloxi, and he located his settlement here, retaining the name, which sprang from the tribe of Biloxians who inhabited the section. For twenty years this place was the capital of the province. Sauvolle the brother of Iberville, and the first Governor of Louisiana, was killed here by the Indians. The late historian, Gayarre, identified his tomb on the site of the old French fort. When Bienville founded the new town of Biloxi on the other side of the bay, this point became known as Old Biloxi. It retained this name for over a hundred and fifty years. The modern town sprang up about 1854, when several prominent New Orleans gentlemen purchased large properties there, and sought to bring its merits as a watering place into notice. The name "Ocean Springs" was given to the old town, the name being taken from several springs thought to have curative properties which are located on the estate of the late William B. Schmidt, who was one of the leading citizens of New Orleans. The town is very pretty and picturesque. There are some very beautiful homes and several fine hotels. The oldest hotel was established in 1835. The population of Ocean Springs is about 1,400. The town is eighty-three miles from New Orleans.

Scranton

Is the only other stopping-place that the train makes before crossing into the State of Alabama. The place is really a part of the old town of Pascagoula, which comprised Pascagoula proper, as the old French settlement along the seacoast is called, Scranton, the county seat, and Moss Point, a pretty little town on Dog River, about four miles from Scranton

Scranton was named in honor of a former official of the railroad which brought the town into existence about thirty years ago. The population is about 2,000. The town possesses many saw mills and ship yards; an admirable harbor afforded by the Pascagoula River has brought the place considerable foreign commerce. Scranton is ninety-nine miles from New Orleans. A mile drive from Scranton to the seashore brings the visitor to the ancient town of

Pascagoula.

The drive leads through wild and pisturesque scenery that is very romantic. Pascagoula is an old Indian village, deriving its name from the famous tribe that inhabited this section. Indian mounds of considerable extent, it is said, are still to be seen in the vicinity. Soon after Iberville settled at Old Biloxi or Ocean Springs, the colonists established a branch station here. This was the beginning of the present town. When Louisiana was ceded to Spain all Pascagoula was granted by the King of Spain to Colonel Krebs, a distinguished officer in the Spanish army, in recognition of important services. Here he settled, and along the banks of the bay and river his descendents have lived from generation to generation. When the depredations of the Indians necessitated the settlers banding together for their protection, Colonel Krebs built a strong fort, the walls of which were twelve feet thick, just at the junction of the Pascagoula River and Bay. Years afterwards his descendants built a beautiful home on the spot, retaining the old historic fort as a part of the residence. A magnificent avenue of live oaks leads up to this old home, which is a point of interest to all visitors.

Hard by the ancient fortress home is heard the famous "mysterious music," which comes up from the mouth of the river. No explanation of this wierd melody has ever been adduced, but it is a positive fact that at certain hours strange singing notes emanate from the water. Many strange legends are, of course, connected with it, one of which is that the sounds are the wails of an Indian girl moaning for her lover, who was drowned at this point; she sprang in after him, and, failing to save his life, has never ceased to bemoan his fate. Another is that in a feud that arose between the Biloxi and Pascagoula Indians the former surprised the latter one dark and stormy night. Rather than fall into the hands of the hated enemy the entire tribe, men, women and children, sprang into the waters with the warwhoop still lingering on their lips, and this is the weird echo which from that day to this haunts the spot.

Crossing the Alabama line, the train stops at Grand Bay and St. Elmo, both thriving little towns, located, respectively, 115 and 120.8 miles from New Orleans.

Mobile

Is reached in an hour. This important Southern city, the older French sister of New Orleans, is 140.5 miles distant from the great metropolis. Mobile was founded by Bienville in 1702, when he built a fort and established a colony near the site of the present city. It derives its name from the tribe of Mobile Indians that inhabited the section. In 1785 Galvez took the first census, and found that it had a population of 746. The number steadily increased, and in 1788 there were 1330 inhabitants. After this period the importance of the place diminished, and in 1803 there were only 803 inhabitants. In 1813 it was surrendered to the Americans by Gayetaud Perez; the population had still further declined to 500. In 1814 Mobile was incorporated as a town, and in 1819 as a city. The rise of the city was remarkable after that. It grew in strength and importance, and became a leading Southern port. Its commerce was very great. The population at present is about 50,000. In 1864 the Federal fleet, under Admiral Farragut, fought a celebrated battle in the bay against the Confederate fleet, under Admiral Buchanan. In March and April, 1865, the city was besieged by the Federals, under General E. S. Canby, and, after a desperate defense by the Confederates, led by General D. H. Maury, was compelled to surrender. Mobile contains many interesting buildings and fine churches and hotels. Nearby is Springhill, with its famous old college. The city has a fine harbor and a constantly increasing commerce, especially with Cuba and Central America.

CHAPTER XXII.

Hunting and Fishing Near New Orleans.

Sportsmen from the frozen North who come down to delightful New Orleans, to learn the art of enjoyment, often go away without taking advantage of an opportunity to hunt over the most wonderfully varied shooting grounds in the country. There is no section of the United States where a greater variety of game can be had with less trouble and expense. Within half a dozen miles of the heart of the city deer roam their native woods; quail can be found only a little further away; while, within a radius of twenty-five miles, every variety of land and water game, known to the semi-tropics is found and killed, and brought back as evidence, too, of the huntsman's prowess.

Northern huntsmen who are accustomed to travel miles and pay large sums for the privilege of shooting, have no idea of the sport which Louisianians secure with little effort. To say that a band of deer hunters will leave the city on a morning train and return that night, with two, three or four deer, which have cost an outlay of about $2 each, seems incredible; but, nevertheless, it is true. Unlike the sportsmen away up in the cold section, the Louisiana hunters have fine shooting for months at a time. The season is not limited to two weeks, but includes four months of good shooting.

The distinctly unusual formation of the land around New Orleans furnishes almost every variety of territory. Within a few miles of the river, Lake Pontchartrain laps the edge of a dense swamp, which narrows down to the eastward into twenty-five miles of unbroken marsh land, often designated as the "trembling prairie."

In this prairie wild duck and geese find their feeding grounds. They come south with the first sign of cold in October, and remain faithful to the semi-tropics until the midde of March. The blue-winged teal and the wood ducks arrive earlier, and leave for the Mexican coast during the coldest of the winter months, returning toward the end of February, and then remain here until as late as May. During the winter months, ducks furnish the great sport for the local marksmen and their Northern frineds. Across Lake Pontchartrain are high lands, clothed with thick bay and gum woods, in which excellent quail, turkey and squirrel shooting is found. On both sides of the Mississippi, about five miles back from the levee, there are miles of cypress swamps which are populated by the cotton-tail deer.

The farthest east of the shooting grounds of Louisiana is called

English Lookout.

Pearl River, the eastward boundary of the State, flows through Lookout on its way to the sea. In this river, during the summer months, the fishermen have great sport, landing bull redfish, speckled trout, sheepshead and the jackfish, the latter being a small edition of the California tuna and just as game. The tuna is, of course, five times as large as the jackfish, which is rarely exceeds 40 pounds in weight. But these 40-pounds are sufficient to furnish two hours' hard work to the most skilled angler, so valiant and determined is the struggle this fish puts up to avoid capture.

In the bayous and lagoons up Pearl River the anglers find half a dozen varieties of perch, and the black bass, which is the best of all Southern fresh water fish.

In order to have a day's sport at Lookout, it would be necessary for a stranger to secure a card to one of its many small private clubs, for there are no public fishing camps at this point. The shooting at Lookout in recent years has not been exceptionally good, although in the spring of the year and late winter plenty of snipe are found in the eastward prairies, on a neck of land which reaches out into the sea and ends at St. Joe Lighthouse.

At the

Rigolets,

just five miles to the westward, the natural conditions are magnificent for fishermen, and hunters, too, have plenty of assistance from nature. Just to the west of the Rigolets is a vast stretch of territory known to hunters as the "Seven Ponds." It extends nearly to the railroad tracks and back to the edge of the open sea. The "Seven Ponds" country is famous. A few years ago the entire area was purchased by a good hunter, and is now a preserve. No hunter not connected with the camp is allowed to shoot in it without having first secured permission; but strangers, properly introduced, have no trouble in securing permission to shoot in the grounds.

If the hunter cares only for snipe shooting, this permit would not be necessary, for there are miles of open country where the snipe feed. It is only the choicest of ponds which come under the protection of the preesrves.

Lake Catherine,

the best duck-hunting ground in this section, is only three miles away from the Rigolets, and here hunters can be accommodated with excellent quarters, boats, decoys and guides. As the season advances, though there are thousands of birds, they become very wise and it requires the services of a good guide to locate them.

Of all sporting points along the Gulf coast, Lake Catherine seems the best situated and best equipped. There are hundreds of lagoons which are filled with wild fowl, scores of bayous teeming with bass and perch, and the open sea water near at hand affords, during the warms months, all kinds of sea fishing. To the stranger, Lake Catherine and Chef Menteur, just twenty miles from New Orleans, would be the most desirable visiting points.

There are two public camps at Lake Catherine. Jacquet, a veteran sportsman, operates a sportsman's hotel, and he has become famous all along the line of clubhouses for his cooking. At this camp a hunter can hire everything needed, excepting the gun.

Chef Menteur.

Chef Menteur is a fishing ground which has long since won a reputation in the South. In the summer months this locality is frequented by scores of anglers and every variety of fish known in Louisiana is landed. Until the winds change to the southward and bring in the salt water from the sea, the fishermen find none of the sea fish for which the State is noted. They find bass in the bayous, however, and this fish, to a Louisiana angler, furnishes all the sport and choice food desired. There are bayous near the Chef where an angler can be reasonably certain of good sport. In addition to the sport, there are accommodations for as many fishermen as care to run out of the city for a day in the open. Several public camps are operated by competent professional fishermen, who know every foot of the country and are the very best guides. The Chef is, in addition, the home of half a dozen of the largest fishing clubs in the State.

At this point the marsh lands end and the swamp begins, to terminate finally in the high lands of what is called "Metarie Ridge." Along the slopes of this ride the cotton-tail deer are found in large numbers, while rabbits make their warrens everywhere.

St. Bernard and Plaquemine Parishes.

To the south of the city, along the line of the Fort Jackson and Grand Isle Road, which runs down as far as Buras, and along the line of the New Orleans and Southern Road, which ends at Shell Beach, on Lake Borgne, the game is equally as plentiful.

During the months of February and March, especially, the marsh lands, some fifty miles down the Grand Isle Road, present the most inviting country to the stranger. In these marshes can be found a world of snipe and rail, known to the local hunters as marsh hens. They are not difficult to get at and still furnish plenty of fine shooting. Near Shell Beach is located the famous Bayou San Malo, where some of the largest green trout in this section have been landed. Closer to the city, near Shell Beach, the sportsman could make a trip in a couple of days and find accommodations and guides. Closer to the city, too, back of the cane fields, there are miles of country where the cotton-tail deer are very plentiful. In Louisiana the deer seems the most common of all classes of game.

To a party of hunters, or to the solitary hunter who wishes to make a journey into an ideal duck and goose country, the Head of the Passes, at the very mouth of the river offers the best shooting in the South. On the westward bank of the river, some twenty miles below the forts, is a pass known as the Jump, which leads from the river to the marshes bordering on the sea. On the east bank is Cubitt's Gap, which also leads from the river to the sea.

The Jump.

In the Jump there are plenty of professionals who will look after visitors for a consideration, and at Empire Postoffice, in Plaquemines, lives Captain Tony Rodriques, a guide, who is noted throughout that entire section of the country. Bay Adam, with fine sea fishing all the year round, is located on the Grand Isle Road. Bay Adam is known to the people of New Orleans not only as a hunting and fishing quarter, but as the pass which leads to the mouth of Bayou Cook and the famous oyster beds. Both in the bay and at the mouth of the bayou are oyster beds which extend over miles of territory and which furnish a majority of the oysters for the local market.

In February the tarpon fishing begins. Tarpon in this part of Louisiana are as plentiful as in any section of Florida and are much easier to reach. By leaving the city in the morning the fisherman can reach the tarpon grounds in time to make his first cast the same afternoon. With good luck, he can be back the next day with a silver fish, king of the Southern waters. In recent years many successful catches have been made, by both local and visiting fishermen; but, of course, to find the proper grounds one will need a guide.

On the eastward bank of the river, at a point called St. Sophie, teal duck shooting is magnificent.

St. Tammany Parish.

To the north of the city, across the big Lake Pontchartrain and on the line of three railroads, an entirely different kind of hunting can be found. At present, the easiest of these localities to reach is St. Tammany Parish, on the line of the East Louisiana Road. St. Tammany, although close to the city, is high, and, in places, a rolling country. Here are found quail in big covies; turkeys frequent the bottom lands along Pearl River, and the Bogue Falla, Bogue Chitto and Amite Rivers. East and West Pearl Rivers inclose what is called Honey Island. This densely overgrown stretch of land is filled with big and small game.

The stranger who goes hunting in St. Tammany should travel on the East Louisiana to Abita Springs, there secure the services of a guide, and strike out into the country. Both quail and woodcocks are fairly plentiful, and a good shot ought to bag twenty to thirty quail and a dozen woodcock in a day.

All along the line of the railroad, as far down as Pearl River, where the junction with the Queen and Crescent line is made, quail are thick. A few years of good protection have allowed the covies to multiply until the country is fairly filled with birds. In the gum swamps the gray squirrels frolic on every tree, and, to the eastward of Covington, and throughout the entire parish, in fact, the foxes are "driven" by the enterprising marksman. All these points can be reached in an hour or two from New Orleans.

- Tangipahoa Parish.

The Illinois Central Road, from a point ten miles outside the city, furnishes excellent shooting grounds. At Bayou La Branche, Owl Bayou, Pass Manchac, and further on in the high lands of Tangipahoa Parish, at Hammond, Amite City, Ponchatoula, as far as the Mississippi line, the quail have long made the country famous.

Formerly turkeys were very plentiful in Tangipahoa, but in recent years the parish authorities have checked the hunters, as the birds were being rapidly exterminated.

The beautiful Tangipahoa River furnishes fine bass fishing, in addition to quail shooting. By traveling up the Illinois Central to Pontchatoula, and driving out to Davis' Ferry, visiting anglers will find the black bass and rock bass plentiful enough to furnish amusement for a couple of days.

If the hunter desires to penetrate the dense undergrowth of Honey Island for deer, turkey and bears, the services of a guide will be absolutely necessary. Often men have been "lost" in this famous island. Guides, however, may be secured at Pearl River Station, and the trip will pay the stranger.

He will see a virgin forest which rivals the jungles of the tropics in thickness. The very denseness of the island has made it famous in past years as the home of fugitive criminals. It was to this island that Bunch, the train robber, who terrorized the South for years, went for safety after each hold-up. He was, in fact, killed amid the umbrageous coverts of this little-explored locality.

Along Lake Pontchartrain.

Both the Queen and Crescent and East Louisiana Roads cross Lake Pontchartrain on one of the longest railroad bridges in America. It is thirteen miles from shore to shore, and on both of these shores there are good hunting grounds, while the lake itself furnishes plenty of game fish. At the south end of the bridge, called South Point, Phil Geiger operates a comfortable public camp, which is fully equipped. The bayous which come out of the marshes have plenty of black bass and perch, and toward the close of winter these fish are exceptionally good eating.

Just as soon as the first signs of warm weather make themselves felt the fish come through the passes from the sea and are found at South Point. Strange undercurrents seem to affect this point more readily than any other locality, and as a result the fishing begins there earlier and the sport is good for months longer than in any other quarter of the lake.

At the north end, famaliarly termed

North Shore,

of the big bridge, are situated two handsome private clubs. Visiting anglers can find no accommodations there unless by special invitation. Once admitted as a guest of either of the clubs, they will find a way open to one of the best duck and snipe shooting grounds near New Orleans. The clubs, some time ago, combined to purchase the marsh lands and turn them into preserves. Only members of these two clubs are allowed to shoot upon these private grounds. Salt Bayou, which runs through the marshes, upholds a record as one of the best black bass waters within miles of the city. In addition to its natural advantages, the North Shore has the further feature of being close to the city. Anglers or hunters can leave New Orleans on one evening train and return on the next.

Game Laws.

The laws of the State and city are liberal. No restrictions are placed upon the number of deer, ducks, quail or turkeys killed, as in other States.

The deer season is open five months in the year and one man may kill as many as his good fortune and skill will allow. There is an unwritten law which prohibits his killing game at night, however. He may shoot and bring back to the city from any of the surrounding parishes all the ducks, quail and turkeys that he can find. In St. Tamany Parish, however, he will not be allowed to sell any game killed. The State law furnishing protection to game has been passed with a view to promoting the sport, not restricting it.

It must be a sportsman, however, for no vagrant, professional or pot hunter can operate in this State under the law.

The laws granting protection to the fishing interests are purely local. Each parish passes its own regulations, which are intended to meet the conditions existing in that particular locality. All these laws, however, have fixed Feb. 15, of each years, as the date for the closing of the open green trout or black bass season.

There is so little really cold weather in Louisiana that the bass spawn much earlier than they do in the North, and it is necessary to close the season before the warm days of spring arrive in order to secure the proper protection. Anglers are fortunate, however, for they have perch fishing in the fresh water streams all the time and very early sea fishing in the spring, which leaves only a few weeks during which fishermen are debarred from their favorite pursuit.

In catching the black bass there is but one thing of which the stranger must be careful; he must not keep bass that are smaller than 10 inches in length. A special ordinance prohibits the catching of such small fish. They are not fit for food and only serve to spoil a good fish for next season.

New Orleans

offers opportunities to visiting sportsmen which are nowhere excelled. Where else can a locality be found in which deer are killed daily within ten miles of the heart of such a city, or where duck grounds, which will furnish forty and fifty birds to a single gun in a morning, lie within twenty miles of thickly-populated centers? The hunters of New Orleans are numbered by the hundreds, simply for the reason that they can leave on Saturday afternoon and return on Sunday with plenty of game. Time is, of course, the great factor, but the question of economy plays an important part. Almost any hunting ground mentioned here can be visited at a cost of not more than $5 per man, including railway fare.

Liberality, generosity and good fellowship seem the three main charactertistics of Louisiana fishing and hunting. If the laws of the State are liberal, the sportsmen, too, will be found generous in the extreme, and the very best of fellowship prevails, even among the most bitter rivals in the championship ranks. To lovers of the rod and gun from the far off North, the field in Louisiana will prove a revelation, and no true sportsman should leave New Orleans without testing the great advantages offered by every acre of land, and almost every waterway, within fifty miles of the city.

CHAPTER XXIII.

The Commerce of New Orleans.

The commercial year of New Orleans begins on September 1, and; of course, terminates August 31. The reason for this is obvious, as all the staple crops of this section begin to move freely after the opening of September. It is not possible in a brief article to accurately describe the volume and scope of the commerce of so important a business community as New Orleans, but the presentation of some of the leading statistics will furnish the average businessman with an accurate idea of the general character of the city's trade.

THE BANK CLEARINGS.

The following total of clearings of the associated banks for the past year, as compared with the previous four seasons, will show more clearly than any other means the volume of the local trade:

Season 1902-1903	$859,472,855
Season 1901-1902	650,573,548
Season 1900-1901	608,750,307
Season 1899-1900	500,671,071
Season 1898-1899	434,956,301
Season 1897-1898	447,673,946

If the figures for the calendar year 1903 be taken the showing is even better:

Clearings, calendar year 1903..............................$927,710,850
Clearings, calendar year 1902.............................. 672,360,577

Increase, 1903 over 1902..............................$255,350,273

The following data, taken from a recently prepared summary of the condition of the local banks, will furnish an accurate idea of the local banking movement:

Loans and discounts, etc.............................$45,076,220
Capital, surplus, etc............................. 15,566,794
Deposits.. 58,079,600

COMMERCE OF THE PORT.

According to the official statistics, as compiled by the local customs officials, the foreign trade of New Orleans makes the following showing:
Statement of the number and tonnage of vessels entered at the port of New Orleans:

	Vessels.	Tons.
Total 1902-1903	1,877	2,386,044
Total 1901-1902	1,438	2,572,501
Total 1900-1901	1,622	2,702,485
Total 1899-1900	1,564	2,367.354

Statement of the number and tonnage of vessels cleared from the port of New Orleans:

	Vessels.	Tons.
Total 1902-1903	1,300	2,183.229
Total 1901-1902	1,439	2,004,041
Total 1900-1901	1,575	2,673,989
Total 1899-1900	1,530	2,345,754

TOTAL IMPORTS.

	Free.	Dutiable.	Total.
1902-1903	$15,427,647	$13,486,900	$28,914,556
1901-1902	14,011,988	10,054,361	24,066,349
1900-1901	9,771,447	11,322,458	21,093,905

TOTAL DOMESTIC EXPORTS.

	American Vessels.	Foreign Vessels.	Total.
1902-1903	$2,735,903	$143,157,865	$145,893,768
1901-1902	3,046,524	127,244,327	130,290,851
1900-1901	2,953,378	148,706,390	151,659,678

Exports to Porto Rico, amounting to $2,875,861, are not included in above table.

TOTAL EXPORTS OF COTTON.

Country—	Bales.	Pounds.	Values.
England	867,263	446,032,824	$39,869,953
France	351,398	177,043,469	15,737,279
Germany	314,504	157,114,555	13,930,763
Italy	226,632	114,696,703	20,357,542
Spain	132,951	66,938,034	6,419,474
Russia on the Baltic	85,346	44,512,843	3,958,096
Denmark	28,123	14,130,585	1,251,350
Austria	25,647	12,810,893	1,163,819
Belgium	25,266	12,728,328	1,139,975
Mexico	21,279	10,923,744	1,027,330
Netherlands	21,028	10,423,051	904,524
Portugal	7,995	4,096,594	348,928
Sweden	4,242	2,225,002	191,687
Ireland	2,365	1,266,070	113,113
Scotland	800	433,491	37,118
Norway	400	215,103	23,279
Greece	200	101,200	10,879
Japan	100	48,846	4,107
British East Indies	70	38,104	3,360
Total 1902-1903	1,115,627	1,075,779,439	$96,492,576
" 1901-1902	1,964,150	992,905,885	$81,643,121
1900-01	2,015,597	1,021,767,618	94,850,944

EXPORTS OF GRAIN AND FLOUR.

	Wheat— bushels.	Corn— bushels.	Flour— bbls.
1902-1903	16,452,435	14,382,006	1,085,928
1901-1902	17,952,195	2,085,447	580,232
1900-1901	17,122,727	20,425,946	589,544

IMPORTS OF COFFEE.

Last year again witnessed the breaking of all records in Coffee Imports. According to the official figures the showing for the coffee year, ending June 30, 1903, is as follows:

	Bags	
	1902-03.	1901-02.
Brazilians	894,447	806,034
Mexicans	38,076	52,611
Miscellaneous	8,530	8,251
Total bags	940,053	866,896

The total imports of Brazilian coffee alone, for the calendar year 1903, were 1,052,937 bags, as against 769,595 for the calendar year 1902.

STAPLE ARTICLES OF COMMERCE.

While New Orleans enjoys a large general trade, her main commercial activity centers in the marketing of the staple crops of this section, such as cotton, sugar and rice. The cotton receipts at this port for a long series of years have been:

Season	Receipts at N. O.	Av. price per bale.	Total value.
1870-71	1,584,136	$65.25	$101,015,780
1872-73	1,407,821	84.37	118,760,758
1874-75	1,157,597	55.40	75,706,842
1875-76	1,604,441	52.65	84,473,819
1876-77	1,385,774	53.00	72,268,248
1877-78	1,689,483	40.95	81,189,658
1878-79	1,426,081	43.00	61,221,484
1879-80	1,712,999	55.00	94,313,845
1880-81	1,800,087	50.00	93,044,350
1881-82	1,462,814	55.00	74,958,070
1882-83	1,999,598	45.00	89,981,910
1883-84	1,694,657	50.00	84,732,950
1884-85	1,689,760	50.00	84,478,000
1885-86	1,946,037	45.00	87,571,665
1886-87	1,919,187	45.00	87,463,414
1887-88	1,912,228	46.25	88,640,145
1888-89	1,838,047	48.30	88,777,670
1889-90	2,148,301	51.00	109,563,351
1890-91	2,270,190	46.00	104,428,920
1891-92	2,713,425	35.00	94,967,875
1892-93	1,734,528	41.87	72,628,687
1893-94	2,060,311	37.50	77,261,662
1894-95	2,702,931	31.00	83,790,861
1895-96	1,911,281	40.00	76,451,240
1896-97	2,249,223	36.00	80,972,028
1897-98	2,815,599	29.00	81,650,921
1898-99	2,278,627	26.00	59,244,302
1899-00	1,913,846	39.00	74,639,004
1900-01	2,498,553	44.00	109,936,882
1901-02	2,326,906	43.00	99,626,958
1902-03	2,880,431	50.00	119,024,050

SUGAR AND MOLASSES RECEIPTS.

	Sugar		Molasses
	Hhds.	Bbls.	Bbls.
2-03	2,635	1,772,228	356,184
1901-02	3,346	1,831,668	359,871
1900-01	5,628	1,450,088	228,362
1899-00	3,235	734,392	232,579
1898-99	10,513	1,325,745	288,211
1897-98	23,523	1,567,342	232,026
1896-97	38,420	1,394,014	235,369
1895-96	55,572	1,082,458	202,590

RICE RECEIPTS.

	Rough, sacks.	Clean, barrels.
1877-78	233,707	15,682
1878-79	279,611	21,152
1879-80	182,999	11,152
1880-81	445,397	29,812

1881-82	....	435,692	39,390
1882-83	....	392,750	37,736
1883-84	....	459,559	41,055
1884-85	....	333,693	32,383
1885-86	....	889,212	57,983
1886-87	....	838,476	48,566
1887-88	....	626,811	23,263
1888-89	....	737,075	29,227
1889-90	....	777,742	7,441
1890-91	....	892,374	4,115
1891-92	....	1,052,331	5,640
1892-93	....	1,972,946	6,490
1893-94	....	921,515	6,295
1894-95	....	789,889	1,650
1895-96	....	1,305,139	7,482
1896-97	....	422,498	9,816
1897-98	....	527,326	8,081
1898-99	....	767,006	12,403
1899-00	....	973,851	18,015
1900-01	....	932,664	277,637
1901-02	....	1,180,192	*577,569
1902-03	....	985,218	*660,110

*Pockets.

TONNAGE OF THE RAILROADS.

The following table shows the volume of freight forwarded and received over the various trunk lines of railroads centering here:

	Forwarded, pounds.	Received, pounds.
Southern Pacific............................	1,923,630,000	1,710,778,000
Texas and Pacific.........................	464,082,544	2,029,634,058
Loutsville and Nashville...................	559,398,700	735,463,200
Illinois Central............................	1,351,116,000	3,111,950,000
Mississippi Valley.........................	359,662,000	1,163,190,000
N. O. & N. E.............................	580,681,315	1,037,006,486
Total 1902-03.......................	5,238,570,559	9,793,021,744
Total 1901-02.......................	4,638,129,705	8,835,478,232

Business.

NEW ORLEANS' FUTURE PROSPECTS.

No city in the country has made greater strides towards commercial greatness, during the last few years, than New Orleans. Not being a new town, nor a boom town, this progress has not startled the country as something new and unlooked for, but the statistics of business growth, the enormous increase in bank clearings, the larger foreign commerce and the great development of banking capital tell a tale of substantial expansion to all students of commercial and financial affairs.

The good prices realized by the South for the past two cotton crops and the present unprecedented price for the fleecy staple have made this entire section prosperous and money plentiful. This condition of prosperity has naturally had a most beneficial effect upon the trade of this City. With the farmers out of debt and the country merchants enjoying a period of business success, such as they never before have experienced, it is but natural that every branch of trade and industry in this, the Southern metropolis, should be greatly benefited.

The development of the oil fields of this and the neighboring State of Texas has attracted the attention of investors and capitalists in this direction and created a demand for supplies of all sorts which has been favorably felt here. It is generally recognized that the oil fields of this section are only in the infancy of their true development and their successful working means much in the way of industrial growth in this City in years to come.

Within the past year or two many fine business buildings have been added to the facilities of this City. Hotel accommodations have been increased and further additions of the same sort are contemplated to accommodate the larger travel in this direction as well as the constantly growing number of winter tourists who seek this City in preference to the tamer attractions of Florida. With a climate equally as mild, and with all the diversions of a metropolitan City, New Orleans offers many attractions to winter visitors from the North which the Florida resorts do not afford.

Situated as New Orleans is, at the gateway of the Mississippi Valley, this City has long enjoyed a considerable volume of foreign trade, but as soon as the Panama Canal is built, and its building is now measurably in sight, this traffic can be safely counted on to increase many fold. This port is nearer to the Eastern entrance of the canal than any of the other large ports of the country and the products of the vast Mississippi Valley, which are needed on the West coast of South America and in the Orient, will naturally seek tide water at New Orleans for reshipment by sea via the Isthmian Canal. The passage of vast fleets of vessels through the canal will also give rise to a great demand for all sorts of supplies at the entrance to the waterway, such as provisions, ship chandlery, naval stores and coal. This Port will be the natural and best shipping point for such supplies, as well as the point of departure and arrival for passengers going to or returning from South American countries, via the Panama Canal. In a word, the Canal means a great deal for this City.

In anticipation of this increased trade, and to accommodate the constantly increasing size of ships, the Government is opening up a channel to the sea through the great Southwest Pass of the Mississippi River, which will give a minimum depth of 35 feet at low water and possibly as much as 40 feet. This improvement is now under way and will be completed long before the Panama Canal can be opened to traffic. With that improvement New Orleans will be the finest deep water port in the world.

MUNICIPAL IMPROVEMENTS.

Not only has New Orleans taken on a new life in the matter of commercial affairs, but a spirit of improvement and enterprise has permeated the community in the interest of modern public conveniences and improvements. Not only have miles of streets been paved, but the people have also imposed upon themselves a special tax to secure adequate drainage and public water and sewerage systems. Fully $18,000,000 are being invested in these improvements, for which all the plans have been prepared. The drainage work has been already completed to a large extent, and although litigation somewhat delayed the sewerage work, it is now making good progress in every district of the city, and in a few more years New Orleans will not only be one of the best drained, but one of the best sewered cities in the country.

The drainage and sewering of a city situated as is New Orleans, in a flat, alluvial country, actually below the flood level of the Mississippi River, presented serious problems not encountered in other cities. These problems have been fully worked out, however, and a system prepared which will overcome all the topographical difficulties that faced the engineers.

During the past three years New Orleans has been one of the most healthy cities in the country. There is no doubt that as soon as the drainage and sewerage systems are complete its healthfulness will be further improved, and the advantages of

NEW ORLEANS AS A HEALTH RESORT.

will become generally recognized. The following article, which appeared in the Picayune of October 27, under the above caption, is pertinent:

"There is every reason why New Orleans should be the winter resort of the country between the north polar ocean and the Gulf of Mexico. Its mild and genial climate; its ample and thorough accommodations for visitors, either in hotels or in private families; its cuisine, famous in every country where the art of dining is cultivated and appreciated; its varied and all-embracing means of amusement and diversion, and its charming social circles, which are open to all visitors who are worthy and are properly introduced, combine to make New Orleans a most delightful place to visit, while its sanitary condition, as shown by its small mortality returns, completes its claims as the winter health resort for the people of North America.

The Picayune prints a testimonial on the subject from one of the most eminent medical authorities on the American Hemisphere, Dr. Charles Alfred Lee

Reed, of Cincinnati, physician, surgeon, medical author, litterateur of world-wide celebrity, and President of the recent Pan-American Medical Congress at the City of Mexico. The verdict of this eminent authority is so important that it is repeated here. He says:

"It has been my custom for a number of years to send certain of my patients to New Orleans to spend a part of the winter season, and I myself have occasionally taken the same prescription. The Crescent City offers peculiar attractions to the winter tourist, and particularly to such of them as are forced, by ill health, to escape the rigors of a Northern Winter. This is a consideration of no little importance to persons who may require the services of a physician or surgeon. In the next place, that city offers peculiar physical comforts to the sojourner; for the hotels are numerous and excellent. It is located far enough away from the seaboard to be free from the unpleasant features of a maritime climate. These features of the seashore, notably, sudden vacillations of temperature, with a maximum of humidity, are frequently inimical to the welfare of physically sensitive people. Those whom I have sent to New Orleans never complain of the ennui so frequently experienced at isolated resorts, but find wholesome occupation for mind and body in the varied attractions of one of the most individual and charming cities of the Continent. I look upon this feature as one of great importance, and insist upon it, whenever possible, in sending patients from home.

"Interested capitalists have made Florida famous as a destination for winter tourists who are rather more pleasure-seekers than invalids. For all such New Orleans offers all that can be found in Florida for health, and a vast deal more for pleasure, in which latter regard this city may well be classed as the Paris of America."

Although New Orleans covers an immense area for a city of 300,000 inhabitants, there is still ample room for expansion. The city limits include many times the area actually built up, so that there is space for growth in all directions, without having to extend the already recognized circumscription. There is sufficient area here, conveniently situated with respect to the older portions of the city, to accommodate several millions of inhabitants. While it would be overambitious to expect any such immediate gain as to warrant the hope that the next census will show anything like a million people, nevertheless there is a rapid growth of the population in progress, and it need surprise no one to find the population of New Orleans doubled by 1910.

CHAPTER XXIV.

Supplementary Street Guide—Car Routes.

The following street guide is based upon the excellent one compiled by Mr. L. Soards, and published in his Directory. It is given herewith in order to assist the visitor in locating any desired point of interest. Four streets have been selected—St. Charles and Rampart, Canal and Esplanade. All streets running up and down town are parallel, respectively, to St. Charles and Rampart; all streets running across town are parallel, respectively, to Canal and Esplanade. Therefore the house numbering on any of these four streets will correspond to the numbering on any other street which may run in a corresponding direction. To find a number on any street other than these four, it suffices to find the nearest number of these streets, which will give the inquirer the nearest street corner to the place he wishes to locate. In order to find out which way a street runs, it suffices to consult any one of the following four tables; if it appears among the names of the "intersecting streets" on St. Charles, it indicates that the thoroughfare in question lies across town, and, therefore, parallel with Canal, and so on. By locating places in this way, and a reference to the map which accompanies this Gudie, the visitor ought to be able to make his way with considerable accuracy about the city. Especially will the street guide herewith presented be found useful in riding on the street cars, as, by reference to these tables, one can give the conductor exactly the place at which it may be desired to have the car stop:

ST. CHARLES, ninth street west of river, from Canal Street to Carrollton Avenue. (Between Canal Street and Howard Avenue the thoroughfare is commonly called St. Charles Street, and from Howard Avenue to Carrollton Avenue it is known as St. Charles Avenue, but for convenience this distinction is here ignored.)

Names of intersecting streets:

	House Numbers.	
	Left.	Right.
Canal	100	101
Common	200	201
Gravier	300	301
Commercial Place	400	....
Perdido	....	401
Poydras	500	501
North	....	....
Lafayette	600	601
South	....	....
Girod	700	701
Julia	800	801
St. Joseph	900	901
Howard Avenue	1000	1001
Calliope	1100	1101
Clio	1200	1201
Erato	1300	1301
Thalia	1400	1401
Melpomene	1500	1501
Terpsichore	1600	1601
Euterpe	1700	1701
Polymnia	....	....
Felicity	1800	1801
St. Mary	1900	1901
St. Andrew	2000	2001
Josephine	2100	2101
Jackson Avenue	2200	2201
Philip	2300	2301
First	2400	2401
Second	2500	2501
Third	2600	2601
Fourth	2700	2701
Washington Avenue	2800	2801
Couery	....	....
Sixth	2900	2901
Seventh	3000	3001
Eighth	3100	3101
Harmony	3200	3201
Pleasant	....	....
Toledano	3300	3301
Louisiana Avenue	3400	3401
Delachaise	....	3501
Aline	3500	....
Foucher	3600	3601
Antonine	....	....
Amelia	3700	3701
Peniston	3800	3801
General Taylor	3900	3901
Constantinople	4000	4001
Marengo	4100	4101
Milan	4200	4201
Berlin	4300	4301
Napoleon Avenue	4400	4401
Jena	4500	4501
Cadiz	4600	4601
Valence	4700	4701
Bordeau	4800	4801
Upperline	4900	4901
Robert	5000	5001
Soniat	5100	5101
Dufossat	5200	5201
Valmout	5300	5301
Leontine	....	....
Peters Avenue	5400	5401
Octavia	5500	5501
Joseph	5600	5601
Arabella	5700	5701
Nashville Avenue	5800	5801
Rosa Park	....	....
Eleonore	5900	5901
State	6000	6001
Webster	6100	6101
Henry Clay Avenue	6200	6201
Calhoun	6300	6301
Exposition Boulevard	....	....
Park Avenue	....	....
Walnut	7000	7001
Audubon Place	....	....
Audubon	7100	7101
Broadway	7200	7201
Pine	7300	7301
Lowerline	7400	7401
Millaudon	....	....
Cherokee	7500	7501
Hilary	7600	7601
Adams	7700	7701
Burdette	7800	7801
Fern	7900	7901
Huso	....	....
Carrollton Avenue	8000	8001

RAMPART STREET (now called North Rampart), thirteenth street west of the Mississippi, from Canal to Columbus, thence east to the City limits.

Names of intersecting streets:

	House Numbers.	
	Right.	Left.
Canal	100	101
Customhouse	200	201
Bienville	300	301
Conti	400	401
St. Louis	500	501
Toulouse	600	601
St. Peter	700	701
Orleans	....	....
St. Ann	800	801
Dumaine	900	901
St. Philip	1000	1001
Ursuline	1100	1101
Hospital	1200	1201
Barracks	1300	1301
Esplanade Avenue	1400	1401
Kerlerec	1700	....
Columbus	....	1701
St. Anthony	1800	1801
Bourbon	1900	1901
Touro	2000	2000
Frenchmen	2100	2101
Elysian Fields	2200	2201
Marigny	2300	2301
Mandeville	2400	2401
Spain	....	....
St. Roch Avenue	2500	2501
Music	....	....
Lafayette Avenue	2600	2601
Port	2700	2701
St. Ferdinand	2800	2801
Press	2900	2901
Montegut	3000	3001
Clouet	3100	3101
Louisa	3200	6201
Piety	3300	3301
Desire	3400	3401
Elmira	3500	3501
Congress	3600	3601
Independence	3700	3701
Pauline	3800	3801
Alvar	3900	3901
Bartholomew	4000	4001
Mazant	4100	4101
France	4200	4201
Lesseps	4300	4301
Poland	4400	4401
Kentucky	4500	4501
Japonica	....	....
Manuel	4600	4601
Sister	4700	4701
Jourdan Avenue	4800	4801
Deslonde	4900	4901
Tennessee	....	....
Reynes	5000	5001
Forstall	5100	5101
Lizardi	5200	5201
Egania	5300	5301
Audry	5400	5401
Flood	5500	5501
Caffin	5600	5601

La Manche	5700	5701
Charbonnet	5800	....
Alabo	5900	5901
Gordon	6000	6001
Tupelo	6100	6101
Hancock	6200	6201
Tricou	6300	....
Delery	....	....

ESPLANADE AVENUE, fourteenth street north of and below Canal Street, from the river to Bayou St. John.

Names of intersecting streets:

	House Numbers.	
	Left.	Right.
North Peters	400	401
Decatur	500	501
Chartres	600	601
Royal	700	701
Bourbon	800	801
Dauphine	900	901
Burgundy	1000	1001
Rampart	1100	1101
St. Claude	1200	1201
Liberty	....	....
Marais	1300	1301
Villere	1400	1401
Robertson	1500	1501
Claiborne	1600	1601
Derbigny	1700	1701
Roman	1800	1801
Prieur	1900	1901
Johnson	2000	2001
Galvez	2100	2101
Miro	2200	2201
Tonti	2300	2301
Rocheblave	2400	2401
Dorgenois	2500	2501
Broad	2600	2601
White	2700	2701
Dupre	2800	2801
Gayoso	2900	2901
Salcedo	3000	3001
Ducayet	....	....
Lopez	3100	3101
Rendon	3200	3201
Labatut	3300	3301
Howe	3400	3401
Bayou St. John	....	....

CANAL STREET, dividing line between First and Second Districts; from the river west to the city limits.

Names of intersecting streets:

	House Numbers.	
	Left.	Right.
Water	....	....
Delta	100	101
Wells	....	....
Front	200	201
Fulton	....	....
Peters	300	301
Tchoupitoulas	400	401
Magazine	500	501
Decatur	....	501
Dorsiere	....	501
Chartres	....	601
Camp	600	....
Exchange Place	....	....
St. Charles	700	....
Royal	....	701
Bourbon	....	801
Carondelet	800	....
Dauphine	....	901
Baronne	900	....
Dryades	1000	....
Burgundy	....	1001
Rampart	1100	1101
Basin	1200	1201
Franklin	1300	1301
Liberty	1400	1101
Marais	....	1501
Howard	1500	....
Villere	....	....
Robertson	1600	1601

Claiborne	1700	1701
Derbigny	1800	1801
Roman	1900	1901
Prieur	2000	2001
Johnson	2100	2101
Galvez	2200	2201
Miro	2300	2301
Tonti	2400	2401
Rocheblave	2500	2501
Dorgenois	2600	2601
Broad	2700	2701
White	2800	801
Dupre	2900	2901
Gayoso	3000	3001
Salcedo	3100	3101
Lopez	3200	3201
Rendon	3300	3301
Hagan Avenue	3400	3401
Clark	3500	3501
Genois	3600	3601
Telemachus	3700	3701
Cortez	3800	3801
Scott	3900	3901
Pierce	4000	4001
Carrollton Avenue	4100	4101
David	....	....
Solomon	4200	4201
Hennessy	4300	4301
Alexander	4400	4401
Murat	4500	4501
Olympia	4600	4601
St. Patrick	4700	4701
Bernadotte	4800	4801
Anthony	4900	4901
Helena	5000	5001

TABLE OF DISTANCES.

	Miles.
Along the city front, from the Barracks to the city limits above Carrollton	12.02
Head of Canal Street to the Barracks	3.79
Head of Canal Street to Carrollton	8.23
Head of Canal Street to Metairie Road	3.73
Head of Canal Street to West End, along the line of the railroad	6.63
From Canal Street up St. Charles to Lee Place	.70
From Canal Street up St. Charles to Jackson Avenue	1.51
From Canal Street up St. Charles to Napoleon Avenue	2.95
From Canal Street up St. Charles to Audubon Park	4.27
From Canal Street up St. Charles to Carrollton	4.67
From Canal and Royal, via Rampart, to Esplanade	1.07
From Canal and Royal, via Rampart and Esplanade, to the Louisiana Jockey Club	2.93
Width of the Mississippi from bank at Jackson Square to bank at Algiers Point	.36
Total area within the city limits, square miles	196.25
Total area of city within the levees, square miles	39.00
Total area of drained portion of city, square miles	21.00
Total miles of streets opened	700.00
Total miles of streets paved	200.00
Street railways, including those to West End and Spanish Fort	173.20
The Mississippi River discharge at high water, in cubic feet, per second	1,500,000
Average velocity of the river at New Orleans, in miles, per hour	4.00

HACKS AND CABS.

The following is a regular tariff of charges fixed by city ordinance (No. 1357, A. S.) for hacks and cabs, and the stranger should see that he is not imposed on by unscrupulous drivers, and would confer a benefit on the public by reporting to the police all cases of overcharging:

For carriages drawn by two horses, any distance not exceeding one mile, or twelve squares, for one or two persons, $1 each.

For every such carriage hired by the hour, $3 for the first hour, and $2 for each succeeding hour or fraction thereof, for the use of the entire carriage.

For cabs or carriages drawn by one horse, any distance not exceeding one mile, or twelve squares, for one or two persons, 75 cents each, and for each succeeding mile or less, 50 cents.

For every such cab or carriage hired by the hour, $2 for the first hour, and $1.50 for each succeeding hour or fraction thereof, for the entire cab or carriage. These rates apply from sunrise to midnight. From midnight to sunrise the rates shall be fixed by agreement, but in no case shall double the rates be exceeded.

All public vehicles are compelled to carry numbers on their lamps."

There are, however, few parts of the city that are worth seeing which may not be reached by street cars.

Car Routes.

BELT LINES.

St. Charles Belt.—The "Show" line of the City. Starts on Canal, near Levee, runs out Canal to Baronne, to Howard Avenue, to St. Charles Avenue, to Carrollton Avenue, to the terminus at Jeannette and Dublin, on through Carrollton, passing Athletic Park, to Tulane Avenue, to Canal, to starting point. Transfers to Jackson Avenue and Napoleon Avenue lines and Southport.

Esplanade Belt.—Direct to Fair Grounds, Race Track and City Park, via Bayou St. John to Half-way House and Cemeteries, in Canal Street. Starts at foot of Canal Street, runs by Canal to Rampart, to Esplanade Avenue, to Bayou St. John and Metairie Avenue, to Canal Street, to the river. Transfers to Villere, Dauphine and French Market lines.

Canal Belt.—Starts on Canal Street, near the Levee; runs out Canal, direct to the Cemeteries and the Half-way House, through Metairie Avenue, to Bayou St. John, to Esplanade Avenue (passing the race track and Fair Grounds), to Rampart, to Canal, to starting point; transfers to Villere and Dauphine lines.

Tulane Belt.—Reverse side of St. Charles Belt. Direct line to Charity Hospital and Athletic Park. Starts on Canal, near the Levee; runs by Canal to South Rampart, to Tulane Avenue, to Carrollton Avenue, to St. Charles Avenue, to Howard Avenue, to Baronne, to Canal, to starting point. Transfers to Jackson Avenue and Napoleon Avenue lines and Southport.

Uptown Lines.

Jackson Avenue Line.—Starts on Canal, near Levee; runs by Canal to Baronne, to Howard Avenue, to St. Charles Avenue, to Jackson Avenue, to Gretna Ferry Landing. Transfers to St. Charles Avenue and Tulane Avenue Belts.

Napoleon Avenue Line.—Starts at corner of St. Charles and Napoleon Avenue, and run out the avenue to the river. Returns by same route. Transfers to and from St. Charles and Tulane Belts, up or down town, at intersection of St. Charles Belt.

Prytania Line.—Direct to Picayune and other newspaper offices, City Library, Memorial Hall, Howard Library, Margaret Monument, passing Lee Monument and thence through a magnificent residence section to Audubon Park. Starts on Canal, near Carondelet; runs by Camp to Prytania, to Joseph, to Hurst, to Audubon Park. Returns to Canal Street by same route.

Magazine Line.—Direct to Lafayette Square, Memorial Hall, City and Howard Library and Stuyvesant Docks. Starts on Canal and Basin Streets; runs by Canal to Camp, to Old Camp, to Magazine, to Louisiana Avenue, to

Laurel, to Audubon Park. Returns by Laurel, to Valmont, to Constance, to Louisiana Avenue, to Canal, to starting point.

Coliseum Line.—Louisville and Nashville Depot. Direct to Audubon Park, Carrollton and Southport. Starts on Canal, at Louisville and Nashville Depot, runs by Canal to Carondelet, to Clio, to Coliseum, to Felicity, to Chestnut, to Louisiana Avenue, to Magazine, to Broadway, to Maple, to Carrollton Avenue. Returns by Carrollton Avenue, to Maple, to Broadway, to Magazine, to Calliope, to St. Charles, to Canal, to starting point.

Henry Clay Avenue.—Starts on Canal, near Levee; runs out Canal to Carondelet, to St. Andrew, to Brainard, to Baronne, to Louisiana Avenue, to Camp, to Henry Clay Avenue; transfers to Audubon Park and Carrollton. Returns by Henry Clay Avenue, to Coliseum, to Louisiana Avenue, to Dryades, to Julia, to St. Charles, to Canal, to starting point. Transfers to Coliseum line for points beyond Henry Clay Avenue; also to Villere line on Canal Street for down town points. Runs by Louisville and Nashville Depot.

Dryades and Ferry Line.—Direct to Ferry Landing at Canal Street; passing Union Depot. Starts at Canal Street Ferry Landing; runs out Canal Street to St. Charles, to Lee Circle, to Howard Avenue, to Dryades, to St. Andrew, to Baronne, to Eighth. Returns by Rampart, to Philip, to Dryades, to Felicity, to Rampart, to Canal, to ferry at foot of Canal Street.

Peters Avenue Line.—Passes Illinois Central, Yazoo and Mississippi Valley, Southern Pacific and Louisville & Nashville Depots. Starts on Canal, near Levee, runs out Canal to South Rampart, to Calliope, to Franklin, to Jackson Avenue, to Freret, to Louisiana Avenue, to Dryades, to Peters Avenue, out Peters Avenue to Magazine, to Arabella Barn. Returns by Constance, to Peters Avenue, to Dryades, to Dufossat, to Baronne, to Louisiana Avenue, to Howard, to Jackson Avenue, to Franklin, to Calliope, to Dryades, to Canal, to starting point. Transfers to Coliseum line for Audubon Park and points beyond.

Annunciation Line.—Passes St. Charles Hotel, Lee Monument, Margaret Statue and Cotton Press District. Starts on Canal, near the Levee; runs out Canal to Carondelet, to Clio, to Coliseum, to Erato, to Annunciation, to Toledano, to Tchoupitoulas. Returns by Toledano to Tchoupitoulas, to Race, to Annunciation, to Erato, to Camp, to Calliope, to St. Charles, to Canal, to starting point. Transfers to Tchoupitoulas line for Stuyvesant Dock, Audubon Park and Carrollton.

South Peters Line.—Starts on Canal at Camp; runs by Canal to Tchoupitoulas, to Annunciation, to Toledano, to Tchoupitoulas; transfers to Audubon Park cars. Returns by Toledano, to Chippewa, to Race, to Annunciation, to Howard Avenue, to South Peters, to Canal, to starting point at Camp Street.

Tchoupitoulas Line.—Direct to Stuyvesant Docks, giving five view of shipping district and levees. Starts on Canal at Camp; runs by Canal to Tchoupitoulas, to Audubon Park. Returns by Tchoupitoulas to South Peters, to Canal, to Camp. Transfers to Peters Avenue and Coliseum lines.

New Orleans and Jefferson Line.—This is a new line recently constructed, and traverses the upper section of the city. It is operated as a crosstown line, starting at the river, on Napoleon Avenue, and out via Washington and Carrollton Avenue to Half-way House and Cemeteries, where close connections are made for West End and City Park. Transfers to Carondelet line.

Southport Line.—Connects the St. Charles and Tulane Belt Lines with Upper Carrollton and Southport, giving a fine view of the great levee system, along the Mississippi above the city proper, where these immense embankments tower above all the surrounding country. This route has been nicknamed the "Klondyke Route."

Downtown Lines.

Levee and Barracks Line.—Direct to French Market, U. S. Mint and N. O. and Northeastern Depots Starts on Canal Street, opposite the United States Custom-house; runs by Canal to North Peters, to Lafayette Avenue, to Chartres Street, to Poland, to Rampart; transfers to Dauphine Line for United States Barracks. Returns by Poland to Royal, to Lafayette Avenue, to North Peters, to Canal, to starting point.

Dauphine Line.—Direct line to Ursuline Convent, United States Barracks, Slaughter House, and all extreme down town points; also to Queen and Crescent, Pontchartrain and Shell Beach Railroad Depots. Starts at foot of

Canal Street; runs by Canal to Rampart, to Esplanade Avenue, to Dauphine, to Flood, to North Peters, to the Slaughter House. Returns by North Peters to Delery, to Dauphine, to Poland, to Rampart, to Canal to starting point. ansfers at intersection of Esplanade Avenue for Esplanade Belt.

Esplanade Avenue and French Market Line.—Direct to Jackson Square Cathedral and French Market. Starts on Canal Street, opposite the United States Custom-house; runs to North Peters, to French Market, to Esplanade Avenue, to Villere Street; transfers here to Esplanade Avenue car for Bayou St. John and City Park. Returns from Villere by same route to starting point.

Claiborne Line.—Direct to old French Cemeteries. Starts on Canal, near the Levee; runs by Canal to Claiborne Avenue, to Elysian Fields, to St. Claude, to Lafayette Avenue. Returns by Urquhart to Elysian Fields, to Claiborne, to Canal, to starting point.

Villere Line.—Direct to St. Roch's Chapel and Cemetery. Starts on Canal near Levee; runs by Canal to Villere, to Lafayette Avenue, to St. Claude. Returns by same route. This route is the most convenient to St. Roch's Cemetery and Chapel. Transfers to Canal and Esplanade Belt lines, and Henry Clay Avenue and Peters Avenue lines.'

Broad Street Line.—Starts on Canal, near Camp; runs by Canal to Dauphine, to Broad, to Laharpe, to Gentilly Road; transfers for Fair Grounds. Returns by Bayou Road, to Broad, to St. Peter, to Burgundy, to Canal, to starting point. Transfers to Henry Clay Avenue and Peters Avenue lines on Canal Street.

Bayou St. John Line.—Starts on Canal Street, near Camp; runs by Canal to Dauphine, to Dumaine, to Bayou St. John, to Grand Route St. John, to Sauvage, to Fair Grounds. Returns by Sauvage to Grand Route St. John, to Bayou Road, to Broad, to Ursulines, to Burgundy, to Canal, to starting point. Transfers to Henry Clay Avenue and Peters Avenue lines on Canal Street.

Up and Downtown Lines.

Clio Line.—Direct to Union Depot and French Opera House. Starts on Elysian Fields, at Decatur; runs out Elysian Fields to Royal, to Canal, to Lee Circle and Howard Avenue, to Rampart, to Clio, to Magnolia. Returns by Erato to Carondelet, to Canal, to Bourbon (passing French Opera House en route), to Esplanade Avenue, to Decatur, to Elysian Fields.

Carondelet Line.—Direct to French Opera House. Passes City Hall and Cathedral. Starts on Louisa Street, near Chartres; runs out Louisa to Royal, to Canal, to Lee Circle, to Howard Avenue, to Baronne, to Philip, to Carondelet, to Napoleon Avenue. Returns by Carondelet to Canal, to Bourbon (passing French Opera House), to Esplanade, to Decatur, to Elysian Fields, to Chartres, to Louisa (passing Queen and Crescent Depot). Transfers to Orleans and Jefferson lines.

West End Railroad.

West End Line.—Starts on Canal, near Baronne; runs by Canal to the Cemeteries and Half-way House, along the New Basin Canal to West End, along Lake Pontchartrain. This line is equipped with modern electric express trains. The route is one of the most beautiful suburban trips that New Orleans offers. The cars return over the same route.

The Last Mule Car Line.

Algiers and Gretna Line.—Starts in Algiers, from First and Second District Ferry Landings; runs by Bouny to Pelican Avenue, to Powder, to Opelousas Avenue, to Brooklyn Avenue, to Periander, to the river, along the river to upper line of Gretna, along upper line to First Street, to Copernicus Avenue, near Jefferson Avenue Ferry. Returns by same route.'

Steam Lines.

Spanish Fort Line.—Starts on North Basin, at Canal Street; runs by North Basin and Bienville Streets to St. Patrick Street, to Metairie Road and the City Park, and by Orleans Avenue and the Lake shore to Spanish Fort. Returns by the same route.

Pontchartrain Railroad Line.—Starts on Elysian Fields Avenue, near Decatur; runs out Elysian Fields Avenue direct to Milneburg and Old Lake.

Ferries Crossing the Mississippi.

New Orleans has an excellent system of ferries, that ply between the city proper and the suburb of Algiers, or rather the Fifth Municipal District. It will be seen from the subjoined list that communication with Algiers may be had from every section of New Orleans.

The First District Ferry runs from ferry house, at foot of Canal Street, to Algiers.

The Third District Ferry runs from ferry house, at foot of Esplanade Avenue, to Algiers.

The Fourth District Ferry runs from ferry house, at foot of Jackson Avenue, to Gretna.

The Sixth District Ferry runs from ferry house, at foot of Louisiana Avenue, to Harvey's Canal.

The Richard Street Ferry runs from Richard Street to Freetown.

Besides these ferries there are three licensed skiffs that run respectively from Upperline, from Carrollton and from the Barracks to Algiers.

Steam Railroad Depots—Trunk Lines.

The Illinois Central, the Yazoo and Mississippi Valley and the Southern Pacific Railroads have their passenger depot at the Union Depot, on South Rampart Street, corner of Howard Avenue. The Clio and Peters Avenue cars pass directly in front of the depot. The Dryades car passes within one square.

The Louisville and Nashville Depot is at the head of Canal Street. Most of the cars in the city pass near by.

The Queen and Crescent or Northeastern Railroad Depot is located at the head of Peters Street, on the river. The Levee and Barracks car and the Carondelet furnish the most convenient routes.

The Texas and Pacific Railroad Depot is on the river bank, at the head of Terpsichore Street. The Tchoupitoulas car will bring the visitor within three squares of the depot.

The Pontchartrain Depot is on Elysian Fields Street, not far from the river, and is reached by the Rampart and Dauphine cars, the Clio and the Carondelet.

The Shell Beach Depot is on Elysian Fields Avenue, corner of St. Claude Street. The New Orleans and Western Railroad uses the same depot. The Spanish Fort Depot is at the corner of Canal and Basin Streets.

CHAPTER XXV.

Creole Cookery.

New Orleans is noted for its excellent cooking. The fame of the Creole Cuisine has so often been the theme of song and story, and has received such flattering tributes from some of the world's greatest minds, that a brief allusion to the noble art seems a fitting conclusion to a Guide Book, whose object has been to give the stranger true glimpses of life in New Orleans.

Creole cookery is not the least part of this life. It has come down as a precious inheritance through long generations of model housewives, and realizing this, THE PICAYUNE proposes in this chapter to lead the tourist right into the heart of the Creole kitchen, by giving selected extracts from the introductions to the recent editions of THE PICAYUNE'S Creole Cook Book, carefully compiled from recipes that have given to the Creole cuisine the unique and interesting and helpful place it occupies in the world's cookery.

INTRODUCTION TO THE FIRST EDITION OF THE PICAYUNE'S CREOLE COOK BOOK.

In presenting to the public this Creole Cook Book, THE PICAYUNE is actuated by the desire to fill a want that has been long felt, not only in New Orleans, where the art of good cooking was long ago reduced to a positive

TANTE ZABELLE'S TRIUMPH—GUMBO FILE.

science, but in many sections of the country where the fame of our Creole cuisine has spread, and where with slight modifications incident to local supplies of food articles, many of our most delightful recipes may be adapted by the intelligent housekeeper with profit and pleasure. * * * *

The Creole negro cooks of nearly two hundred years ago, carefully instructed and directed by their white Creole mistresses, who received their inheritance of gastronomic lore from France, where the art of good cooking first had birth, faithfully transmitted their knowledge to their progeny, and these, quick to appreciate and understand, and with a keen intelligence and zeal born of the desire to please, improvised and improved upon the products of the cuisine of Louisiana's mother country; then came the Spanish domination, with its influx of rich and stately dishes, brought over by the grand dames of Spain of a century and a half ago; after that came the gradual amalgamation of the two races on Louisiana soil, and with this was evolved a new school of cookery, partaking of the best elements of the French and Spanish cuisines, and yet peculiarly distinct from either; a system of cookery that has held its own through succeeding generations and which drew from even such a learned authority as Thackeray, that noted tribute to New Orleans, "the old French-Spanish city on the banks of the Mississippi, where, of all the cities in the world, you can eat the most and suffer the least, where claret is as good as at Bordeaux, and where a 'ragout' and a 'bouillabaisse' can be had, the like of which was never eaten in Marseilles or Paris."

But the Civil War, with its vast upheavals of social conditions, wrought great changes in the household economy of New Orleans, as it did throughout the South; here, as elsewhere, she who had ruled as the mistress of yesterday became her own cook of today; in nine cases out of ten the younger darkies accepted their freedom with alacrity, but in many ancient families the older Creole "négresses," as they were called, were slow to leave the haunts of the old cuisine and the families of which they felt themselves an integral part. Many lingered on, and the young girls who grew up after that period had opportunities that will never again come to the Creole girls of New Orleans. * *

But soon will the last of the olden negro cooks of ante-bellum days have passed away and their places will not be supplied. The only remedy is for the ladies of the present day to do as their grandmothers did, acquaint themselves thoroughly with the art of cooking in all its important and minutest details, and learn how to properly apply them. To assist them in this, to preserve to future generations the many excellent and matchless recipes of our New Orleans cuisine, to gather these up from the lips of the old Creole negro cooks and the grand old housekeepers who survive, ere they, too, pass away, and Creole cookery, with all its delightful combinations and possibilities, will have become a lost art, is, in a measure, the object of this book.

But far and above this, THE PICAYUNE, in compiling this book, has been animated by the laudable desire to teach the great mass of the public how to live cheaply and well. The moral influences of good cooking cannot be too forcibly insisted upon. There is an old saying that "the way to a man's heart is through his stomach." Every housewife knows the importance of setting a well-cooked meal before her husband if she wishes him to preserve his equanimity of temper. Every mother should know the importance of preparing good, nutritious dishes for her children in the most palatable and appetizing manner, if she would give them that most precious of all gifts "a healthy mind in a healthy body." People are the better, the happier and the longer lived for the good, wholesome, well cooked daily meal. * * * *

It is proposed in this book to assist housekeepers generally to set a dainty and appetizing table at a moderate outlay; to give recipes clearly and accurately with simplicity and exactness, so that the problem of "how to live" may become easier of solution and even the most ignorant and inexperienced cook may be able to prepare a toothsome and nutritious meal with success. The housekeeper is not told "to take some of this, a little of that," and "a pinch" of some other ingredient; she is not left to the chance of guessing accidentally at the proper proportions of component parts of any dish, but the relative proportions of all ingredients are given with accuracy, the proper length of time required in cooking is specified to a nicety, and the relative heat of the fire required for cooking different dishes. In all the recipes the quantities are given for dishes for a family of six. The intelligent housekeeper will thus be able to form a happy medium and increase or reduce proportionately according to the size of her family, the number of invited guests, etc.

THE PICAYUNE CREOLE COOK BOOK is not designed for chefs of cusines; it has been prepared with special appreciation of the wants of the household and of that immense class of housekeepers who, thrown upon their own resources and anxious to learn, are yet ignorant of the simplest details of good cooking, and who, as a rule, have yet to learn that in a well regulated kitchen nothing is ever wasted, but with careful preparation even the "rough ends" of a beef steak may be made into a wholesome, tender and appetizing dish; that "stale bread" may be used in the most delicious "desserts" and "farcies," and "left-over" food from the day before need not be thrown in the trash-box, but may be made into an endless variety of wholesome and nutritious dishes.

Hence, especial care has been taken to rescue from oblivion many fine old-fashioned dishes, and bring them back into general use—dishes whose places can never be equaled by elegant novelties or fancifully extravagant recipes; special attention has been given to the simple, every-day home dishes of the Creole household, while those that tempted the gourmet and epicureans in the palmiest days of old Creole cookery have not been admitted. THE PICAYUNE points with pride to the famous "soupes," "gumbos," "ragouts," "entremets," "hors-d'oeuvres," "jambalayas" and "deserts," that in turn receive particular attention. A special chapter has been devoted to the science of making

THE PICAYUNE'S FROG—"A VOTRE SERVICE, MESDAMES ET MESSIEURS."

good coffee "à la Créole," and one to the modes of cooking Louisiana rice. Our Calas," our "Pralines," and "Pacane Amandes," our "Marrons Glacés" and ices, our "Méringues," and our delicious ways of serving Louisiana oranges peculiar to ourselves alone, are given in respective order. The history of many dishes is also given, thus affording a glimpse into old Creole hospitality, customs and traditions. Commendable features are the series of menus for holidays and daily suggestions for the table, as also the thoroughly classified list of seasonable foods.

Throughout this work THE PICAYUNE has had but one desire at heart, and that is to reach the wants of every household in our cosmopolitan community; to show the earnest housekeeper how the best food may be prepared at the least cost, and how it is possible for every family from the palace to the cottage, to keep a good table and at the same time an economical one.

"Whatever is worth doing at all is worth doing well." If this is true of other things, how much more of cooking, upon which the life and health of the family depend. The kitchen should not be looked upon as a place of drudgery; a poet once sung of

"Making drudgery divine;
Who sweeps a room as to God's laws,
Makes that and the action fine."

The benefits that will ultimately accrue to every family, morally and physically, from paying greater attention to the proper preparation of food can not be over-estimated; the fact that good cooking operates to the greatest extent in the preservation of the domestic peace and happiness of a family cannot be gainsaid. * * *

INTRODUCTION TO THE SECOND EDITION.

The universal favor with which the First Edition of THE PICAYUNE'S Creole Cook Book was received throughout the United States, the remarkably short time in which the edition was exhausted, and the numerous demands for copies that are continually coming in from all sections, have impelled the publishers to issue a Second Edition of this work.

In yielding thus to the popular demand, THE PICAYUNE feels that it can justly claim that this enlarged and amended edition of its Cook Book more fully represents the progress and perfection of culinary art than any existing work.

The Revised Edition has been prepared with great care. Each recipe that has been added has been tried and tested and is given as the result of personal practical experience and success in the Creole Kitchen. The topics have been more conveniently and systematically classified and arranged, the methods of preparation and manipulation, in many instances simplified, and the edition, in its entirety, will therefore be found far more complete, comprehensive and valuable than its predecessor. The book has been bound in cloth to render it more serviceable and durable.

With these explanations THE PICAYUNE sends forth the Second Edition of the Creole Cook Book. Its name tells its story and bespeaks its value. It is the only book of the kind.

By Registered Mail to any part of the United States........$1.25
Retail price in Picayune Counting Room 1.00

CHAPTER XXVI.

"Lagniappe."

"Lagniappe" is a local institution of long standing like "picayune." Indeed as far as traditional customs go, the two are intimately united, the coin itself calling always for a bonus in kind with every purchase, while the readers of the staunch old journal "The Picayune," receive a generous lagniappe of infinite variety and interest with every number. And so following the long established usage, here is a chapter of Lagniappe for the readers of the Picayune Guide.

SEATING CAPACITY OF VARIOUS CHURCHES, THEATRES AND PUBLIC BUILDINGS.

CHURCHES.	Seating Capacity.
Carondelet St. Church (Meth.)....	900
Christ Church Cathedral (Epis.)..	800
Christ Church Chapel (J. L. Harris Memorial)	300
Felicity St. (Meth.)	500
First Presbyterian Church (Dr. Palmer's)	1,500
Free Church of the Annunciation (Episcopal)	800
Lafayette Presbyterian (Dr. Markham's)	700
Jesuits' Church (Cath.)	1,400
Prytania Street (Pres.)	1,500
St. Alphonsus (Cath.)	1,200
St. Anna's (Epis.)	700
St. Anna's (Epis.) Chapel	300
St. George's (Epis.)	900
St. John the Baptist (Cath.)	1,116
St. Joseph (Cath.)	1,900
St. Louis Cathedral (Cath.)	1,364
St. Mary's Assumption (Cath.)....	1,000

St. Patrick (Cath.) 1,200
St. Paul's (Epis.) 800
St. Stephen's (Cath.) 1,200
Temple Sinai (Hebrew) 1,150
Touro Synagogue (Hebrew) 950
Trinity Church (Epis.) 1,200

THEATRES.

Audubon (burned Feb. 11, 1903) 1,800
Crescent 1,800
Elysium 1,400
Grand Opera House (not including
　　stockholders' seats) 1,800
French Opera House 2,300
St. Charles Orpheum 2,064
Tulane 1,700

PUBLIC HALLS.

Athenaeum (Young Men's Hebrew
　　Association) 900
Boys' High School Alumni Hall
　　(Boys' High School) 600
Tulane Hall (upper and lower
　　floors) 2,100
Temperance Union Hall (Rampart
　　and Spain) 500
United Confederate Veterans Hall,
　　Fair Grounds 15,000
Union Francaise Hall (Rampart
　　Street) 1,200
Washington Artillery Hall (includ-
　　ing upper and lower floors and
　　supper hall) 6,500
Young Men's Christian Association
　　(Y. M. C. A. Building) 600

PRIVATE HALLS.

H. Sophie Newcomb Memorial
　　Hall (upper floor College Build-
　　ing) 750
Gibson Hall (Tulane University) .. 350
Jesuit Alumni Hall 486

The above halls, though belonging to private institut'ons, are often loaned for public meetings.

HEIGHTH OF TALLEST BUILDINGS IN NEW ORLEANS.

	Feet.
American Sugar Refinery Company....	148
Hennen Building........................	150
Hibernia Bank and Trust Company,	
above sidewalk,	180
Illinois Central R. R. Dock Elevator,	
[old]............................	148
Illinois Central R. R. Dock Elevator,	
[new]..............................	175
Liverpool and London and Globe In-	
surance Company.................	108
Lyons Building.......................	110
Morris Building.......................	101
Shot Tower...........................	196
St. Charles Hotel Annex..............	168
St. Patrick's Church Tower.........	
plus the pinnacles,	170
Tulane Educational Fund.............	115

POPULATION OF NEW ORLEANS, 1722-1900.

Year.	Population.
1722	300
1727	1,600
1745	2,900
1790	7,000
1810	17,242
1820	27,176
1830	29,737
1840	102,103
1850	116,375
1860	168,675
1870	191,418
1880	216,090
1890	242,079
1900	287,104

ILLUSTRATORS OF THE PICAYUNE GUIDE BOOK.

The ilustrations in this book are without exception the work of New Orleans artists. The two views, entitled respectively, "Type of Old Courtyard—Royal Street," and "Old Courtyard in Chartres Street." are reproductions of original paintings from the brush of Mrs. Walter Saxon, a talented artist who kindly loaned the Picayune these beautiful glimpses of old New Orleans. In like manner the cut representing "View of Old Court, Faubourg Marigny, Royal, Near Port Street," is a repro- duction of a painting by the charming artist, Mrs. A. Moore, who lives within the old Court.

Glimpses of peculiar characters and street criers, group of Indians, and other typical sketches are from the pencil of the Picayune's able artist, Mr. Louis A. Winterhalder. The other illustrations, with the exception of those marked Rivoire, and several unmarked, are the work of Mr. Louis E. Cormier. an artistic member of the Picayune staff, who gave of the results of his ex- perience with the camera toward the beautifying of these pages.

LANDING OF THE URSULINES.

The picture on Page 6, entitled "Landing of the Ursuline Nuns," deserves more than a passing notice. It is the most historic picture in Louisiana, being the only glimpse taken of New Orleans in that early period. It is a reproduc- tion of a sketch made by Madeleine Hauchard, a young Ursuline novice, at the moment of the landing of the community on Louisiana soil. From the day of the departure of the Sisterhood from France, Madeleine Hauchard, who was far ahead of her day and generation, began to keep a diary of the order. As the nuns landed in New Orleans, and were met by Bienville and the other Government officials, and clergy, Madeleine Hauchard paused and rapidly sketched the group, for as she afterward told her superioress, "The landing was historical." This original sketch, faithfully preserved by the Ursulines, and still to be seen in the old Convent, was subsequently enlarged by Madeleine Hauchard, and hangs in the Convent parlors within the strict enclosure. On completing the picture, she placed herself among the Sisterhood; she may be easily recognized by the tall, white novice's cap that she wears, and the cat that she bears in her arms. She brought this pet cat all the way from her old home. The picture has never been seen outside of the Convent walls, and it is now given to the public for the first time by The Picayune, through the courtesy of the Ursuline Nuns. Madeleine Hauchard, it may be added, took the black veil of the Ursulines and for nearly forty years, up to the time of her death, devoted herself to the work of religion, education and charity in Louisiana. For upwards of thirty-eight years she kept the daily record of all the events that happened in the colony, and this diary, still faithfully preserved in the old Convent, is the only record extant of those early days. Madeleine Hauchard was of a bright, vivacious, generous nature; it is recorded in the order that she was the life and heart of the community from the time that it set sail on the unknown seas in 1727 to her death. Her cheery, sunny temperament is revealed in every page of her diary, and one may imagine what a tower of strength such a sweet, sturdy, optimistic character must have been to that brave band of pioneer women-workers in Louisiana.

THE PICAYUNE FROG.

When the "Frog" first made its advent in New Orleans as the "Weather Prophet" of the Picayune, and appeared daily at the head of our "Guide to the Weather" column, arrayed in various garbs, indicating the kind of weather one might expect for the next twenty-four hours, enthusiasm for the "Picayune Frog," as our prophet was immediately dubbed, was very great. Not only did the great popular heart go out to Froggie, but the most exclusive circles caught the idea, and "Picayune Frog Teas," "Picayune Frog Pins," "Picayune Frog Calendars," menu cards, etc., with the pictures of Froggie in his amusing garbs became the fashion of the hour. No entertainment, no reunion, no fair, or children's party was considered complete without the presence of the Picayune Frog. The Frog soon became the "mascot" of every charitable and philanthropic entertainment, the booths at which he was invited to take up his headquarters generally carrying the fair. Cakes and drinks and fashionable dishes were named in his honor, and so great was his popularity that a famous old chef in the French Quarter, unable to control his enthusiasm for the little frog, who had left the bayous and swamps of this old Creole State to take up his abode in a great newspaper office, complimented him with an original dish named in his honor, "Picayune Frogs à la Créole." Froggie, always ready to adapt himself to circumstances, at once responded the next day by appearing as a waiter serving the dish. Subsequently, on occasions of great festivals in New Orleans, such as Thanksgiving, Christmas, New Years, etc., Froggie always appeared in this conventional garb, ready, as he said, for duty. And so, when the Picayune published its Creole Cook Book, Froggie, "who," as distinguished critics aver, "is able to do all things and do them well," delighted the public by offering to serve the dishes which the old Creole Cook so faithfully portrayed in the cut presented for their delectation. Froggie appears in the chapter on "Creole Cookery," of this Guide, "A Votre Service, Mesdames et Messieurs!"

SAYINGS OF JOHN McDONOGH.

Reference has been made in this Guide to John McDonogh, who spent all the years of his life in solitude, and who died leaving his vast estates for the benefit of public education in New Orleans and Baltimore. At the close of his remarkable will, written in McDonogh's own hand, and which covered over eighty pages of foolscap paper, a testament which seemed in reality a defense of his own life—there occur the following passages, which gave the public the first glimpse into the inner heart of the man:

"I have preferred as a revenue of the earth as a part of the solid globe. One thing is certain, it will not take wings and fly away as silver and gold and Government bonds and stocks often do. It is the only thing in this world that approaches to anything like permanency."

"The love of singing given me by my mother in my youth, has been the delight and charm of my life throughout all its subsequent periods and trials. Still has its love and charm pervaded my existence and gilded my path to comparative happiness below, and I firmly believe led me to what little virtues I have practiced."

"And all I ask in return is that the little children should sometimes come and plant a few flowers above my grave."

Upon the old granite tomb, on the Algiers side of New Orleans, in the old plantation of McDonoghville, where the remains of the philanthropist reposed previous to final interment in Baltimore, may be seen the following inscriptions, written by himself and placed there, at his request, by his friend and executor, Christian Roselius, the eminent lawyer.

INSCRIPTION ON THE SOUTH SIDE OF TOMB.

"Rules Written for My Guidance in Life—1804."

"Remember always that labor is one of the conditions of our existence.

"Time is gold—throw not one minute away, but place each one to account.

"Do unto all men as you would be done by.

"Never put off till to-morrow what you can do to-day.

"Never bid another do what you can do yourself.

"Never covet what is not your own.

"Never think any matter so trivial as not to deserve notice.

"Never give out that which does not first come in.

"Never spend but to produce.

"Study in your course of life to do the greatest possible amount of good."

INSCRIPTION ON NORTH SIDE OF TOMB.

."Deprive yourself of nothing necessary to your comfort, but live in an honorable simplicity and frugality. Labor then to the last moment of your existence. Pursue strictly the above rules, and the Divine blessing and riches of every kind will flow upon you, to your heart's content; but first of all, remember, that the chief and greatest study of your life should be to tend by all the means in your power to the honor and glory of the Divine Creator.
New Orleans, March 2, 1804.   "JOHN McDONOGH."

"The conclusion at which I have arrived is, that without temperance there is no health—without virtue no order—without religion no happiness—and the sum of our being is to live wisely, soberly and rigteously."

NEW ORLEANS.

The Picayune closes this Guide with the following beautiful tribute to New Orleans from the pen of the gifted poetess, "Pearl Rivers," the late Mrs. E. J. Nicholson.

She floats within her sunlit seas,
  A languorous lily dreaming,
Her green hair trailed about her knees,
  And sweet beyond all seeming;
I can not say how fair she is—
  I may not say it nearly;
She's like a radiant girl to me,
  And I,—I love her dearly.

T. Fitzwilliam & Co.,

LIMITED.

One of the landmarks of Camp Street is the building occupied by the firm of T. Fitzwilliam & Co., Ltd., Manufacturing Stationers, Lithographers and Printers. The reader may turn to the illustration elsewhere in this book, which shows The Picayune office and the adjoining buildings. On the left of the picture he will see a portion of the establishment of T. Fitzwilliam & Co., Ltd. The building may easily be identified by the name of the firm reproduced in the engraving. This location, at No. 324 Camp Street, is exceedingly advantageous, as it is in the very heart of the business quarter, and within convenient access to all the large business houses and office buildings of the city. The building is four stories high and extends through the block to Bank Alley, on which there is a rear entrance, at 321.

The building contains an extensive plant for the manufacture of blank books for merchants and corporations; also for job printing, which in completeness can hardly be equaled even beyond New Orleans. In addition to which the firm possess an elaborate lithographic plant, where the most modern methods are employed in the execution of the highest grades of the work.

For twenty years past, The Picayune has intrusted to the firm of T. Fitzwilliam & Co., Ltd., the task of preparing the lithographic work of the Carnival editions of that paper. The widespread popularity of these brilliantly illustrated papers evinces the merit of the firm's work, and each year finds them acquitting themselves of this congenial task with greater skill and higher artistic perfection. The firm also carries an extensive stock of general office stationery and supplies of all kinds. In fact, the lower floor of their building contains a perfect assortment of articles used in offices, and an inspection of the stock is interesting and instructive, as it reveals how much ingenuity is devoted in these days to ministering to the comfort of clerks, book-keepers and others who are occupied in business offices. In this connection, the firm manufactures and sells patent flat-opening blank books, which are very popular and give entire satisfaction. It also prints all kinds of bankruptcy and other legal blanks, the forms of which have been scanned by competent authorities and found to be entirely in consonance with the soundest practices of the local bar. A competent staff of binders, printers and engravers enables the firm to turn out at short notice the most attractive examples of work.

As an adjunct to the large business carried on by this house in its various branches, the firm has acquired the sole agency for the celebrated Edison Oscillatory Memeograph.

The house was established forty-four years ago, and is to-day conducted by the same management as directed its affairs in the early period of its development. It stands very high in the estimation of the community, having shown itself eminently worthy of the confidence which its numerous customers continue to repose in it.

STEAMBOAT LANDING—FOOT OF CANAL STREET.

LOADING COTTON ON THE LEVEE.

THE COUNTRY CLUB, NEAR THE BAYOU ST. JOHN.

THE SPIRIT OF THE CONFEDERACY.

Proof

27225952R00133

Made in the USA
Charleston, SC
03 March 2014